Families of
Halifax County, Virginia

By M. Secrist

2012

ISBN-13: 978-1475188769
ISBN-10: 1475188765

PREFACE

This work consists of biographical and genealogical sketches of Halifax County, Virginia families. Many of the family sketches contain abstracts of wills, lists of marriages and other vital information. For ease of the reader they are arranged in alphabetical order.

Please be forgiving if you find mistakes. It would be unrealistic to expect any work of this nature to be error free. But, I did go through great methodical lengths to assure the accuracy of facts presented here. Of course, I can only strive to be as accurate as the sources these sketches are derived from, which are also fallible.

I hope this publication is valuable to all of those with roots connected to Halifax County, Virginia. I enjoyed learning about the people that chose to make Halifax County their home. I encourage the reader to read beyond their personal ancestors' sketches alone, as the other people mentioned here may have been their in-law, neighbor, partner in business or close personal friend.

ADAMS family is of Welsh extraction, and the first American ancestor of whom we have any reliable account was John Adams, who came from Wales during the first half of the eighteenth century, and settled in Maryland, whence he came to Virginia. He had three sons, Sylvester, Philip and John. This second John Adams came to Halifax County, Virginia, about the time of its organization (1752). He married Susan Wood, daughter of Richard Wood, of Brunswick County, as shown by his will recorded April 24 and proved September 4, 1746, in Brunswick County. Many of the descendants of the Adams family migrated to Tennessee, Texas, Missouri and other States.

William Adams, the eldest son of John and Susan (Wood) Adams, was born in Halifax County about 1756. He died September 10, 1839, aged 83. He was a soldier in the Revolutionary War, and in his old age delighted to recur to the stirring events of that period in which he had participated.

Three Adams brothers married daughters of George Boyd. William married Elizabeth Boyd, Sylvester married Rebecca, and Richard married Hannah Boyd. John Richard Adams (son of Richard, son of William, son of John, son of John the emigrant) was born in Chesterfield County, but moved to Halifax, where in 1849 he married Amanda Wade, daughter of Richard and Sarah (Chappell) Wade. Amanda (Wade) Adams died in 1853, and in 1855 John Richard Adams married Mary A. Stanford, a daughter of Saurin Stanford, of Orange County, North Carolina. She was a niece of his first wife and granddaughter of Sarah Wade. She was also a granddaughter of Richard Stanford, of Person County, N. C., who came to that State from Maryland in 1790, and married a daughter of General Stephen Moore, of Revolutionary fame, and an uncle of Bishop Channing Moore.

Stanford was elected to Congress from North Carolina in 1796, and served continuously in that body for twenty years. His wife, Mary Moore, was a lineal descendant of Sir John Moore, of Fawley, Berkshire, England, who was knighted by King Charles I, May 21, 1627. Richard Stanford before being elected to Congress founded Hawfield's Academy in Alamance County, N. C., and had many pupils who became distinguished citizens.

Richard Stanford was born in Vienna, Md., March 5, 1768, and was the son of Richard Stanford, whose father, Richard Stanford the 1st emigrated from Gravesend, England, in 1684; although the family is Scotch, the name being derived from Stoneford, the Scotch being "Stane-ford."

Mary (Moore) Stanford was the twelfth generation from John Moore, of Fawley, Berkshire, England, who was knighted by King Charles I; and her mother was Grizelda Phillips, of Boston, of the well-known family to which Oliver Wendall Phillips belonged.

The above Mary Ann Stanford was the mother of Samuel L. Adams, of Cluster Springs and South Boston, a man who knows more about his native county than any one with whom we have talked. He was a quiet, dignified gentleman, kept his own counsel, and ordered his life by its circumstances. He was an attorney in Halifax County, and was highly regarded for his integrity and honesty. Mr. Adams married Alice, a daughter of Captain John A. Mitchell, of the Virginia State Guard, before the Civil War, and during the war he served in Wright's battery of heavy artillery. She had three brothers, Gus E. Mitchell, a merchant of Natalie; Dr. John H. Mitchell, a prominent physician of Buckingham County; and J. R. Mitchell, associate justice of the Supreme Court of the State of Washington; and one sister, Mrs. Mary M. Owen (widow of Mr. John Owen), of South Boston. Mrs. Alice Mitchell Adams died September 25, 1923, at the Halcyon Hospital, South Boston. She was survived by her husband, four sons and one daughter—John R., Philip C., Mary, William J. and Gus C. Adams. *[A History of Halifax County, by Wirt Johnson Carrington]*

More about Hon. Samuel Lee Adams and his family (with slightly different information) from *History of Virginia*, Vol. IV, published in 1924:

Hon. Samuel L. Adams was born near Black Walnut in Halifax County, October 31, 1863, and was a member of an old American family of Revolutionary stock. His first American ancestor was John F. Adams, a native of Wales, who came to Virginia when about twenty-four years of age and settled in Lunenburg County, where he became a planter and where he died in 1750. He married Susan Wood, a native of Lunenburg County. Their son, William Adams, great-grandfather of Hon. Samuel L. Adams, was born in Halifax County in 1748, and devoted his active career to the management of his farming interests. He was a slave owner. He was the Revolutionary ancestor, serving as a private in a company commanded by Capt. George Rogers Clark. He died in Halifax County in 1812. His wife was Martha A. Boyd, who was born in Halifax County in 1751, and died there in 1810.

Richard Adams, grandfather of Samuel L., was born in Halifax County in 1792, and also had a military record, in the War of 1812, being a member of Capt. Edmund Randolph Cocke's Company. He was a farmer, and for many years a resident of Powhatan County. He died in Chesterfield County in 1841. His wife was Ann B. Tucker, who was born in Powhatan County in 1796, and died in Chesterfield County in 1842.

Their son, John R. Adams, was born in Powhatan County, May 10, 1822, was reared there and in Chesterfield County, and as a young man settled near Black Walnut in Halifax County. He became known for his extensive interests as a tobacco grower. He was one of the first growers of bright leaf tobacco in Southern Virginia. He spent the rest of his years near Black Walnut, where he

6

died May 27, 1887. He was a democrat, was a member of the Methodist Episcopal Church, South, and of the Masonic fraternity, and during the War Between the States was an enrolling officer for the Confederacy and participated in the Staunton River Bridge Fight. His first wife was Amada Wade, whom he married in 1847. She was a native of Halifax County and died at Black Walnut in 1850. By this union there were two children: Luther C, a farmer, who died in Halifax County in 1909; and Sallie Chappell, who died in Halifax County in 1910, wife of George C. Oliver, a farmer, who died in 1914.

In May, 1852, John R. Adams married Mary Stanford, who was born in Orange County, North Carolina, in 1834 and was a graduate of the Greensboro Female College in that State. She died at her home near Black Walnut July 3, 1873. Her grandfather, Richard Stanford, founded in 1790 Hawfields Academy in Alamance, then a part of Orange County, North Carolina. In 1796 Richard Stanford was elected to Congress, being then twenty-eight years of age, and he continued to represent the Hillsboro District of North Carolina in Congress until his death about twenty years later. He had the distinction of being the first member of Congress, and was called "the Father of the House," being so referred to by John Randolph of Roanoke. The children of John R. Adams and his wife, Mary Stanford, were: Richard A., resided at DeLand, Florida; Theophilus A., a farmer and merchant who died in Halifax County, January 31, 1918; Samuel Lee; William H., a merchant at Smithfield, Isle of Wight County, Virginia; Thomas Tucker, a lumber dealer at Danville; Walter E., who was an employe of the Atlantic Coast Line Railway Company and died at Richmond January 4, 1918; Mary S., who died at Semora, North Carolina, October 10, 1917, wife of Zachariah T. Pointer, a farmer who died in June, 1915; and Adella, resided at DeLand, Florida.

Samuel Lee Adams grew up on his father's tobacco plantation in Halifax County, attended private and public schools, and at the age of nineteen left the farm to go to Richmond, with the purpose of working and continuing his higher education in night schools. His health failed after two months, and he then returned to the home farm for several years, but continued his studies. From 1884 until 1888 Mr. Adams was in the mercantile business near South Boston, and in the meantime was studying law. On leaving Halifax County he was in the life insurance business with headquarters at Elam College, North Carolina, until 1896. In June of that year he was admitted to the bar, and he began practice at Alton in Halifax County, but since 1904 his home offices were at South Boston with a general civil and criminal practice.

From 1907 to 1922 Mr. Adams served as school trustee of the Black Walnut District. He was elected to the House of Delegates, to represent Halifax County, in November, 1921, and served in the regular session in 1922, and the special session of 1923. He is a strong prohibitionist, and has been interested in all legislation to strengthen the moral standards of the state. He served on the committee of moral and social welfare, was also the champion of nearly all measures of moral and social reform, and was chief patron of the bill for the Moving Picture Censorship, which he safely piloted through the House of Delegates, where it was strongly opposed. He was also one of the patrons of the bill for cooperative marketing. Mr. Adams has always taken a keen interest in the Confederate Veterans of his county and state, and was the patron, of the bill increasing pensions for Confederate Veterans and their widows at the regular session of 1922. He has also been an active member of the Sons of Confederate Veterans, and was commander of the Virginia Division of that organization from 1917 to 1921. Mr. Adams was a lay leader in the Methodist Episcopal Church, South, and for at least twenty years taught a Sunday school class. Mr. Adams is affiliated with the Masons, Odd Fellows, Knights of Pythias, and a member of the Virginia State Bar Association.

He and his family resided in the country, on a farm owned by himself and wife six miles south of South Boston. During the World war Mr. Adams acted as local counsel for the Veterans Bureau, and he and his son Samuel L., Jr., gave practically an entire year to handling work involved in filling out questionnaires, and cases of exemptions and investigations. From the strain and responsibility of this work his son's health broke, and it was as a direct result of the service that he died June 29, 1922.

Mr. Adams married in Caswell County, North Carolina, January 12, 1887, Miss Alice Mitchell, daughter of Capt. John A. and Mary (Pringle) Mitchell. Her father was a farmer and fire insurance man, and died in Halifax County, Virginia, in 1906, and her mother died there in 1902. Mrs. Adams was educated in the South Boston Female Institute. Among her brothers one is John R. Mitchell, associate Supreme Court justice in the State of Washington; another is Dr. Joseph H. Mitchell of Dillwyn, Buckingham County, Virginia; and another is Gus E. Mitchell, a merchant at Alchie, Virginia. She had a sister, Mary M., who was a resident of South Boston and widow of John S. Owen, who was a merchant.

To the marriage of Mr. and Mrs. Adams were born six children: John R., Samuel Lee, Jr., Mary, Philip C., William J. and Gus C.

Some Adams marriages in Halifax County, Virginia:

Amey Adams and Edward Oakes, 23 December 1823.

E. Adams and William Bartlett, 9 January 1817.

E. Adams and Edward Rudder, 8 November 1820.

Gideon Adams and E. A. Moorefield, 8 November 1839.

Hannah Adams and Peter Puryear, 30 November 1802.

J. Adams and Susan Y. Flora, 29 July 1841.

James M. Adams and Rachel Hanes, 28 August 1800.

James W. Adams and Elvira Foulks, 28 September 1837.

John Adams and Mary Thompson, 27 October 1781.

John Adams and Prudence Thornton, 31 August 1791.

John Adams and E. McGriger, 21 December 1795.

John Adams and Lucy Owen, 1 March 1810.

John Adams and N. M. Craddock, 30 December 1819.

John Adams and Rebecca Martin, 5 January 1828.

Joseph Adams and Elizabeth Watkins, 24 September 1799.

Margaret Adams and R. Wade, 23 February 1842.

Margaret Adams and J. D. Chandler, October 1850.

Martha Adams and Thomas Dickson, 20 December 1771.

Martha Adams and Isaac Palmore, 7 April 1823.

Mary Adams and Joseph Overton, 18 February 1789.

Mary R. Adams and Robert W. Vaden, 16 December 1851.

Moses Adams and Mary A. Buckner, 13 October 1842.

Moza Adams and Polly George, 26 June 1797.

N. Adams and John Ragland, 14 November 1812.

Nancy Adams and James Powell, 13 February 1800.

Nipper Adams and Polly Farmer, 17 December 1785.

Nipper Adams and Obedience Farmer, 16 June 1791.

Nipper Adams and Frances Carter, 1 July 1795.

Phillip Adams and Martha Beadles, 12 November 1818.

Polly Adams and Absalom Jones, 6 November 1811.

R. C. Adams and Judith Chandler, 23 November 1837.

Rednor W. Adams and Martha W. Wilburn, August 1847.

Richard Adams and E. Prewett, 13 September 1781.

Richard Adams and S. McDowell, 22 January 1851.

S. Adams (wife) and Currie Barnett, 8 April 1811.

S. Adams (wife) and C. Scott, 11 January 1837.

Sarah Adams and Patrick Boyd, 20 November 1785.

Susan Adams and Joseph Pointer, 4 September 1835.

Susannah Adams and Richard Ball, 3 November 1798.

Sylvester Adams and Rebecca Boyd, 9 February 1792.

Thomas Adams and Rachel Nobles 11 November 1782.

Thomas Adams and Martha Jordan, 30 November 1825.

William Adams and America H. Wilburn, 16 October 1839.

William W. Adams and Susan A. Wilson, 2 March 1852.

ANDERSON family: Will of Andrew Anderson, 27 May 1839, Halifax County. Sons: Andrew, Pauldin, Isaac. "To my beloved wife" (does not state name). Daughters: Elizabeth, Melissa Jane Anderson, Parthenia Tune, Eliza Chaney. Son, Andrew, executor.

20 December 1841, Will of Orpha Anderson, of Halifax County, Virginia:

"I give to my brother, John K. Anderson, two hundred dollars, the balance to be divided among my brother-in-law's children (William Powell), and William W. Powell to act as their agent." Witnesses: Edward P. Williams, Thomas A. Powell and Watson T. Powell.

"At a court held for Halifax County, January 24, 1842, the within writing, purporting to be the nuncupative will of Orpha A. Anderson, deceased, was exhibited in court by William A. Powell for probate, and thereupon ordered that Anna Denton, formerly Anna Anderson and Mary Anderson, be summoned to appear here on the fourth Monday in March next to contest the same, if they please, and it appearing to the court that the said Anna Denton and Mary Anderson are not inhabitants of the Commonwealth, it was ordered that a copy of this order be inserted in the Danville Reporter for four weeks successively. Later sworn to by Watson T. Powell and Thomas A. Powell and recorded."

ARMISTEAD, Judge Edward W., was born in Halifax County, Virginia, in May, 1855. His father was William H. Armistead, who was born in Petersburg, Virginia. His mother, who was Miss Sarah Henry before marriage, is the granddaughter of Patrick Henry. The early education of Judge Armistead was received at Hampden-Sidney College. In 1876 he entered the Washington and Lee University, and was graduated from the Law Course there in 1878. Several years afterward he entered into practice in South Boston. From 1881 to 1885 he was judge of Halifax County court. *[Virginia and Virginians, Vol. II]*

ARMSTRONG family: 20 May 1779, Halifax County, Will of John Armstrong:

"Sister, Jane Burton (whose first husband was Stephen Norton); my mother, Jane Armstrong; my nephew, John Norton.

"I give and bequeath unto my late wife's youngest son, David Boyd, &c.

"John Armstrong."

Executors: Joseph Penir, Charles Burton, David Boyd. Securities: Isaac Cole, George Boyd, Jr., Richard Gwinn, Wright Bond, John Irvine and James Le Grand.

In the Halifax County marriage records John Armstrong married Margaret Boyd on 1 January 1759. On 12 December 1764 is the marriage of Micajah Watkins and Mary Boyd (daughter by first marriage. Order by her mother signed Margaret Armstrong).

ARNETT, Eugene S., was born at Brooklyn, Halifax County, Virginia, on January 30, 1847, son of W. W. Arnett, a Virginian by birth, later a resident of Saline County, Missouri, and Martha A. Strickland. He had an elder brother in the Confederate States Army, W. W. Arnett., Jr. The first wife of Mr. Arnett was Sallie A. Hatchett, who died on July 25, 1880, leaving him one son, Willie P., born December 14, 1872. He married secondly Miss M. H. Dixon, of Pittsylvania County, their marriage solemnized December 6, 1881. Their children are two sons: Eugene W. and Alvah H. Mr. Arnett received a common school education in his native county, and went to Danville where he began business at the age of 22 years, in 1869, as leaf tobacco dealer. From 1876 to 1886 he was connected with the firms of Arnett & Wemple, and Arnett, Wemple & Ellyson. On January 1, 1886, the firm as last named was dissolved, and Mr. Arnett entered into a co-partnership in the firm of Arnett, Snellings & Co., proprietors of the Martha Washington Tobacco Works, on High Street, in Danville. *[Virginia and Virginians, Vol. II]*

Halifax County marriage records shows William W. Arnette married Martha Strickland on 19 December 1833.

ATKISSON family were of Scotch ancestry. We do not know when they came to the Colony, but they were in Halifax County as early as 1799

(December 15), when Jesse Atkisson married Jinny Medley. Their son, Clement Mayo Atkisson, born at Cluster Springs, married in January, 1849, Mary W. Sydnor. They had only one child, William Sydnor Atkisson, who married Minnie Brown, daughter of Dr. A. B. Brown and Sallie Henry (Wimbish) Brown. Their children were: (1) Sallie Wimbish Atkisson, born July 4, 1898, married Wilbur Hardman Ryland; (2) William Atkisson, Jr., born November 15, 1907.

The Atkissons are related to the Wimbishes, Brooks, Medleys, Barksdales and other leading families in the county, and through the Sydnors to the Colemans and Clarks. Susan Coleman Barksdale, daughter of Major Peter Barksdale and Elizabeth Watlington, married William Sydnor, and their children were Beverly S., Peter, Alex, William, Giles (the father of Mrs. Carrie Clark, relict of Dr. A. Trent Clark, who served the people of South Boston for more than a quarter of a century as the dear "old family doctor"), Fannie, Betsy, Judy and Mary Webb Sydnor. The Sydnors were people of wealth and position, holding offices of honor and trust. *[A History of Halifax County, by Wirt Johnson Carrington]*

Some Atkisson marriages in Halifax County, Virginia:

Clement M. Adkinson and Mary W. Sydnor, ___ Jan. 1849.

E. Atkinson (wife) and Albert Warren, 10 Feb. 1837.

J. Atkinson (husband) and S. Picket (wife), 16 Oct. 1800.

J. Adkisson (husband) and J. C. Callahan (wife), 15 Jan. 1839.

Jane Atkisson and John Ladd, 22 Nov. 1836.

Jesse Atkisson and Jinny Medley, 15 Dec. 1799.

John Atkerson and Sally Watkins, 13 Nov. 1795.

Josiah Atkinson and Susannah Wall, 22 June 1789.

Martha E. Adkisson and Asa B. Cabaniss, 26 Sept. 1848.

Mary W. Adkisson and James Young, 14 Jan. 1852.

N. Adkisson (wife) and James Singleton, 12 May 1825.

Sally Atkinson and Wyatt Howell, 13 March 1786.

Samuel Atkinson and Nancy Torian, 13 Oct. 1831.

Sarah Adkinson and James F. Brooks, 31 May 1827.

Thomas Adkison and Rachel Link, 7 Nov. 1799.

BALLOU, Charles A., is a descendant of one of the Huguenot families who escaped from religious persecution in France by emigration to America, and founded a line in Virginia. His father, also named Charles A. Ballou, was born in Cumberland County, Virginia, and his mother, Rebecca A. Medley, was born in Halifax County, Virginia. The father's death occurred in 1865, in his 73rd year. The subject of this sketch was born in Halifax County, December 4, 1833. He was twice married. His first marriage was solemnized at McMinnville. Tennessee, where on February 2, 1859, Mary G. Tate of Roanoke County, Virginia, became his wife. She died in 1866, leaving him two daughters, Kate P. and Mary G. He married secondly Annie P. Talley of Clarksville, Virginia, who died in January, 1885. Their children were: Natalie, Charles A., Jr., James E., N. Talley, Sallie T. and Alice R.

James E. Ballou, brother of Charles A., serving in the Confederate States Army, was killed at Balls Bluff. Charles A. Ballou was in service, 1864-5, in the quartermaster's department. His early school years were passed in Halifax County, and his education completed at the Washington and Lee University. In 1856 he accepted position as civil engineer on the M. C. & T. R. R., and except for the time he was in military service he followed this profession on various railroads until he made his home in Danville, in 1873, and was city civil engineer. He also ably filled other city offices: Superintendent of water works, superintendent of electric lights, superintendent of gas works, etc. *[Virginia and Virginians, Vol. II]*

26 June 1809--Inventory of the estate of Thomas Ballow (Ballou), Gent., farm, household furniture and farm utensils and twelve Negroes. Appraisers: Robert Chappell, Beverly Borum, John Wood.

Will of Charles A. Ballow/Ballou (son of Thomas).

"I, Charles A. Ballow, of the county of Halifax, State of Virginia, do make and publish this my last will and testament.

"First--I desire all of my just debts to be paid.

"Second--I give to my wife, Rebecca A. Ballow, all my household and kitchen furniture. I give to her two horses or mules as she may select, a wagon, two sets of plough geers, one-half of my plantation tools, one-half of my stock of cattle, one-half of my stock of hogs, and all of my flock of sheep, and one ox cart. This I give to her to dispose of as she may think proper. I also give to her to be held in dower during her natural life all of my lands lying south of the road immediately in front of my dwelling house and west of the road running from Union Church to Medley's Mill, on to the creek on Headspeth's line and down to the upper end of the land given to her by her father, lying on the creek and Medley's Mill pond, which line includes my dwelling and other houses. At her decease this land is to be divided between all of my children. "In testimony whereof I hereby set my hand and seal this 30th day of June, 1865.

"Charles A. Ballow."

Witnesses: R. A. Tucker, George C. Carrington.

"I appoint William H. Morton, Jr. (my son-in-law), of Clarksville, Virginia, executor to my last will and testament."

Codicil No. 1: "The Negroes which I have given to my children heretofore shall not be counted in any future division of my property, as the fortune of war has taken them from their possession and set them at liberty.

"This codicil signed by me this third day of July, 1865.

"Charles A. Ballow."

Mrs. Charles A. Ballow's securities, Charles A. Ballow, Jr., J. T. Ballow and James Medley, gave bond for $8,000. Teste: James D. Clay, C.

[Will book 29]

BARKSDALE family: The first record of the Barksdale family we can find in this county is the will of Nathaniel Barksdale, who married Mourning Dickerson. His will was recorded July 21, 1789, in which he left a goodly estate to be divided among his eight children—four sons and four daughters and wife, Mourning.

His eldest son, Peter Barksdale, married Elizabeth Watlington, January 11, 1781, and their son, Nathaniel Barksdale, married Patsy Hurt in 1805 (they were married by Rev. Robert Hurt, a distinguished Baptist minister of the well-known ministerial family of Hurts).

Their son, Elisha Barksdale, married Judith A. Barksdale, October 22, 1835, and their son, the subject of this sketch, William Randolph Barksdale, born January 6, 1848, in Halifax County; married first Miss Hallie (or Harriet) Bailey Craddock, who was born in Halifax County, and died at Richmond, Virginia, while on a visit, in 1900.

They had the following children:

(1) William Randolph Barksdale, Jr., married Miss Mary Jane Morgan.

(2) Fannie Poindexter Barksdale, married first Mr. H. Vaughan. Their children were Henry, Frances, Catherine, Bird and Barksdale. She married, second, Mr. Edward C. Craddock.

(3) Charles Craddock Barksdale, born at Halifax Court House, Virginia, November 6, 1878; married Miss Avis Walker Grant, daughter of Percy S. and Avis (Walker) Grant.

(4) Dr. Elisha Barksdale, married Miss Rosa McWane.

(5) Louise Jasper Barksdale, married Mr. Tucker Carrington Watkins, Jr., son of William J. Watkins and Elizabeth (Coles) Watkins, of Charlotte County. William J. Watkins was a son of William M. Watkins, of Charlotte, and Elizabeth W. (Venable) Watkins (daughter of Col. S. W. Venable, of "Springfield"). William M. Watkins was a son of Joel Watkins, proverbial for his honesty, integrity and piety, and Agnes (Morton) Watkins, of Charlotte County. (See Watkins.) Mr. Tucker Watkins' ancestors belong to Charlotte County, but for many years he has been a progressive, eminent and conspicuous citizen of South Boston, where he has a beautiful modern home, but being a controlling member of the Co-operative Tobacco Association, he, with his family, are living pro tern. in Richmond, Va. They have three children: (1) William, (2) Tucker, (3) Mary.

(6) Helen Barksdale married Mr. John Martin, a prominent lawyer of Halifax He is the son of Miles Macon Martin and Edmonia Blair (Read) Martin (born at "Ingleside" November 23, 1851). She is the daughter of William Watkins Read and Pauline E. (Carrington) Read. Born at "Retirement" October 22, 1825. Miles Macon Martin is the son of Rev. Alexander Martin and Elizabeth (Macon) Martin.

(7) Mary Owen Barksdale.

(8) Alfred Dickerson Barksdale, an attorney of Lynchburg, and a veteran of the World War, who served as captain of Company M, Twenty-ninth Division, was in France over a year, serving in the Meuse-Argonne and other offensive and defensive sectors, and winning the Croix de Guerre, Legion of Honor Modal and Distinguished Service Cross.

(9) John Craddock Barksdale.

Judge Barksdale married for his second wife Miss Virginia Douglas Watkins, sister of Mr. Hal Watkins, superintendent of public schools for this county.

Judge Barksdale was born in Halifax County near Meadville. He attended Powell's school at the Court House and at Leighwood, taught by Mr. John Henry Powell, father of the celebrated John Powell, pianist. In 1870, he took the M. A. degree at the University of Virginia and began the practice of law the following year. Was made judge in 1874.

The Barksdales are professional and educational people, and have always been prominent in the progress of the county. They have been considerable land and slave owners, and their influence in politics and religion is well established, Judge Barksdale being a representative member of the Baptist denomination in this county.

In the Land Office, Richmond, Va., we find one John Barksdale, subaltern of Continental line three years. He received a land grant for 666 2-3 acres issued to William Barksdale, his heir. This John Barksdale was dead in 1784. The Revolutionary War roster for Virginia gives Nathaniel Barksdale, (auditor's account), Peter, Joseph, John, Daniel, Claiborne and Samuel Barksdale. So we find them representative fighters as well as adjusters of the law. The family is extensive by virtue of intermarriage with many of the leading people of the county, and the kinship, though interesting, is difficult when it comes to connecting the various lines. *[A History of Halifax County, by Wirt Johnson Carrington; and History of Virginia, Vol. IV, 1924]*

Some Barksdale marriages in Halifax County, Virginia:

Armistead Barksdale and Judith Sydner, 1805.

Beverly Barksdale and Judy Womack, 1801.

Claiborne W. Barksdale and E. W. Whitlock, 14 Dec. 1831.

Cornelia Barksdale and John Quarles, 30 Aug. 1830.

Elisha Barksdale and Judith A. Barksdale, 22 Oct. 1835.

Frances Barksdale and William M. Williams, 28 March 1809.

J. H. Barksdale (husband) and Wilmouth M. Irby, 23 Nov. 1841.

John Barksdale and Anne P. Green, 1805.

John Barksdale and Hannah C. Watkins, 28 Feb. 1832.

John L. Barksdale and Obedience Owen, 17 June 1844.

Nathaniel Barksdale and Patsey Hurt, 1805 (by Rev. Robert Hurt).

Martha Ann Barksdale and James S. Lovelace, 22 Nov. 1849.

Martha W. Barksdale and John H. Caldwell, 16 May 1838.

Mary A. Barksdale and Robert Easley, 24 Feb. 1836.

Mary Barksdale and David Johnson, 3 Jan. 1782.

Peter Barkesdale and E. Watlington, 11 Jan. 1781.

Polly Barksdale and John Logan, 27 Dec. 1809.

S. T. Barksdale (wife) and Armsted M. Lacy, 25 July 1843.

Susannah Barksdale and Thomas Thweatt, 15 Nov. 1792.

Thomas E. Barksdale and Sallie E. Edmunds, 1 May 1850.

BAYNHAM family has a good deal of romance in their history. John Baynham, Sr., Duke of Baynham, married at Inverness, Scotland, in 1780, Elizabeth Eggleston (sister of the Earl of Eggleston). He was condemned to death for his radical religious and political views, but escaped and came to America on a sailing boat and landed at Old Point Comfort, Virginia.

Dr. C. W. Baynham, of Fort Smith, Ark., wrote the following letter to his relative, Mrs. Mary Jordan Faulkner, wife of Garland Faulkner, of South Boston:

"My great-grandfather, John Baynham, came to this country about 1790 and settled in Virginia. About 1830, his three sons, Grief, John, Jr., and William, came west and settled in Missouri. My father was John, named for his grandfather.

"I have traced our family back to Mary Queen of Scots. Sir Walter Scott married Mary Baynham and wrote a poem on Baynham Castle (which you will find on reading his works, and I am sending you a picture of the castle).

"I will leave here April 30th and sail from New York May 4th on the S. S. Cedric for Liverpool. Am going to Scotland to establish my claims, etc., etc."

From Fort Smith, Ark., dispatch to the New York Herald, 1912: "Within a few months Fort Smith is to be the home of a real live duke, for the Duke of Baynham, of Scotland, will then take up his residence here.

"The duke-to-be is Dr. C. W. Baynham, of Fort Smith, who will leave in April for Glasgow, where he will receive his title and come into possession of the castle with its large estate upon the northeast coast of Scotland. The estate is situated between Inverness and Romarty on the Irish channel.

"The story of the inheritance of this estate by the Fort Smith physician is an interesting one. The estate has been unoccupied and supported by the government for many years. The great-great-grandfather of Dr. Baynham was the last Duke of Baynham. He, with his son and grandson, who was the father of Dr. Baynham, left Scotland in 1801 for America. The old Duke died at sea, but the others landed at Old Point Comfort, Virginia, April 18, 1801.

"In 1890, the father of Dr. Baynham, who was then living at Fairplay, Missouri, made an attempt to get the estate and title, which rightfully belonged to him by inheritance,

"He wrote to the Antiquarian Society of Salem, Mass., for the record of his family, and found that it could be traced back to Mary Queen of Scots, but was dumfounded to find that the record showed his father and grandfather had been beheaded.

"Knowing this part of the record to be false, the elder Baynham secured the affidavits of several who had come over on the same ship with them, showing that the old duke died at sea, but that others of the family landed in this country and were not beheaded. The Court of Royal Judges found that the claim was correct.

"The elder Baynham then prepared to go before the Secretary for Scotland to receive his title and property, but died before the date set for his appearance. Two months later his home was destroyed by fire and all the papers and other proofs of kinship were destroyed.

"Five years ago Dr. Baynham took up the matter where it had been left by his father, only to find that the court records of the time the father had sent in his claim had not been properly kept and he would have to furnish new proof of his rights. The papers of the elder Baynham being destroyed and all the men who had come from Scotland with him now dead, this was a difficult task, but with the assistance of a Scotch attorney he was enabled to gather such proof as the judges required, and his case has been favorably acted upon. Only the sanction of the Court of Royal Judges, which meets in April, remains to be obtained, and this has been promised."

Elizabeth Eggleston Baynham, born in Kyle, Scotland, married George Boxley, Jr., October 3, 1816. Mary Baynham Boxley married Reuben Fourqurean. She was born in Halifax County, November 7, 1818, and died April 15, 1868.

Reuben Fourqurean was born in Halifax County, February, 1812; married January 19, 1835; died May 25, 1851. Their daughter, Elizabeth Baynham Fourqurean, born October 17,1835; married Robert E. Jordan, Sr., born March 3, 1828. *[A History of Halifax County, by Wirt Johnson Carrington]*

Some Baynham marriages in Halifax County, Virginia:

Charles Baynham and Emily M. Morgan, 17 Aug. 1842.

E. E. T. W. Baynham and George Boxley, 3 Oct. 1816.

Elizabeth Baynham and Branch J. Drinkard, 4 Dec. 1833.

John Baynham and Salley Blackwell, 1 Jan. 1805.

Kezia Baynham and Ephraim Blane, 19 Jan. 1826.

Polly Baynham and John Holt, 4 March 1824.

William Baynham and N. Faulkner, 15 Oct. 1803.

BEAN family: In 1752 William Bean purchased land in the new county of Halifax. In 1753 William Bean was appointed with others to lay off a road "from William Bean's to the Court House." That seems to have been the last service William Bean performed for Halifax County, for we next find him in 1768-69 pushing on with the tide of emigration that settled on Boone's Creek in East Tennessee, where his wife was captured by the Indians, but subsequently released through the interposition of Nancy Ward, the beloved woman of the Indian tribe and the friend of the white man. His son, Russell Bean, was the first white child born in Tennessee.

BELT family: When Humphrey Belt came from Scotland to Maryland, where he received a patent of land of several hundred acres on June 30, 1663, in right of himself, John, Sarah and Ann Belt, he brought his "Seal" with him. He had three sons, Joseph, John and Benjamin.

The Belts of Maryland married the daughters of the most distinguished Colonial officials of their generation. Colonel Joseph Belt, to whom the fine old estate of Chevy Chase was patented in the year 1722, married twice, his first wife being Esther, daughter of Col. Ninnian Beale, that grand old Indian fighter from the Highlands of Scotland.

While the Belts were proud of their Scotch origin and did largely intermarry with those of their same ilk, where love was concerned the question of nationality did not count with them; hence it is not surprising to find Anne Belt, the wife of Basil Brashears, a descendant of the early Huguenot refugee of 1658.

Some of the descendants of John and Benjamin Belt came to the Eastern Shore of Virginia from Maryland and meandered this way until they reached Pittsylvania and Halifax Counties, where we find our Dr. Humphrey Singleton Belt, of South Boston, Virginia.

Dr. Humphrey S. Belt, son of Humphrey S. Belt, and his wife, Mollie Angeline Daniel, was born in Pittsylvania County March 1, 1869, and was educated at the Pittsylvania High School, the University of Virginia and the University of Maryland. He graduated in the medical profession and began its practice in 1891; and in 1893, November 14th, he settled in South Boston, where his success as surgeon and physician steadily increased.

On December 19, 1894, he married Annie, daughter of Colonel Henry and Nannie Preston (Owen) Easley, of South Boston, by whom he had two sons, Henry Belt and Humphrey Singleton Belt, Jr.

Dr. Belt began the practice of his profession in moderate circumstances and has earned through hard labor the substantial position he holds in the community and the warm place he will ever hold in the hearts of all who know him. Nevertheless, the masses did not fully realize what a blessing they had in his services and in the Halcyon Hospital, which he established in South Boston in 1910.

Patients coming to him from all sections, he early recognized the need of a place to minister to them, and while the enterprise was expensive and unparalleled for such a small town, he had no lack of faith and pushed the work to completion as rapidly as possible to meet the demands of those then waiting to come in. And so it has progressed, most of the time filled to its capacity, never without patients; and some of the most difficult and wonderful operations have been performed by Dr. Belt there.

Few laymen can understand the amount of money, the constant struggle, the wear and tear on body and mind it takes to keep a comparatively small hospital in good running order, to employ in it first-class nurses, etc.; but that is what has been accomplished in the Halcyon Hospital. The faithful and unfailing service of Miss Virginia C. Duncan, the superintendent, and her efficient corps of nurses make the Halcyon Hospital a solid success and a comfort to all who enter its doors.

In connection with it is the nurses' home, a large commodious building adjoining the hospital, where the nurses have really a comfortable home in which to rest.

Then there is the hospital farm of six hundred acres, two hundred and seventy-five acres under cultivation, furnishing all that is needed at the hospital and the home of Dr. Belt in the way of vegetables, fruits, fowls and other meats, butter, cream and plenty of rich milk.

Wile Dr. Belt finds pleasure and rest in visiting the farm and overlooking it, the real work is managed by Mr. E. A. Onsrud, a man of Norwegian ancestry, whose clear-cut features bear the impress of integrity and fidelity, just what is necessary in his position. Besides the well equipped dwelling house on the farm, there is a private bungalow built for rest and recreation, for the doctor and his friends when they have the opportunity to avail themselves of it.

The young people have enjoyed some pleasant dances in the hall of the bungalow, which means a good deal in the lives of the younger set when it comes to terpsichorean relaxation. *[A History of Halifax County, by Wirt Johnson Carrington, 1924]*

BENNETT family: In Halifax County will book 1, on 5 October, 1781, is the will of Robert Bennett:

"I leave to my beloved wife, Anne Bennett, all and every part of my whole estate during her widowhood, if that continues her life. At the expiration of widowhood all estate to be divided between my children, to-wit: John,

Stephen, Mary, Nancy Bennett. My wife being now with child, that child to share equal with the other children in my estate.

"Executors and executrix: Thomas Dobson, Moses Hendrick, 'my wife, Anne Bennett.'

(Signed) Robert (X) Bennett."

Witnesses: James Hendricks, Joshua Irby, John Irby.

In Halifax County will book 14, is the will of Richard E. Bennett, 9 February, 1827:

"I, Richard E. Bennett, County of Halifax, &c. All of my debts to be paid which can speedily be done by collecting debts due me, and a crop of tobacco now on hand. My mercantile business to be continued in the names of my executors for the benefit of my estate, and that my son, John Bennett, shall continue in the business to assist in the management thereof until he arrives to the age of 21 years, immediately after which an inventory of the stock of goods on hand shall be taken, and he, my son, John, to come in as a partner, if he thinks proper to do so, &c., until my youngest son, William Waller Bennett, arrives to lawful age. I desire the same privileges given by executors to my sons, Richard E. Bennett and Theoderick A. Bennett, each as they arrive at age. I wish all my sons Richard, Theoderick and William, with all my children to live with their mother, and in common upon my estate, so far as their support and education is concerned, until they marry or arrive to lawfnl age.

"I wish Mary W. Bennett to be educated as well as her sisters have been, and Richard E. Bennett, after he has been one or two years more at school, to live with his mother and manage the affairs of the plantation, for which she may allow him a reasonable compensation.

"I wish my son, Theoderick, to study law and my son, William Waller Bennett, to study physics, and have my books or such of them as treat on law or physics equally divided between them.

"I give to my daughter, Eliza Ann Bennett, one negro woman, &c., to be delivered to her when she marries or becomes of lawful age.

"To my daughter, Ann E. Bennett, same as above.

"To my daughter, Mary W. Bennett, same as above.

"To my seven children, John, Theoderick, Richard, William, Elizabeth, Ann, Mary.

"Executrix, my wife, Ann; executors, my son, John Bennett, and my friend, Samuel Williams.

(Signed) "Richard E. Bennett,"

Securities: Elisha Botts, Phil. Howerton, James Howerton, Jonathan McCarys, Edward Carrington, Alex Irvine.

BLACKWELL family: Thomas Blackwell came to Halifax County in 1780. The Blackwells emigrated from England and were prominent in Northumberland County as early as 1680. Many of them were soldiers in the Revolution, the Civil War and the War of 1812.

Some Blackwell marriages in Halifax County, Virginia:

Anne Blackwell and Andrew Torian, 29 March 1785.

James Blackwell and Elizabeth McCarty, 9 Oct. 1799.

James L. Blackwell and Lucy H. Betts, 24 Jan. 1811.

James Blackwell and Betsy E. Cole, 19 Jan. 1812.

Louisa W. Blackwell and Richard H. Webb, 21 Dec. 1843.

M. Blackwell and Samuel B. Mood, 13 Oct. 1841.

M. F. Blackwell and Robert Oliver, 12 Jan. 1841.

Martha Blackwell and John Nelson, 17 Aug. 1826.

Moses Blackwell and Sucky Wall, 2 Jan. 1786.

N. Blackwell and Ephraim Guthrey, 22 Dec. 1809.

Robert Blackwell and Charrety Stone, 19 Oct. 1799.

Salley Blackwell and John Baynham, 1 Jan. 1805.

Sally Blackwell and William Link, 23 Feb. 1808.

Susan Blackwell and James T. Jones, 1 March 1833.

William Blackwell and Mary McCarty, 14 July 1787.

William Blackwell and Martha Nelson, 24 July 1823.

BOOKER family is one of the earliest on the records of Halifax County. In 1759, December 7th, there is recorded an indenture between Edward Booker and William Cook, both of Halifax County. The names of those who signed this indenture were Mary Booker, Edward Booker and William Cook.

26 July 1760: Edward Booker buys from Joseph Laws, 200 acres of land on north side of Banister River.

31 December 1760: John Bates sells to Edward Booker, for five hundred and fifty pounds, 261 acres in Halifax County lying on Staunton River, in separate patents, 129 acres on the river low-grounds, bearing the date August 20, 1741, and the remainder being adjacent to high land, held by patent bearing the date June 6, 1753. Witnesses: Jas. Murdock, Parham Booker and Thos. McMahan.

10 September 1767: Will of Edward Booker. "I, Edward Booker, of the County of Halifax, make this my last will and testament in manner following: "I leave and bequeath to my wife, Henerica Booker, one negro fellow named Joe during her life, and likewise an equal part of my estate after the legacies are paid."

"Daughters, Eliza and Rebecca; son (name not mentioned), land and negroes.

"My brother, John Booker."

Wife, Henerica, executrix, and Colonels Thomas Tabb (of Amelia County), Joshua Morris and James Bates, executors. Witnesses: Richard Booker, Parham Booker and James Murdoch. Robert Munford, Clerk. He is called Edward Booker, Gent. Thomas Tabb could not act as administrator, Paul Carrington and Peter Johnston, Gents., took oath and served as securities. Later records state Richard Edward Booker, Rebecca Booker, and Elizabeth Mary Anne Booker as orphans of Edward Booker, decd.

25 April 1781: Will of Parham Booker. Sons, Richard and James; daughter, Susannah. Beloved wife, Frances, executrix, and James McCraw, Sr., executor. Recorded September 21, 1786. Securities: William Oliver, Gilbert Hunt, Jacob Kilby.

14 June 1783: William Hunt, of Charlotte County, sells to John Booker, of Lunenburg County, 145 acres on the south side of Staunton River.

25 December 1786: Pinkethman Davis Booker, of Amelia County, sells to Shields Booker, of Halifax County, 370 acres on Difficult Creek, south side. Witnesses: William Pride, William Hawkins, John Booker, Thomas Booker, Susannah Booker and Mary Pride.

20 April 1787: William Townes, of Halifax County, sells to Richard Booker, of Amelia County, 350 acres on Staunton River.

11 August 1785: Jos. Scott and Elizabeth, his wife, sell to Richard Edward Booker, for 140 pounds, lands on south side of Stanton River, called and known as "Booker's Ferry," 210 acres adjoining the said river, and the lands of Richard E. Booker and Thomas Youille. Received money at the hands of his guardian, Benjamin Lankford.

1800, January Court: Indenture between Benjamin Lankford and Henrietta, his wife, late widow and relict of Edward Booker, of Halifax County, Jos. Scott and Elizabeth, his wife, daughter and legatee of the said Edward

Booker, William DeJarnette and Rebecca, his wife, daughter and legatee of the said Edward Booker, and Richard Edward Booker, son and heir-at-law of the said Edward Booker, of the one part, and Sarah Yuille and Thomas Yuille, of the county of Halifax, of the other part.

"Whereas, Edward Booker aforesaid did by his last will and testament, direct that a certain parcel of land be sold to pay his debts, and appointed his wife, the aforesaid Henrietta, his executrix, and Thomas Tabb and others his executors, all of whom declined to execute his will and administer on his estate."

An administration on the estate with the will annexed was granted to John Esdale, a creditor, by the court, from which he got the power to sell, with the consent of the children, and secure his debt. The land was sold and Thos. Yuille bought it at 517 pounds. He kept it until his death, and devised it to his wife, Sarah, for her lifetime, and then to his son, Thomas Yuille, Jr., and if no heirs, to his brother George Yuille, of Dartmouth, in North Britain, and the said Benjamin Lankford and his wife, and the said daughters and son of the said Edward Booker, many years since of lawful age, and willing to convey and confirm to Sarah and Thomas Yuille, Jr., the land.

Benjamin Lankford and his wife, Henrietta, of Pittsylvania County; Joseph Scott and his wife, Elizabeth, of Campbell County; William Dixon and his wife, of Pittsylvania County, and Richard Edward Booker and his wife, Elizabeth, of Halifax County, for 571 pounds, accounted for by John Esdale, in his administration account, and applied to payments of Edward Booker's debts, and the payment of one Spanish milled dollar, in hand paid by Sarah and Thomas Yuille, Jr., acknowledged, satisfied, etc., etc.

Witnesses: Achilles Allen, L. B. Allen, Isaac Hill, John Gilfoy, Gross Scruggs, Priscilla Craddock, Kittie Lankford, Stephen Lanford, Robert Moore, William Robertson, Charles Winfree, Robert Bumpass, John Norton, James DeJarnette and William Royall.

23 January 1802: James Booker, son of Parham Booker, gives mortgage, on Negroes, for debt he owes Williamson Price, of Charlotte County. The indebtedness not being satisfied, he sells to Price all of that tract of land on south side of Stanton River, in Halifax County—it being the land devised from Parham Booker to James Booker, beginning at the River Stanton up the Richard Booker's line to Miller's line.

17 October 1802: James Booker and Susannah sell to Williamson Price a parcel of land on Staunton River opposite Scott's Landing. Susannah Booker relinquishes her dower right.

1802, December Court: Whereas the Commonwealth of Virginia. To James DeJarnette, William Jennings and William Royall, gentlemen, Justices of the County of Halifax, Greeting; Whereas Richard Booker and Ridley Booker, his wife, by their certain indenture of bargain and sale, bearing date 16th day of June, 1802, sold and conveyed to Williamson Price 471 acres of land in the County of Halifax, and whereas the said Ridley cannot conveniently travel to our court, of ye said county, to make acknowledgments of, &c. Jas. DeJarnette and William Jennings wait upon her and she relinquishes her dower right.

20 November 1797: This indenture between John Booker, William Marshall Booker and Elizabeth Booker, his wife, of Amelia County, of one part, and Patrick Henry, of Charlotte County, of the other. Whereas, William Claiborne and Susannah Taylor, executors, &c., of William Taylor, deceased, lately in the high court of chancery recovered a large sum of money against the said John and William M. Booker to the amount of 500 pounds, more or less as their part of the portion given by their father, Richard Booker, deceased, to his daughter, Annie, their sister, who intermarried with the said Taylor, and by means whereof the said portion with its accumulated interests and costs have been lately recovered against them and other legatees and devisees of the said Richard Booker, deceased, and the said John and William M. Booker being desirous to discharge the said judgment against them, have agreed by writing under their hands to sell to the said Patrick Henry a tract of land called the Seven Islands, at the price of five hundred pounds, on the south side of Staunton River. Resigned all title and claims under the will of their father, the said Richard Booker, deceased, or under the will of their brother, Edward Booker, deceased. Witnesses: Jas. Townes, Jr., Jno. Roberts, Edward Roberts, Edward T. Townes, James Booker, Thos. Worsham, and John Pride.

Some Booker marriages in Halifax County, Virginia:

Henrica Booker, widow, and B. Lankford, 10 Jan. 1771.

Parham Booker and Frances Martin, 4 April 1770.

Patsey Booker and William Wall, 20 Sept. 1792.

Richard E. Booker and Elizabeth Moore, 6 Oct. 1788.

Richard M. Booker and E. Palmer, 2 Nov. 1770.

Shields Booker and Ann Pride, 15 Dec. 1785.

Susanna Booker and Williamson Price, 31 May 1786.

Thomas Booker and Fanny Terrell, 25 Dec. 1795.

BORUM family: In 1763, July 19--William Borum and his wife, Frances, appears on the records, sells land to William Shackleford, and in 1771 sells land to Roger Atkinson (of Dinwiddie county).

1775--William Borum buys land, or establishes his right to it, through William Byrd, and his attorney, Robert Munford. For 16 shillings he bought the land from Robert Wade, and Wade died without signing or making the title legal, for one thousand and forty acres in Halifax County, with all the rights and titles. The witnesses: Thomas Twitty, Reuben Morgan, John McKie, Christopher Watson, Henry Clift and John Whit.

In 1779, William Borroum and Fanny, his wife, of Halifax County, sell to Willia Collier, of Halifax, and George Isbel, of Caroline County.

1810, August 27--Judith Borum, of Highland County, Ohio, sells land in Halifax County, on Pole Cat Creek, to John Hughes. Witnesses: Beverly Hughes, Obed Hendricks and Thomas Burgess (Quakers).

1794 (Halifax Court records)--"John Borum manumitted his slaves."

1814, November 3--Obed Heridricks, administrator for John Borum, deceased, and attorney in fact for Sarah Borum.

1813, June--Indenture between Obed A. Borum for himself and attorney in fact for his sister, Catherine B. Borum, of the County of Highland, Ohio, sells their land on Pole Cat Creek.

Some Borum marriages in Halifax County, Virginia:

Beverly Borum, Jr., and Martha C. Tucker, 12 Jan. 1828.

Elvira H. Borum and Thomas J. Green, 18 Dec. 1851.

George Borum and Peggy Murphy, 4 Feb. 1783.

George R. Borum and Parmelia A. Jennett, 28 Oct. 1829.

John Borum and Judith Hendrick, 17 Jan. 1788.

Martha W. Borum and James H. Edmundson, 22 Dec. 1853.

Susan Borum and Johnston Daniel, 12 Jan. 1819.

BOSTICK family: 1781, November 26--Halifax County--Will of Charles Bostick. Wife, Betty; sons, William, John, Moses and Absolom; daughters, Ann, Elizabeth and Mary. Witnesses: Thomas Yuille, Roger Scott, John Scott, John Adams and Archie Robinson.

Some Bostick marriages in Halifax County, Virginia:

Absalom Bostick and Bethenia Perkins, 22 June 1762.

Absalom Bostick and Mary Petty, 30 Aug. 1788.

Absolom Bostick and Margaret W. Roberts, 20 Dec. 1832.

Absolom Bostick and Martha M. Carter, 1 Jan. 1850.

Obediah Bostick and Nancy Colquitt, 27 June 1787.

Richard Bostick and Anne Link, 20 Jan. 1798.

BOXLEY: Will of Benjamin Boxley, Sr., 4 January 1809, Halifax County:

"I, Benjamin Boxley, Halifax County, Virginia, planter.

"My son, Joseph Spiller Boxley, son Harrison Boxley, land which he sold to William Faulkner.

"My son, George Boxley, my son, Benjamin Boxley, Jr., the land I purchased of James Palmer (the tract whereon I now live, Blue Wing Creek), on Boyd Pinson's line; my daughter, Mary Wade, land on Willis' Creek; daughters, Wilmoth Boxley and Lucy Boxley.

"I lend to my beloved wife, Tabitha Boxley, &c.

"Benjamin Boxley."

Executors: Joseph Spiller Boxley and George Boxley. Witnesses: Jacob Faulkner, Joseph Griffin, Thomas McCarler, John Goode, Elizabeth Goode, Martha Willis.

Some Boxley marriages in Halifax County, Virginia:

Benajmin Boxley and Tabitha Irby, 22 Nov. 1769.

Eliza E. Boxley and William F. Fourqurean, 24 Aug. 1837.

George Boxley and E. E. T. W. Baynham, 3 Oct. 1816.

Harrison Boxley and N. Haynes, 7 May 1799.

John Boxley and Elmira T. Young, 5 Dec. 1833.

Joseph Boxley and Susannah Boyd, 28 March 1799.

Joseph Boxley and N. Blane, 28 Dec. 1825.

Mary B. Boxley and Reuben D. Fourqurean, 10 Jan. 1835.

M. J. Boxley (wife) and Claiborne Whitlow, Oct. 1851.

Polly Boxley and Allen Wade, 13 March 1794.

S. Boxley (wife) and Benj. B. Wade, 29 Dec 1825.

Thomas Boxley and Elizabeth Boxley, 26 Jan. 1820.

William Boxley and Elizabeth Bennett, 18 June 1799.

William Boxley and Jane S. Jones, 31 May 1827.

BOYD family were early settlers in Halifax, and there were several families apparently not related.

John Boyd, of Lunenburg County, left a will dated July 2, 1748; wife, Margaret; sons, John, James, George and William.

On January 1, 1759, John Armstrong marries Margaret Boyd (widow), and a license for the marriage of Mary Boyd (daughter of Margaret) was issued as follows:

"I, Robert Munford, clerk of Halifax County Court, do hereby certify that sufficient security has been given in my office for a license to issue for the marriage of Micajah Watkins with Mary Boyd, this 12th day of January, 1764.

"These are to license and permit you to join together in the holy state of matrimony Micajah Watkins and Mary Boyd, according to rights and ceremonies of the Church of England, and for so doing this shall be your warrant. Given under my hand and seal this 11 of October, 1764. To the Rev. Mr. Alexander Gordon, minister of Antrim Parish, or any other authorized minister of the Church of England."

"I do hereby certify that my daughter, Mary Boyd, who is not registered, is of full age, and I have no objection to her being married to Micajah Watkins.

"Given under my hand and seal this 12th day of December, 1764."

X (her mark)

Witnesses: George Boyd, Jr., Isabel Wade and John Sullins

Marriage Bond: Know ye all men by these presents that we, Micajah Watkins and John Armstrong, of the County of Halifax, are held and firmly bound unto Our Sovereign, King George III, in the sum of fifty pounds, current money, of Virginia, to be paid to our said Lord the King, his heirs and successors, to which payment will, and truly to be made, to our said Lord the King his heirs and successors, we bind ourselves, our heirs and executors and administrators by by these presents sealed with our seals and dated this 11 day of December, 1764.

Whereas there is a marriage depending, and by God's permission is suddenly intended and itemized between the above bound Micajah Watkins and Mary

Boyd, of the county aforesaid. Now the conditions of the above obligation is such that if there is no lawful cause to obstruct the said marriage, then the above obligations to be void, otherwise to remain in full force and virtue.

Sealed and delivered in the presence of the jury.

(Signed)   Micajah Watkins   (Seal)

John Armstrong   (Seal)

This Micajah Watkins had a son, Micajah Watkins, Jr., who married Sarah Williams. Their married life was very transient, for he died just before the birth of their only daughter, Mourning Watkins.

Micajah Watkins, Sr., with Nathaniel Terry, was a member of the Convention of 1776 from Halifax County, and also a member of the last House of Burgesses that enacted anything, June, 1775. [*Virginia Historical Magazine.*]

1762, January 26--Nuncupative will of George Boyd. Wife, Ann; sons, Richard and Henry, not yet of age.

1803, January 9--Will of George Boyd, Sr.; wife, Amey; daughter, Mary Wade.

[A History of Halifax County, by Wirt Johnson Carrington, 1924]

BRANDON family: 16 March 1769, Halifax County, Will of David Brandon. Wife, Rebecca; sons, William and Thomas; daughters, Elizabeth, Margaret, Mary and Agnes, children all under age and to be educated. Executors: John Lawson and William Edwards. Witnesses: William Brandon, Frances B. Brandon and John Brandon.

Some Brandon marriages in Halifax County, Virginia:

Agnes Brandon and Abner Rodden, 1791.

Agnes Brandon and Joseph Pulliam, 4 Jan. 1798.

Amy Brandon and Henry Stimson, __ Dec. 1822.

Ann Brandon and Thos. Crawley, 24 Dec. 1806.

Ann Brandon and James W. Featherston, 22 Dec. 1831.

Catherine Brandon and James Stuart Warren, 12 Feb. 1795.

Catherine Brandon and Richard Carter, 19 July 1822.

David Brandon and Catherine Irvine, 17 May 1785.

Eliza Brandon and Joel A. Kirby, 9 Jan. 1821.

Francis S. Brandon and Eliza Stanfield, __ Aug. 1822.

Green Brandon and Ann Scott, 14 April 1836.

Irvine Brandon and Mary Lawson, 27 Dec. 1810.

M. Brandon (wife) and Mordica Burgess, 25 Oct. 1790.

Martha Brandon and Jas. Chambers, 7 Jan. 1821.

N. D. Brandon (wife) and J. B. Scott (husband), 22 Dec. 1836.

Robert Brandon and Jane Holt, 17 Jan. 1811.

Sarah Brandon and Thomas Stimson, __ Jan. 1822.

T. Brandon (husband) and M. Brandon, 28 Nov. 1835.

Tabitha Brandon and David Irvine, 14 Sept. 1826.

Thomas Brandon and Margaret Irvine, 19 Feb. 1782.

Thomas Brandon and Agnes Warren, 28 May 1789.

Thomas Brandon and Betsy Lawson, 9 Nov. 1797.

William Brandon and Hannah Thomas, 1805.

William A. Brandon and Mary A. Brandon, 27 March 1851.

BRUCE family: Charles Bruce resided at "Soldiers' Rest," Orange County, Virginia. The farm was a large and valuable one. It was situated near Kelly's Ford, on the Rapidan, a spot well known in the history of the War Between the States. The dwelling was built before the Revolution, and in its time was looked upon as a fine establishment. It was a quaint colonial mansion, with its long sloping roof, narrow porch, and tall chimneys at either end. The nails used in its construction were made by hand of wrought iron, probably in a shop on the estate by one of the owner's smiths.

An account of Charles Bruce, of "Soldiers' Rest," by a contemporary represents him as "physically under the average with a fair complexion, sandy hair, blue eyes, and a constitution of durable fibre. He was a man of great vigor of intellect and of controlling influence in his neighborhood and county, but without any political ambition." The name of his residence suggests military tastes, and it is not surprising to find that he was an officer (captain) in the Revolution, and for his services received a grant of land (Records, Register's Office, Richmond, Virginia).

Among the soldiers enlisting at Winchester, Va., in 1754, for the great French and Indian War was a Charles Bruce, who was about the age of Charles Bruce, of "Soldiers' Rest," at that time. He was enrolled as a native of Scotland. It is possible that this was Charles Bruce, of "Soldiers' Rest," who may have come over with his father, James Bruce, the emigrant, from Scotland. Charles of "Soldiers' Rest" died in 1792. Among the items of his personal property were forty-seven slaves, a considerable holding at that time, and about two hundred head of live stock. The value of the personalty was 1,735 pounds. A careful examination of the records of Culpeper, Orange and Spotsylvania Counties will give additional information as to this Charles Bruce and his father, James, the emigrant. Of the children of Charles (2), Thomas, William and Henry may have died young, as nothing is known of them. Charles (3), the third son, removed to Halifax County, Virginia, and resided at "Tarover," a house which he built on the model of "Soldiers' Rest." He died unmarried, leaving a handsome fortune. Elizabeth, the only daughter of Charles Bruce, of "Soldiers' Rest," married James Williams, a captain in the Continental army and a major general in the War of 1812.

James Bruce (3), the eldest son of Charles (2), of "Soldiers' Rest," would have inherited the "Soldiers' Rest" estate, but early in life developed a taste for mercantile pursuits. Having received an ordinary school education, he secured at the age of sixteen a situation at Petersburg, Va., with Mr. Colquhoun, who carried on an extensive business in buying tobacco from the planters and selling them goods which he had imported from England. James by his industrious habits, honest character and capacity for business soon won the confidence of his employer, to such an extent that he was sent to establish a branch house in Amelia County. In this he became a partner. In a few years, finding that the more remote county of Halifax offered greater business advantages, he removed there and made it his permanent home during the rest of his life.

By a system of country stores, which supplied the wants of the planters, and by judicious purchases of land and tobacco, he accumulated one of the largest fortunes of his day. At his death his estate was valued at over fifteen hundred thousand dollars, probably the greatest in the United States at that time after those of John Jacob Astor and Stephen Gerard, who had a much wider and more profitable field in which to work. On at least one occasion in a public speech, Mr. Randolph classed Mr. Bruce with these two famous merchants. At the beginning of the war his estate was valued at nearly four million of dollars. It included in one item over three thousand slaves.

The only glimpse we have of James Bruce in early life is to be had through a diary kept during the latter part of the eighteenth century by the father or grandfather of Major Richard Venable. The writer of this diary states that he spent a night under the same roof with James Bruce and Archibald Alexander —afterwards president of Princeton College—both very young men at the time. The impression which they made on Mr. Venable by these few hours of intercourse was such that he prophesies that they will each attain unusual prominence before many years shall have passed.

Mr. Bruce was not simply successful from a pecuniary point of view in his own part of Virginia; indeed, wherever he was known, his name was a synonym for integrity and liberality. A letter from a distinguished contemporary, who was well able to judge, pronounces him to have been "the justest and most honorable man" the writer ever knew. Added to this, he had a temper of such serenity that no one ever saw it ruffled.

Soon after settling in Halifax County, James Bruce married, August 1, 1799, Miss Sally Coles, daughter of Walter Coles, of the well-known Coles family of Virginia. The ceremony took place at "Mildendo," the home of Miss Coles' guardian, near Coles' Ferry on Staunton River. The marriage was hastily celebrated in order to gratify the last wish of the bride's only near living relative, a brother, who was then dying. Mr. Bruce's second wife, who was then a widow, Mrs. Patrick Henry, Jr., happened to be present, and the ring used during the ceremony was taken from her finger.

Sally (Coles) Bruce died May 21, 1806, and on April 20, 1819, Mr. Bruce married Elvira Cabell, daughter of William Cabell, of "Union Hill," Nelson County, Va., and widow of Patrick Henry, Jr., who died only a few months after their marriage. The only child of this marriage was Elvira Henry, afterwards Mrs. William H. Clark, of "Banister Lodge," in Halifax County.

The second Mrs. James Bruce was a woman of unusual intelligence and charm of manner. Her conversation was especially remarkable for quaint humor. In appearance she strongly resembled the Cabells—black hair, large dark eyes, swarthy complexion and aquiline nose, a notable representative of a family long distinguished for beauty and talent. After her marriage she and Mr. Bruce resided for many years at "Woodburn," near Halifax Court House. The house was destroyed by fire after the war. James Bruce died in Philadelphia, May 12, 1837, where he had gone for his health, and was buried in the yard of St. Andrew's Church.

After his death his widow removed to Richmond, where she built the house which was later the central part of the University College of Medicine. In its time it was one of the finest residences in the city, and noted for its charming and generous hospitality. Mrs. Bruce was a woman of strong and unaffected piety. She gave liberally to charity, both public and private, and was one of the largest contributors to the fund raised for the erection of St. Paul's Church in Richmond, where she worshiped until her death.

What was known in the Episcopal Church of Virginia as the "Bruce Fund" was a sum which her children gave in accordance with a desire which she frequently expressed but which on account of her extreme sickness she had no opportunity of leaving to the church in the form of a legal bequest. She died in October, 1859, and was buried in Hollywood.

The children of James (2) and Sally (Coles) Bruce were James Coles (4) Bruce, Charles (4) and Mildred (4). The last two died in infancy. James Coles Bruce (4) was born January 26, 1806. He received his education at Chapel Hill and Harvard Colleges and the University of Virginia. In early life he was elected a member of the General Assembly which came within a few votes, three by the record, one by tradition, probably at a secret session not recorded, of abolishing slavery in Virginia. This was shortly after the Turner insurrection (1831), which had raised a great commotion.

Not long before he died Mr. Bruce expressed much regret that he had voted for the perpetuation of slavery. In after life he favored gradual emancipation, though one of the largest slave-holders in the South. In an address delivered at Danville, which attracted general attention at the time, he took an advanced position on the subject. He declared that the greatest harm of slavery was to the white people, and that it "cheated the planters with a semblance of wealth." There is an extended reference to this address in a note to "Howerson's History of Virginia."

Mr. Bruce was a Whig in politics, and as that party was in the minority in Virginia, and he himself without political ambition, and owing to his great wealth, without strong motive for exertion, he never sought high office, though a finished public speaker, and a man whose extraordinary talents were generally recognized.

As the foremost citizen of his county and the Union candidate, he was elected a member of the Secession Convention. He was an active opponent of secession, but voted in favor of it when Lincoln called for troops. He was considered to be one of the ablest debaters in the convention.

Among the casual addresses of Mr. Bruce was one delivered before the students of Chapel Hill, N. C., at the commencement of 1841; another before the alumni of the University of Virginia. Both are marked by vigorous thought, brilliant expression and high literary finish. Mr. Bruce resided at "Berry Hill," Halifax County, Virginia, which had formerly been a part of the estate of the second William Byrd and afterwards of General Edward Carrington. The house which he erected was considered to be one of the finest models of the colonial style in the South, if not in the United States. Among the other valuable contents of the house was an extraordinary quantity of silver of the finest designs. Even the basins, pitchers, etc., of the sleeping rooms were made of this material. Here Mr. Bruce lived, like the lord of an English manor, in the midst of hundreds of slaves and adherents of all kinds— a sort of feudal chief on his great landed estate.

He died in 1865, just before the close of the war. He said on his death-bed that he "felt a grim satisfaction in leaving the world at that time, as he knew that nothing but ruin was in store for his class." Though originally a Union man, his contributions for the advancement of the cause of the Confederacy had amounted to at least fifty thousand dollars.

Few of the present inhabitants of Halifax County know when James Bruce, the richest and, judging from the records, one of the best and purest of men, settled in this county. He left a most remarkable will, which is recorded at the court house. He died in Philadelphia, whither he had gone for his health. He was reputed to be the largest slave-holder in Virginia and one of the richest men in America at that period.

Will of James Bruce:

No man that lived in Halifax County left a more carefully written will than James Bruce. It evinced a broad mind, a generous heart and a wonderful spirit of humility for a man with such an extensive estate. He gives to James C. Bruce, his son, besides other large endowments, "a tract of land in Halifax County called 'Boyd's Tract,' now tenanted by John Juniel—the same tract of land I hold as heir to my brother, Charles, who owned, I think, a good equitable title under George Carrington, who purchased it from Archie Boyd, the title of the same being warranted by the said George Carrington, John Carrington and Paul Carrington, deceased, by a bond made for that purpose. The said James C. must look for the title, with all the powers that I am invested being hereby invested in him."

"I give to my son, Charles Bruce, a tract of land purchased through Gerard Banks, Jr., and Co., who purchased through William M. Irby and wife, and James Smith, the trustee of said Irby; also my lots and improvements, in the town of Banister, near Halifax Court House; also my store and lott, and every of the appertencies, adjoining Halifax Court House lott. One lumber house in the town of Lynchburg purchased of Charles Johnston and lying on Blackwater, adjoining the Cotton Factory."

He leaves to his friends, James Atkisson, William Penick and James S. Easley, five hundred dollars each. "James C. Bruce shall continue to act as guardian for all of my said infant children unless the said act shall be too oppressively inconvenient to him, in that event he must use his efforts to ordain some reputable and responsible and friendly person or persons to aid him in guardianship, who will, of course, give bond and security under the direction of the court.

"I do hereby appoint and constitute my very dear son, Jas. C. Bruce, Executor of my last Will and Testament, without giving any sort of security, as I have decided confidence in him, and owe but little comparatively.

"James Bruce."

Witnesses: William Penick, Jas. Atkisson and Thomas J. Green. September 28, 1836.

This will of James Bruce filled several pages, and is a most comprehensive and interesting one, especially when we know that he went to work as a mere youth and by honest work made the third largest fortune in the United States at that period. He bought from Colonel Edward Carrington the tract of land upon which "Berry Hill" was afterwards built by his son, James C. Bruce.

There is a tradition that "Berry Hill" was built after the style and architecture of "Montpelia," Lord George Keeling's seat in Granville, now Vance County, North Carolina, which Lord Keeling had copied after his country seat in Ireland, which he had to leave on account of religious persecution.

Mr. Philip Alexander Bruce, of the University of Virginia, states in a letter the following in regard to "Berry Hill": "The 'Berry Hill' estate was purchased by my uncle, James Coles Bruce, about 1830 from Colonel Edward Carrington. The 'Berry Hill' house was built by my uncle, James Coles Bruce, after his purchase." And in regard to it he adds: "I was told by Professor Fiske Kimball, of the school of architecture at the University of Virginia, that this house is the most remarkable specimen of its kind to be found in the South. Colonel Carrington's residence, a plain one, stood on the same site and was pulled down."

Judge Paul Carrington and his wife are buried in the graveyard at Berry Hill.

James Bruce was a character that no thoughtful person will pass by without taking into consideration the manner of his life and his excellent advice to those who sought it. If one will go carefully through his several volumes of letter books and read his character from the letters therein, it will be easy to understand how he grew to be the richest man in Halifax County and the third richest in the United States at that time. He was a sturdy Scotchman of the Kinloss Clan, and was honest in thought, word and deed. He was an extensive money lender and attended to every detail of his tremendous business with his personal advice and letters through his lawyers and agents, of whom he had many, tested and tried for ability and honesty. Through all his dealings with men, he never lost faith in humanity. Shrewd and close in business as he was, he was no Shylock, nor did he demand his dues, but by gentleness and persuasive measures he obtained what was his.

He was merciful, and when those who had served him had grown old and feeble, he ministered to their necessities so graciously they could not feel their dependence. He disliked above all things to have recourse to the law and never did if it was possible to avoid it. Being honest himself, it was hard for him to understand the long continued delinquencies of a debtor. He gave his honest opinion when his advice was sought, though it may not always have been agreeable to the party seeking it. He had many relatives who suffered losses through misfortune or adventure; he helped them all with financial gifts well seasoned with good advice.

Not one of his many letters give the slightest evidence of self-indulgence, pride, arrogance or display, and this sentiment in one of his letters illustrates the tender sympathy he had for a friend and relative who was in trouble: "They must know that a man under desperate circumstances with a large family has no chance to rise whilst embarrassed with debt, and the greater distance one takes under such circumstances from his friends in a wide world of strangers the worse his situation."

James C. Bruce left his plantation and home (the slaves having been emancipated) to his son, Mr. Alexander Bruce, the father of Mr. Walter Bruce, bachelor, and Mr. Malcolm Bruce, who had been twice married; his first wife was Miss Myrtle Heison, of Chicago, Illinois, by whom he had two daughters, Myrtle and Evelyn Bruce. He married secondly his cousin, Miss Bruce Williams, of Culpeper.

Miss Ellen Bruce, the last of the female line of Bruces at "Berry Hill," married Mr. Charles Crane, III, who after his return from his foreign ministry in Czechoslovakia, purchased "Westover," the celebrated home of the Byrds, where they resided when in Virginia. They had a daughter, Bruce Crane.

Excerpt from a Letter of Mr. James Bruce to Mr. Josiah Abbott,

"Halifax, June 2, 1828.

"Mr. Josiah Abbott.

"Dear Sir: I now send you annexed the names of persons distributors of Henry's estate—the Elder, whose names appear in the Clerk's office signing an address to codicil which consents to a final decree on the principle of the former interlocutory decree admitting the account of Winston's estate to stand as it appears from his account settled by commissioners, which is all he can ask, but if anything is required of him in a way of consent to a final decree you can advise what is necessary for him to say as to my claim in right of my wife, late Elvira A. Henry, who was the widow of Patrick Henry, Jr. I abandon all claim, my chief object being to secure a final decree in favor of her daughter, Elvira A. Henry, now Clark, as she has lately intermarried with William H. Clark, who, I suppose, must, of course, become a party to a final decree.

"Fayette Henry willed his whole estate to his mother, Dorothea Winston, late Henry, and Sarah Scott, late Sarah Campbell (her maiden name Henry, sister of Fayette Henry), who have divided the estate, I believe, in equal proportions and sold the land (the will of Fayette Henry is recorded in Campbell County).

"Edward Henry formerly married Kitty, who was a daughter of Patrick Henry, the elder, who died long since, and also Edward Henry, whose representative is suing the distributors of Patrick Henry, the elder, in the Chancery Court of Lynchburg for an alleged claim on them, a money legacy only.

"I have mentioned all the distributors of the last marriage of Patrick Henry, the elder, with the list balance included. As to others by the first marriage, I suppose they had claims of money legacies which have been probably satisfied. My chief object is to obtain distribution in favor of William H. Clark and Elvira A., late Henry, his wife, and to get out of court, if possible, being willing to abandon my claims as plaintiff in the suit.

"This list is made mainly to refresh your memory:

"James Bruce in right of his wife, late Elvira A. Henry.

"Elvira A. Henry, now Elvira A. Clark.

"John Henry.

"Sarah B. Scott, formerly Sarah B. Henry, in her own right and as distributor of Fayette Henry, deceased,

"Dorothy Winston in her own right and as distributor of Fayette Henry, deceased.

"Alexander S. Henry.

"Nathaniel Henry.

"George D. Winston in right of his wife, late Dorothy Henry.

"Edward Winston, executor of Edward Winston, deceased.

"James Bruce."

"November 14, 1828.

"To Mr. Henry Banks.

"Have this day ordered Mr. Maux & Sons to remit $150 to you in a bank check payable to your order, fifty dollars of which is remitted at the instance of your brother, William.

"You have said nothing in your letter the present year that would have a bearing the least unfavorable to General Jackson. In yours of February 4 last you expressed an inclination of returning to Richmond and residing with your niece, Miss Spottswood, and occasionally visiting your brother and myself. I approve of this resolution and would be pleased if you would withdraw yourself from the public journals, and meddling with elections, such doings though accompanied with the purest patriotism often involve sad results. Governor Giles, formerly a man of high estimation, has lowered his standing considerably by subscribing his name to a great deal of scandal and defamation against characters of high standing.

"Respectfully, James Bruce"

"Halifax, May 30, 1833.

"Mr. Henry E. Watkins.

"Dear Sir: At Clarksville four days since I was informed by Mr. Samuel S. Venable that you were disposed to borrow from me five thousand dollars if it should be convenient. I have to say in answer that I will accommodate you with pleasure, if you will make a bond and add a name merely for the sake of bank form, and made payable in two years, bearing interest, payable semi-annually, and send it to your friend in Richmond to be negotiated, where I shall be from the 25th to the 28th or probably longer, as I think of starting tomorrow and may go with my family from Charlotte C. H. in the stage, which may prevent my having the pleasure of calling on you. Intending to go to Norfolk and the northern cities I may be absent four or five weeks,

"I am with great regard and esteem,

      "Your most obedient servant,

                "James Bruce."

              "Halifax Co., Nov. 7, 1832.

"Messrs. Joseph Marx & Son.

"Gentlemen: Your much esteemed favor, &c. Your remarks on the valuableness of U. States bank-stock, the political effects, the cause of foreign demands for our stock, and the quotations of value of various stocks, and of produce in your market are all instructive, convenient and profitable to me. Our election terminated on Monday and three hundred votes were taken at the C. H. and about six were taken for Clay and Seargeant of that number, and the balance for Jackson for Vice-President and a few for Vanburan. Clay and Seargeant may probably get from the district some 20 or so more. In the election at Court House, Barber had a few scattering votes not worth mentioning.

"Notwithstanding my objection to General Jackson for his bank veto, and other considerations, yet I greatly prefer him to Mr. Clay, being most suitable to represent the Southern interest. Clay I think a great spendthrift of the public funds, in the way of protection for manufactories and public improvements, &c., &c. I fully expect we differ in opinion on this subject of the election, only for the same reason that men of the most honest convictions and the like interests often differ in sentiment on political subjects.

"I am with great regard and esteem,

      "Your most obedient servant,

"James Bruce."

Copy of Letter From William H. Clark to James Bruce.

"Halifax, Dec. 21, 1831.

"Dear James:

"I received a letter yesterday from Mr. John Henry, informing that a part of Long Island tract of land was advertised for sale under the Delinquent Land Act. I saw your father yesterday and consulted him about what was best to be done. He advised me to write to our Servant James and beg of him the favor to attend to this matter for us. Should the time of payment be first of January, 1832, the matter will admit of no delay, but I observe from the papers that the Legislature had taken up that subject and should the time be postponed I will get you to wait till you hear from me again. I should be very glad to see first the list of delinquent lands for Campbell, as it is probable that tract of land belonging to Cabell's estate purchased from Fayette Henry may be the lands advertised to be sold for delinquent taxes. I commit to your care, however, knowing that in so doing I shall receive no detriment.

"I was glad to see your father in his usual good health. They were all well at his house and at yours, as he informed me.

"You and Sims both I see are against anything like emancipation, and Sims, I hear, has made a speech. You have voted no doubt on the popular side, though I differ in opinion with you on that very important subject. Large slave owner as I am, I am clear for taking some steps in that matter which all admit must sooner or later come to pass. Public opinion is not ripe for it at present, though I believe a respectable minority to be, and I have no doubt that public sentiment might be changed by a man of energy and talent who would openly advocate it.

"Be so good as to give my best respects to my friend Sims, and say to him I understand Mr. Madison did not open his mouth in the Legislature for probably the two first sessions he served.

"Nothing interesting in the way of gossip except Miss Banks' wedding, which takes place tomorrow, I understand.

"Remember me to Sims and Preston. I shall be very glad to hear from you at any time, and in turn to be of service to you in Halifax. I have some small expectation of being with you in January.

"I remain,

"Yours very truly,

"Wm. E Clark."

[A History of Halifax County, by Wirt Johnson Carrington, 1924]

"Berry Hill"

The Hall at "Berry Hill"

BUTLER, Martin, was a son of Hudson Butler, of Halifax County, Va., who had a brother Samuel Butler, who migrated south from Halifax County at a very early date; he carried with him, on horseback, a half bushel of silver, and was never heard from again.

Martin Butler was born in Halifax County, Va., 15 May, 1806; moved to Missouri about 1835; married a widow, Emiline Pugh, nee Davis, 18 March, 1847; died at his home near New Bloomfield, Missouri, 1 March, 1863. His parents died when he was a small child, and he was reared by his maternal grandmother, a Mrs. Farmer, of Halifax County. He had a brother, Joel Butler, who lived and died at Peebles, Ohio, leaving descendants; his sister, Jane, married Rev. Apple, of Virginia, and lived at Clarksville, Mecklinburg County; he probably also had a sister named Nancy. His aunt, Edith Farmer, died in 1860, his aunt Boyd died in 1862, and his aunt Nancy was still living in 1867.

Martin Butler was a successful, prominent, leading citizen of his county, and accumulated a fortune in merchandizing, trading and farming. *[The Gentry Family in America, 1676 to 1909, by Richard Gentry]*

Some Butler marriages in Halifax County, Virginia:

Barsheba Butler and John Patterson, 1 Nov. 1792.

Harriett R. Butler and Charles Lovelace, 15 Dec. 1829.

J. T. Butler (wife) and Alfred Apple, 2 Nov. 1837.

John Butler and Nancy Cannaday, 15 Sept. 1787.

John Butler and Suckey Hughes, 19 June 1800.

Joshua Butler and E. Stanfield, 8 Jan. 1807.

Nancy Butler and Joseph Glenn, 18 Nov. 1790.

Obediah Butler and Elizabeth Newbill, 5 Nov. 1833.

Richard Butler and Sally Enroughty, 14 March 1796.

CALLOWAY family: In 1745, Rev. Mr. Stith (the historian) bought 200 acres of land from Francis Calloway of "Poplar Forest," the founder of the Calloway family in the Colonies.

Francis Calloway had sons, Thomas, Richard and William.

Thomas Calloway was born in 1712. He was Vestryman and Church Warden, 1752, of Antrim Parish, Halifax County, Virginia. He was Gentleman Justice and commissioned captain of Militia for that county in the French and Indian

War prior to 1755. He emigrated to North Carolina about 1758, where he was active in church work. In his later years he settled in Wilkes County, Georgia, 1782.

Richard was born in 1722. He was Sergeant, Lieutenant and Colonel in the French and Indian Wars from Bedford County, Virginia; he was trustee for the town of New London in 1761; went to Kentucky with Daniel Boone in 1764; was a Burgess in Virginia in 1777; was killed by the Indians in 1780.

William Calloway was born in 1714. He patented 15,000 acres of land in Lunenburg, Brunswick, Bedford and Halifax Counties. In 1761, William Calloway, gent., made a free gift of a hundred acres of land to the County of Bedford to be settled with a town to be called New London. He married Miss Crawley and had many descendants throughout the South.

William Calloway was Justice of Peace in Bedford County, Va., in 1754. In 1755 he was Major in the French and Indian Wars; and in 1758 was made Colonel. In 1758 he was appointed County Lieutenant by the English Government. *[A History of Halifax County, by Wirt Johnson Carrington. And, The Callaway Clan, by Bessie Callaway Hoffmeyer]*

CARLTON family: The first survey book of Halifax County shows, on page 160, 370 acres of land in the county surveyed by Robert Wooding for Thomas Carlton, Jr., land lying on Straightstone creek, adjoining James Hunt and Benjamin Clements' lines. Dated April, 1757. From this date on the Carltons had many deeds, wills and marriages recorded in the court house. Among the deeds is an indenture made 17 November 1817 *(Book 27, page 83)*.

This indenture between John Holt and Elizabeth, his wife, Jeremiah Boyd and Christian, late Christian Holt, Henry McClarney and Sarah, his wife, late Sarah Holt, Mary Milam, late Mary Holt, and Lawson Royal for himself, claiming under Peter Holt, and his wife, Tabitha, deceased (formerly Tabitha Holt), and her son, Armistead Boyd, of the County of Halifax, of one part; and Edward Carlton, Sr., of said county, of the other part. Witnesseth, that above parties for and in consideration of sum of four hundred dollars paid in hand to them by Edward Carlton, Sr., sell to him 111 1/2 acres on the waters of Wolf creek. Land devised to Richard Holt by Peter Holt.

In 1819, Edward Carlton buys from Nancy Wimbish (executrix of the estate of John Wimbish, her husband, deceased) a certain half acre of land situated in the town of Banister and known as lot No. 35.

In 1819, August 21, Catherine Carlton, executrix of her husband's, Philoman Carlton, estate, for a certain sum of money paid by the legatees, relinquishes her dower right in favor of her children, viz., Edward, James, John, Anthony,

William Fitzgerald, and Elizabeth, his wife, and Thomas Conner, and Lucy, his wife.

The will of Philomon Carlton was probated in 1813, March 23, recording his wife, Catherine, and six children, Edward, James, John, Anthony, Elizabeth Fitzgerald, and Lucy Carlton. He made his wife executrix and son, Edward, and trusty friend, Dr. Charles D. Fontaine, executors.

Edward acknowledged bond in the penalty of twenty-five thousand dollars.

The appraisal of his estate in 1816, August court, showed twenty-six Negroes valued at $3,258, a good landed estate, household furniture and farm implements.

Several wills are recorded leading up to that of Rachel Carlton's estate settlement in 1862.

In 1833, John L. Lewellyn was trustee for Mary C. Carlton and children.

In 1840-45, Henderson Sneed was guardian for Henry H. Carlton, and Emeline Waller, formerly Emeline Carlton.

[A History of Halifax County, by Wirt Johnson Carrington, 1924]

CARRINGTON family: Dr. Paul Carrington, of Barbados, and his second wife, Henningham Codrington, who lies buried in St. Philip's Parish, under a monument thus inscribed: "Hennningham Carrington, widow of Dr. Paul Carrington, Obit, June 28, 1741, Aet, 69." She was born 1673.

Colonel George Carrington, son of Dr. Paul Carrington, married Anne Mayo, daughter of William Mayo, gent., of Goochland County, Va. (He was with Colonel William Byrd in making the survey between Virginia and North Carolina in 1728 and also in 1733.)

Paul Carrington, Sr., was twice married, his first wife being Margaret Read, daughter of Clement Read, of "Bushy Forest." His second wife was Priscilla Sims, daughter of Matthew Sims.

Paul Carrington, Jr., married Mildred H. Coles, daughter of Walter Coles, of "Mildendo," and his wife, Mildred Lightfoot. Walter Coles was born in Hanover County, November 13, 1739. He married Mildred Lightfoot, born at Sandy Point, Charles City County, February 11, 1752. She died May 1, 1799. She was a daughter of Mildred Howell and William Lightfoot. Walter Coles died November 7, 1780, at "Mildendo," his country seat in Halifax County.

Walter Coles Carrington (son of Judge Paul Carrington, Jr., born September 20, 1764, died January 8, 1816, and his wife, Mildred H. Coles, born May 15, 1769, died April 24, 1840, married August 24, 1785) was born March 4, 1794.

He married Alice Cabell, November 15, 1817. She was the 2nd daughter of Dr. George Cabell.

Mrs. Alice Cabell Carrington died leaving four children (sons), viz.: (1) Edward Coles Carrington; (2) George Cabell Carrington; (3) Paul Jones Carrington; (4) Walter Coles Carrington.

Edward Coles Carrington (1) married, first, Mary Coleman, of Williamsburg, Va., and had one child, Thomas Carrington.

George Cabell Carrington (M. D., died 1880) married Sarah Winston Henry and had the following children:

(1) John P. Metteaux Carrington, married Sarah Frances Toot and had one child, Mildred Coles Carrington. (She married Mr. Waddell and had Carrington Waddell.)

(2) Susan Love Carrington, married Rev. A. Y, Hundley. Four children.

(3) Charles Craddock Carrington, married Sarah Henry French. Issue:

(1) Margaret Logan Carrington, married Charles H. Stebbins, cashier of Planters and Merchants National Bank, South Boston.

(2) George Cabell Carrington (civil engineer), married Louise C. Stebbins.

(3) Sarah Henry Carrington, married James F. Dorrier.

(4) Marcellus F. Carrington.

(5) Charles Reid Carrington, married Kizzie McDaniel.

(6) William Lorria Carrington.

(7) Elizabeth F. Carrington.

(8) Alice Cary Carrington, married William B. Settle, attorney, of the firm of Settle & McKinney.

(9) Winifred W. Carrington.

Dr. William W. Carrington, of Halifax, married his cousin, Jane W. Carrington, daughter of Colonel Clement Carrington and Jane (Watkins) Carrington, of Charlotte County, and had eight children: Virginia, Thomas, Clement, Betsey, Susan H., Mary G., Anne R. and William.

Dr. William Carrington owned many slaves. Daniel King and his wife, Katy, were slaves owned by him. Daniel was born about 1822, in Granville County, South Caroline. Katy was born about 1822, in Charlotte County, Virginia. They married 25 December, 1846. Their children were: Paul King, born about 1848; Hampton King, born about 1850; Lewis King, born about 1852; Scylla King, born about 1855; Washington King, born about 1858; Meshack

Washington, born about 1860; John Washington, born about 1862; and Elizabeth Washington, born about 1865.

Henry Paul Carrington, of "Bellevue," was son of John B. Carrington, who, about the year 1825, erected the fine home. This was a beautiful old seat, surrounded by massive oaks, covering extensive grounds, the house built of red brick. A small porch with massive pillars reaching to the top of the second story gave an imposing air to what was once a most attractive and hospitable home. The rooms were large and high-pitch, the walls white and of such hard finish as to have withstood many long years of wear and tear. The mantels were of marble and the "parlor" had the usual frescoed ceiling. It was like almost all of the old Virginia homes, with a large flower garden that leads to the last resting place of those who once reveled amid the evergreens and blooming shrubbery. The following epitaphs from the gravestones were embedded in a tangle of honeysuckle:

"Sacred to the memory of Our Mother,
Judith A., wife of John B. Carrington.
Born Dec. 24, 1804. Died Aug. 31, 1878.
"She is not dead but sleepeth."

"In Memory of Fannie E. Watkins (wife of R. V. Watkins)
Born Dec. 21, 1829. Died Oct. 9, 1882.
"And I will show thee my faith by my works."

"Sacred to the Memory of Henry Paul Carrington
Born Aug. 7, 1848. Died March 29,1900.
"Mark the perfect man, and behold the upright, for the end of that man is peace."

"Bellevue"

Colonel Henry Carrington, of Halifax, married Betsy Morton, and had (1) Agnes Carrington and (2) Henry Carrington.

The Carringtons of Halifax, Charlotte and Prince Edward Counties were all related, and all intermarried with the Mortons, Watkins, Venables, Cabells, Henrys and Frenchs. *[A History of Halifax County, by Wirt Johnson Carrington, 1924]*

George Carrington, of Halifax County, Virginia, was Lieutenant in the Revolutionary War and son of George Carrington, of Barbados. *[Notes on Southside Virginia]*

CARRINGTON, Gene Edward G., was born 4 January, 1790, in Halifax County, Virginia. Died 7 March, 1855, buried in Botetourt County.

CARTER, John, was born August 26th and baptized October 30th, 1737, at St. Peter's Parish, son of Theodrick (second) Carter and his wife Anne (believed to be Anne Wadill), of Prince Edward County. Theodrick Carter is son of Theodrick (first) and Elizabeth Carter.

In the records on file in Halifax County, Va., is a sale of a tract of land of 183 and a half acres, on Dan River, by Theodrick Carter, of Prince Edward County, to his son, John Carter of Halifax County. John Carter's will was drawn 18th of June 1781, and probated in Halifax County on 20th September, 1781. In his will he names his wife, Mary, daughters Ann Waddill, Elizabeth Carter, Mary Carter, Judith Carter, Sally Carter; and sons Richard, Theodrick (fourth), Robert, James and Francis Carter. His wife Mary was executrix and his brothers, Richard and Theodrick (third) Carter, executors.

In his will, John Carter left his "well beloved wife, Mary Carter, during her widowhood for her use and the bringing up and educating my children the land and plantation where on I now live with the use benefit and labour of the following slaves, Jack, Charles, James, Baker, Tainor [or Tamer]." When his youngest son comes of age he gets those slaves with the "future increase." Daughter, Ann Wadill, was given twenty-five shillings; to daughter, Elizabeth Carter, one Negro boy named Sam; to daughter, Mary Carter, one Negro boy named Crafford; to daughter, Judith Carter, one Negro girl named Hannah; to daughter, Salley Carter, twenty-five pounds specia in gold or silver; to the three oldest sons, Richard, Theodrick and Robert Carter, "my creek land I purchased of George Ridley containing 450 acres which I desire may be equally divided between the three brothers," "and in case either of the said three boys should die before they come of age for the surviving said brothers to inherit the land of the deceased by equal division;" to son, James Carter, "the land where on I now live;" and to son, Francis Carter, "two hundred and ninety acres of land lying out on the road adjoining the land of Mr. Hobson." It also states, "in case either of my daughters that is Elizabeth, Mary, Judith or Salley Carter should die before they come of age or marry," suggesting all the children, except Ann Wadill, were minors.

Robert Carter, son of John Carter, was born 22 December, 1770, in Halifax County, Virginia. He married, 1 November, 1792, Unity Cook. They moved to Williamson County, Tenn., in 1805. The children that were born in Halifax County, Va., were: Sarah Venable, Henry Cook, John Blackgrove, Robert Michaux, Polly and Samuel Jefferson Carter. Another son, Alexander Cunningham Carter, was born in Tennessee. Two other children, Mary and Nancy, did not survive infancy. Robert Carter died 9 September, 1839, at Franklin, Williamson County, Tennessee.

Robert Carter

Samuel Jefferson Carter, son of Robert and Unity (Cook) Carter, was born in Halifax County, Virginia, 3 January, 1803, and died suddenly at Carter's Landing, West Tennessee, on 31 March, 1873. He married, as recorded in the family Bible, first, Eliza Staggs, and had three children: Watson M., Jordan B., and Eliza S. Samuel Jefferson Carter married second, Anne Vaulx, and had fourteen children: Warren, Hays, Watkins Leigh, Charles Vaulx, Samuel J., Laura O., Irene M., Samuel Jefferson, William Giles Harding, Anne Catherine, Frank Cook, Ella Watson,Vaulx, Mary Hays.

Samuel Jefferson Carter

There was a considerable migration of Virginians to the new lands to the west and south, and besides Robert Carter and his family, his brothers Richard, James and Francis Watkins Carter, their sister Anne Waddill and Robert's brother-in-law, Henry Cook, left Halifax County with their families and went to seek homes in Tennessee and to the south. Robert and Francis Carter and Henry Cook settled at Franklin, Williamson County, Tennessee. Richard and James Carter and their sister Anne Waddill went to Alabama, as did their kinsmen John and Michaux Cunningham. *[Giles Carter of Virginia, by Gen. Wm. Giles Harding Carter]*

CARTER, John W., was born in Halifax County, Virginia, on March 25, 1851, and was educated in the schools of that county, beginning his business life in 1873. He was the son of Captain Jeduthan Carter, born in Pittsylvania County, who commanded Company F, of the 38th Virginia Infantry, C. S. A., during the late war. His mother, whose maiden name was Ann Hubbard, died on June 8, 1874. His wife was Maggie A., daughter of Frank and Annie E. (Watson) Redd, of Prince Edward County, Virginia. They were married in Danville, December 3, 1879, and had three sons: Warner P., J. Epps and John W., Jr.

In 1873 Mr. Carter clerked for W. P. Robinson, of Danville; from 1874 to 1878 was with John F. Rison & Co., Danville; then went into business with W. P. Hodnet. style of firm Hodnet & Carter; from 1880 to 1885 was in business alone; and in the last-named year organized the first wholesale grocery house in Danville, under the firm style of John W. Carter & Co., wholesale grocers, and jobbers of manufactured tobacco and cigars, 304 Main street. Mr. Carter was also connected with S. P. Wimbish & Co., brokers and commission merchants. *[Virginia and Virginians, Vol. II]*

CHALMERS family: The genealogist, E. C. Meade, said: "These Chalmers are said to be in direct line from James II and through Jenet Hamilton."

David Chalmers inherited most of his father's estate, which was called "Rose Hill," later "Creek Side," which he sold to E. A. Coleman, of Halifax County, and then bought "Springfield," the plantation adjoining, from his brother, Joseph Chalmers, afterwards judge and United States Senator. The brothers, Joseph and John Gordon Chalmers, sold all their lands in Virginia and moved to Holly Springs, Miss.

James Chalmers married Sarah (Lanier Williams) Watkins, in Halifax County, Va., November 13, 1797. The will of James Chalmers was probated in this county in 1826. By the will he left his property to his three sons, plantations, and a number of Negroes to each. The sons were named John, David, and Joseph W. Chalmers, and these are undoubtedly the ancestors of the Chalmers of this county.

James Chalmers had also two other sons, viz., Gordon and James Ronolds, and three daughters, Lucinda, Sarah and Jannett.

Lucinda Chalmers married Thomas Galloway and had three sons and three daughters.

Sarah Chalmers married John Glenn. Had three sons, James, Chalmers, and Archie Glenn.

Jannett Chalmers married Hamilton Bradshaw, of North Carolina. (No children.)

David Chalmers, son of James, married Miss Coleman.

Ronald Chalmers emigrated from Ayreshire, Scotland, to Petersburg, Virginia. He represented a celebrated ancestry, and the Chalmers arms have been borne with honor by the descendants, now living in many Southern States. *[A History of Halifax County, by Wirt Johnson Carrington, 1924]*

CHALMERS, Dr. Henry C., was born at "Springfield," Halifax County, 20 July, 1837. He attended the University of Virginia from 1854-1856. He was Surgeon for the Confederate States Army, died 7 February, 1865. *[The University Memorial Biographical Sketches of Alumni of the University of Virginia who fell in the Confederate War, by Rev. John Lipscomb Johnson]*

CHALMERS, James, was the son of David Chalmers, of Halifax County. He was born at Woodlawn, the residence of his grandfather, Colonel Coleman, on the 21st of September, 1829. As soon as he was old enough to leave home, he was sent to an Episcopal school at Hagerstown, in Maryland, and while there, in his sixteenth year, was confirmed by Bishop Whittingham, and became an active member of the Church of his forefathers. From this primary school he went to Chapel Hill College, in North Carolina. He decided to study law and went to the University of Virginia. Immediately upon leaving the University he opened an office and commenced the practice of his profession in Lynchburg.

On the 8th of December, 1852, he was married to Fannie M. Saunders, the second daughter of Dr. James Saunders, a prominent and wealthy tobacconist of Lynchburg.

In January, 1853, Dr. Saunders found it necessary to have someone to whom he could confide the joint management of his large and varied business. This post he tendered to Mr. Chalmers, making the offer so advantageous as to induce him to abandon his legal profession.

Although in no respect a politician, Mr. Chalmers was a Whig, and was much opposed to the course of those States which first seceded from the Union; but as soon as war became necessity, like all other true men he did not doubt as to where his allegiance was due, and was one of the first to place his name on the list of members of a cavalry company, whose services were to be tendered the Governor of the State for immediate duty in the field. His company was one of the first mustered into the service of the State, and was early ordered to the seat of war. The company, upon reaching Manassas, was assigned to the 2nd Virginia Regiment of Cavalry, then being organized under Colonel Radford, and took its position as the second, or Company B, in that regiment. He was in several skirmishes prior to the battle of Manassas, including one at Vienna, where the Federals under General Schenck were routed, and he displayed himself every inch a soldier in each trial of his mettle. At the battle of Manassas his conduct especially attracted the commendation of his commanding officers. Foremost in the gallant charge made that day by his regiment upon the breaking foe, he was the first, when pursuit was over, to minister to the suffering of the wounded, whether dressed in gray or blue.

After this battle, Company B was sent to the front on picket and vidette duty, camping at various times at Centreville, Falls Church, Annandale and Fairfax C. H. Here the service of the cavalry was exciting and dangerous, the skirmish line under Gen. Stuart running through Munson's and Mason's Hills, and in sight of the dome of the Capitol. This life Chalmers seemed to enjoy very much, and the more dangerous the service the more it attracted him. On Saturday, the 28th of September, the company had been on laborious duty all day, and did not return to camp at Fairfax C. H. until after dark. Scarcely had the men gone to rest before Gen. Longstreet sent an order to the Capt. (Charles M. Blackford), to detail two intelligent and reliable men to go with some important messages to the outposts. Chalmers was one of those on whom the lot fell. On this Saturday, Chalmers was shot and badly wounded. He had been shot while riding between the pickets at Annandale—the ball entered his left arm, crushing both bones, and then passing into the stomach. He rode back some two miles to Annandale before dismounting. From Annandale he was removed first to a tavern, then quartered in Mr. Thomas' law-office. His arm was amputated just below the elbow. But the ball that entered the cavity of the stomach inflicted such an injury that peritonitis ensued, and he died at sunrise on Tuesday morning, the 1st of October. His remains were carried to Lynchburg for interment. *[University Memorial Biographical Sketches of Alumni of the University of Virginia who fell in the Confederate War, by Rev. John Lipscomb Johnson]*

CHALMERS, James R., was born in Halifax County, Va., 11 January, 1831. He was Brigadier General in Confederate States Army. He was appointed from Mississippi 13 February, 1862, to rank from same date; confirmed 17 February, 1862, and 17 February, 1864; paroled at Gainesville, Ala., 10 May, 1865. He died at Memphis, Tenn., 9 April, 1898. *[General Officers of the Confederate Army, by Gen. Marcus J. Wright, 1911]*

CHAPPELL family descendants were very numerous in this county and throughout the United States.

Mr. Phil E. Chappell, of Kansas City, Mo., wrote the genealogy of the Chappells, and he said in regard to them:

"Sufficient evidence will be adduced to satisfy the most skeptical that the American Chappells came from England, and that they sprang from an old and noble family, which had lived in that country for hundreds of years. This is all that we now know, and all that is necessary for us to know, for while this information may be gratifying to our family pride, we must not forget that we are Americans—not English—and the fad that ours is one of the very oldest families in this country is a far greater cause for self-congratulation and honest pride of ancestry than that we sprang originally and remotely from a noble family in England."

Many of the Chappells have gone from Halifax County to the South and West and become prominent men of affairs. *[A History of Halifax County, by Wirt Johnson Carrington, 1924]*

CHASTAIN family descended from the Huguenots, and suffered all the perils and hardships attendant upon a Huguenot refugee. Being compelled to leave home, friends and all earthly possessions in their native land, they came to this colony, barely escaping with their lives.

We find the forebear of the subject of this sketch living in this county at a very early date, with sufficient land upon which to build a simple home, and sufficient thrift, frugality and industry to add to it and provide for a family.

The old home was well built of hewn logs, smooth and square, mortised together after the substantial fashion of most of the primitive homes of people in moderate circumstances of that day. The nails used were evidently made in the blacksmith shop. Through the small panes of glass in the narrow windows several generations have looked out over the broad fields and sloping hills, and two generations were laid to rest in the graveyard close by, around which there is a strong wall and within it on a large slab is the inscription, *"Sacred to the memory of the Chastain family,"* the names following:

"Howell Chastain, born April 3, 1800, died October 30, 1868.

"Elizabeth A. Chastain, born December 25, 1810, died June 18, 1886.

"Mary Gilliam Chastain, born February 28, 1835, died August 30, 1842.

"Richard Cabell Chastain, born September 16, 1852, died December 1, 1859.

"Howell Archer Chastain, born August 28, 1840, died September 12, 1861."

The parents of Howell Chastain are buried at Clover in the old churchyard. The subject of this sketch, their descendant, James Chastain, has had substantial marble stones placed at the head of each grave. He was born and lived through his young life in this county. In later years he went to New York to live, and there met and married a wealthy widow, who died in a few years, leaving him an independent fortune, and one of the most praiseworthy things that he did was to mark with stones the graves of his people and leave an endowment fund with St. John's Church at Halifax for keeping up these graves.

After the death of Captain Henry Edmunds, James Chastain bought his beautiful home that he had built for his wife, who was Susan Edmondson. Mr. Chastain put some improvements on it, and there he lived during his widowhood and entertained with lavish hand his friends and relatives. Generous to a fault, those who knew him best know how many he helped in times of stress, and how bitterly disappointing was his sudden death to those who regarded him as still a man in the prime of life.

His will, recorded at Halifax, a lengthy and liberal one, covers several pages with generous legacies and leaves the home, which he named "Restawhile," to his cousin, Miss Lula Howard Edmondson (with other legacies and no encumbrances as to upkeep, etc., of the large house and grounds) during her lifetime, and after her death to be a home for aged women of gentle birth of Halifax County.

Mr. Chastain's French blood was strongly tinctured with a love of luxury and pleasure, which licensed him to do many things repugnant to the more straight-laced views of the puritanical, but he was so thoroughly unselfish, and generous withal, that the envious alone could have maligned him. He died suddenly in Washington, D. C., while on a pleasure trip to New York and other cities with some of his relatives and friends, and his body was sent to Kentucky to be buried beside that of his wife. He left a large estate, and was considered very liberal to his legatees, but nevertheless there followed some law suits and much wrangling. *[A History of Halifax County, by Wirt Johnson Carrington, 1924]*

CHILES, Paul: Will of Paul Chiles, 2 September 1761, Halifax County:

"To my son Henry, negroes and land on Bottom Town creek in Halifax County.

"To my son, Paul Chiles, negroes and land in Bedford county and in Halifax County.

"To my son, Rowland Chiles (not yet baptized), land I now live on, and after my wife's decease, also 110 acres at mouth of Bottom Town creek, also 70 acres on Sycamore creek in Halifax County, and negroes.

"To my daughter, Elizabeth Chiles, 728 acres on both sides of Smith's River in Halifax County, also negroes.

"To my daughter, Frances Chiles, 200 acres on Mayo's River and 400 acres joining the same not yet cleared, out of the office in Halifax County; also 130 acres on the other fork of the Mayo and 400 acres joining it not yet cleared; one of the offices to be cleared with my estate; also negroes.

"All personal estate sold at public sale, giving six months credit,

"All debts paid from it, and all back lands not mentioned in the will to be sold and equally divided among the children.

"To my loving wife, Anne, 60 pounds to be at her disposal.

"Anne Chiles, my wife, executrix; John Chiles and Captain John Ward, executors.

"Paul (his-X-mark) Chiles."

Witnesses: William Cadwell, R. Robinson Hunt and William W. Glass.

CHRISTIAN family were of Manx descent, settled in Ireland, whence Israel migrated to America in 1740, and settled near Staunton, Virginia, where his son, William, was born in 1742. When in his twentieth year, William commanded a company on Byrd's Cherokee expedition; and again, in 1764, he headed a militia company wherein Henry Pauling and Walter Crockett were his subordinates.

Removing first to Botetourt, then to Fincastle County, William Christian established his home at Dunkard Bottom, on New River, whence he was called to represent his county in the Virginia Assembly in 1774. In Colonel Preston's enforced absence he commanded the Fincastle Regiment during Dunmore's War, arriving at Point Pleasant at midnight after the victory had been won.

In 1775, Christian acted on the committee of safety, and in the following year was chosen second in command of Patrick Henry's Continental regiment. Upon hearing of the danger from the Cherokees, he resigned his commission and enrolled an expedition of seventeen hundred men to advance to the Cherokee towns (1776), which were burned and the savage uprising quelled. In 1781, William acted as one of the commissioners who concluded a lasting peace with this tribe.

Early in 1785, Christian removed to the neighborhood of Louisville, Kentucky, where his advent was eagerly welcomed by the harassed frontier. He did not live to secure its permanent peace, being mortally wounded by a party of marauding Indians, April 9, 1786. His widow, a sister of Patrick Henry, and six children survived him. His only son, John, died while a youth, and all of his daughters married Kentuckians.

[Documentary History of Dunmore's War, 1774, by Reuben Gold Thwaites and Louise Phelps Kellogg; 1905]

CLARK family: To get a clear understanding of the Clarks of Halifax and "Banister Lodge" it will be well to read the will of John Clark, given herein, and dated the 10th of March, 1827. This John Clark was the son of William Clark, of Prince Edward County, Virginia, and his wife, Phoebe Howson. His ancestry was almost, if not entirely, English.

In his will John Clark gives to his son, William H. Clark, "My Banister plantation, with all the stock, tools, and everything belonging to the plantation, including all the Negroes, except Dick Coates and his family." for which he supplied two other slaves. He wished William to take possession of the place and property bequeathed immediately after his demise.

"To my son, John Thomas, I give my Staunton River plantation, which includes the mansion seat, etc., subject to provisions hereinafter mentioned.

"To my son, Charles, a large amount of bank stock, etc., to be invested until Charles becomes of age, etc."

He is very explicit in names of parties from whom he purchased the various parts of the Staunton River plantation. One part from William Thewett and another part from the children of Matthew Sims after the death of Mrs. Sims. (John Clark married for his second wife Priscilla Sims, daughter of Matthew Sims.)

William H. Clark was born in Halifax County, January 23, 1805. He was educated at Hampden-Sidney College, the University of Virginia and Cambridge, Mass. He represented Halifax County in the Legislature and was a planter. He died at his seat, "Banister Lodge," October 20, 1873. He married Elvira Ann Henry (posthumous), daughter of Patrick Henry, Jr. (eldest son of Patrick Henry, the orator), and his wife, Elvira Cabell, daughter of William Cabell, of "Union Hill," Nelson County. Elvira Ann Henry was born at "Union Hill," September 27, 1804, and married at "Woodburn," Halifax County, May 8, 1828. She died at "Banister Lodge," June 21, 1870. It was said of her that she was one of the purest and noblest of women, and that "her life was a living witness to the truth she professed, and by her beautiful example of Christian gentleness and love she allured to brighter worlds and led the way."

The will of John Clark provided that his son, Charles, should have a home when the proper time arrived, and besides the will we have the evidence in the following statement of one of his descendants:

"The will of John Clark stated that a river plantation was to be bought for his son, Charles Adolphas Clark. The only river plantation for sale at that time in Halifax County was 'Rosebank' on the Staunton River, which belonged to the Yuilles. It was purchased and Mr. Charles Clark lived for a while in the old Yuille house.

"He married February 18, 1846, Miss Eliza A. Spraggins. Just before his marriage Mr. Clark had Mr. Howard Cosby, of Halifax Courthouse, to build a brick house for him on the 'public road' about a mile and a quarter from the river. He and his bride moved in shortly after its completion.

"Mr. Clark superintended the laying out of his grounds by the slaves, of whom he had a goody number. To the southwest of the house was situated a deer park. The flower garden, where he himself grafted roses, was approached through cathedral arches of arborvitae which led from the house.

"Mr. Charles Clark bought land and added to the original tract; he called the place 'Hoveloke,' an Indian name. After the Lynchburg and Durham Railroad was built his son, Thomas B. Clark, named the depot 'Clarkton,' and so the whole place has been called ever since.

"Charles Clark contracted tuberculosis when quite young and he traveled a great deal seeking his health in a milder climate. In that day and time the disease was treated very differently from what it is now. He visited the West Indies and spent nearly every winter in New Orleans. In his travels he went North and heard Henry Ward Beecher preach. When he returned home he remarked at a family gathering that abolition had gotten into religion and politics and that slavery was not going to last. He expressed it as his opinion that after slavery was abolished Southern plantations would be worked by the tenant system. His family, complacent and satisfied in their isolation, said 'poor Charles he is losing his mind.'"

Nevertheless, he had his slaves make brick on his place and build six four-roomed tenant houses; they were erected on different parts of his plantation. Charles Clark died at the age of thirty-nine years, two years before the Civil War.

Thomas B. Clark, the son of Charles and Eliza (Spraggins) Clark, being the only child, fell heir to "Clarkton," where he lived and died, and is buried in the family graveyard, a short distance from the mansion house, where the native oaks shelter with protecting shade this well kept "God's Acre," where his parents are also laid to rest under fitting marble stones.

Charles Adolphus Clark, born February 9, 1821, died December 18, 1859.

Eliza A. Clark, born July 24, 1821, died February 1, 1897.

Thomas B. Clark, son of Charles Adolphus and Eliza Ann (Spraggins) Clark. Born February 9, 1851, died July 9, 1919.

Mr. Thomas B. Clark married April 30, 1878, Miss Grace Thomson, of New Orleans. She was the daughter of Adam Thomson, of Belfast, Ireland, one of the old Scotch-Irish clan, and close akin to the Murrys and Allens. He came to America and settled in New Orleans, where he became a large sugar planter and merchant. He spent much of his time abroad, his daughter often traveling with him. When she married Mr. Clark and came to live with him at Clarkton, beautiful as it was, she must have felt the sudden transition from life in a large and gay city, with its varied amusements, to that of a remote plantation in the sylvan shades of Halifax County, but the nearness to several old country seats, homes of royal hospitality and refinement, compensated for the city life. Mrs. Clark was by nature domestic, enjoyed her home and took the greatest delight in having her friends enjoy it with her. She had two accomplished daughters, Anita Grace Clark, wife of Mr. Frank Robertson White (son of Mr. James L. White, and his wife, Kate Robertson, daughter of Governor Wyndham Robertson), they later resided in Washington State, and Miss Elise T. Clark, of Clarkton.

"Clarkton" is a stately old mansion "all in white," with its massive pillars reaching to the roof. Broad piazzas, winding stairways and large square rooms, each exquisitely furnished in "heirloom" mahoganys of many designs, from the ornate tables to the tester beds in "my lady's chamber," not one but six, each vieing with the other in exquisite mechanism. Old portraits, old china and old silver, that did service in "ye olden times," all so beautiful, and the home so perfectly equipped with all that is modern and convenient, one forgets amid such luxury that it is really a country seat. Near by is the little Clarkton church. *[A History of Halifax County, by Wirt Johnson Carrington, 1924]*

"Banister Lodge"

CLARK, Rev. John Thomas, was born 19 September, 1809, in Halifax County, Virginia. Ordered Deacon, Sunday, 25 May, 1834, in Trinity Church, Staunton, Va., by the Rt. Rev. William Mead, Bishop of Virginia. Ordained

Priest, May, 1835, in St. John's Church, Halifax C. H., Virginia, by the Rt. Rev. William Meade.

For many years he was the only P. E. Clergyman (without any pay) in Halifax, Charlotte, Mecklenburg and Campbell Counties, Virginia. From about 1850 to 1877 was in charge of Roanoke Parish, Halifax County, Virginia. From 1877 to his death, was in charge of Reidsville and Leaksville, North Carolina. Rev. John Thomas Clark died on 25th of October, 1886.

CLARK, Dr. Patrick Henry, youngest son of William H. and Elvira A. Clark, of Banister Lodge, Halifax County, Va., and great-grandson of Patrick Henry, was born April 21st, 1837. After careful training at home, he was sent for several years to the excellent school of Mr. Franklin Minor, in Albemarle County. From Mr. Minor's he went in October, 1855, to the University of Virginia, and, in accordance with the wish of his father, entered upon a course of study preparatory to the profession of Medicine.

After leaving the University, Pat. Clark attended lectures in the Medical College at Richmond, during which time he resided with his grandmother, Mrs. Bruce. At the end of the term in 1858, he was graduated Doctor of Medicine. His father now gave him an ancestral estate, situated in Campbell County, and known as "Long Island;" but it could hardly be said that Dr. Clark resided upon it, so much of his time did he spend with his friends in Halifax. In 1859 he went abroad to enlarge the liberal culture he had already received. In Paris he pursued again his professional studies, and then set out for a tour of the Continent. But he had gone no farther than Italy, when he heard of the secession of Virginia; and, true to his proud Revolutionary lineage and his own convictions of duty, he left at once the scenes of enchantment amid which even they who lack the enthusiasm of youth are tempted to linger, and hastened home to aid in defending the land of his birth.

When he reached Virginia, he repaired at once to Campbell, and finding that Captain Alexander had already raised a company of cavalry with which he was hurrying to take the field, he promptly enrolled his name as a private in its ranks, and set about his preparation to accompany it. During the brief space allowed him for this purpose, Mrs. Clark, moved, perhaps, both by her instinctive apprehensions for the personal safety of her son, and by a natural and laudable desire to see him fill that station which his professional studies had so admirably fitted him for, said to him, "Patrick, you have been highly educated; your medical course completed in Paris, where you enjoyed so many advantages. You could now serve so well both your country and your fellow-men as a surgeon." To the appeal, intelligible and eloquent as it doubtless was to him, he replied at once:—" Dear mother, while I love to gratify you in all things, don't ask me to take a surgeon's place. I want to go into the ranks and fight as a common soldier." And thus did he enter the army and fight the first battle of Manassas, in which his gallantry and efficiency were conspicuous. But when the victory was won, he applied himself industriously to the relief of the wounded.

Dr. Clark was not long allowed, however, to remain a private. "His excellent character as a soldier speedily won for him the rank of Orderly Sergeant. In this position his soldierly qualities and his capacity for command soon became so conspicuous that he was urged to raise a company, and procured from the War Department authority for that purpose." In a few weeks he succeeded in raising an artillery company of over one hundred men, who elected him captain by acclamation, and called the command after his plantation, "The Long Island Artillery."

In this new position " he secured alike the respect and the affection and the confidence of his officers and men. In the battles around Richmond his battery was frequently engaged, and he conducted himself with conspicuous gallantry, which elicited the complimentary notice of his commanding general upon the battlefield, and won for him the highest admiration of his compatriots in arms." Through this series of conflicts he passed unscathed by shot or steel; but very soon after he was stricken down with violent disease — the consequence of excessive exposure and privation. At the first symptoms of fever he was warned and urged by his friends to retire from the field; but his devotion to duty would not allow him to do so until he was prostrated and it was too late for safety.

In one of the hospitals, with which the Confederate capital was crowded, he received every attention—all that medical skill or humanity could suggest, was done for his relief. Yet so rapid was the progress of his disease, that even his relatives in the city knew nothing of it until they were stunned by the news of his death, which occurred on the 25th of July, 1862. *[University Memorial Biographical Sketches of Alumni of the University of Virginia who fell in the Confederate War, by Rev. John Lipscomb Johnson]*

COLEMAN family: John Coleman with two brothers came to Virginia from England about the middle of the eighteenth century. They were shipbuilders and settled first at City Point, later one brother went to Pennsylvania, where he and his descendants became wealthy. John Coleman married Sarah Embry, of Gloucester County, Va., and took up lands. Later he removed to Halifax County and purchased a large estate and called his place "Woodlawn," not far from the little town of Clover. John Coleman was a vestryman in the Established Church, Antrim Parish, Halifax County, between the years of 1752-1776 (Bishop Meade). He was present as justice of county court in 1763, and was magistrate in county court in 1776, which tried eight Scotch merchants, factors charged with disaffection to the cause of the Colonies and sentenced to depart. John Coleman was a delegate to the General Assembly in May and October sessions of 1782.

Henry Embry Coleman, son of John and Sarah (Embry) Coleman, was born April 27, 1768, and married Ann Gordon June 13, 1795. He died December 16, 1837. She was born July 13, 1776, and died June 7, 1821. She was the daughter of Thomas Gordon and Peggy Murry, daughter of James Murry and Annie Bolling, daughter of Colonel John Bolling and Mary Kennon, son of Colonel Robert Bolling and Jane Rolph, daughter of Thomas Rolph and Jane Poythress. Thomas Rolph was son of John Rolph and Pocahontas.

Henry E. Coleman and Annie G. Coleman had the following children:

(1) John Coleman, married first Elizabeth Clark, second Mary Love. His only daughter married Mark Alexander, whose only child, Bettie, married Gen. Herbert, of Baltimore, Md.

(2) Thomas Gordon Coleman, born March 23, 1802; married May 6, 1828, Miss Annie Clark. She was born January 27 1807; died January 1899.

(3) Elizabeth Coleman, married Colonel Baskerville.

(4) Henrietta Maria Coleman, married Rev. John Clark.

(5) Margaret Murry Coleman, married Richard Logan.

(6) Sarah Embry Coleman, married David Chalmers.

(7) Ethelbert Algernon Coleman, married first Miss Simms, second Martha Frances Ragsdale.

(8) Jane Catherine Coleman, married a Mr. Hamilton.

(9) Henry Embry Coleman, married first Miss Turner, second Miss Bester, and had Anne Gordon, Lena, Alice and Perrin.

(10) Charles Baskerville Coleman, married first Miss Sarah Eaton and had Col. Henry Eaton; married second Miss Alice Sydnor and had Judith and Carrie.

Dr. Ethelbert Algernon Coleman, born February 12, 1812, died June 14, 1892, had by his second wife Martha Frances (Ragsdale) Coleman twelve children, of whom Nathaniel Ragsdale Coleman was the eldest son.

Nathaniel R. Coleman, was born July 19, 1843, in Halifax County, and died December 30, 1917. He married January 13, 1875, Annie Nelson Page, daughter of Frederick Winston Page and Annie Kinlock Meriwether, his wife, of Albemarle County, Virginia, and had the following children:

(1) Francis Coleman; born July 25, 1876, married Roger H. Williams.

(2) Natalie Coleman, born February 10, 1878, married Rev. George McLaren Brydon.

Henry Embry Coleman inherited "Woodlawn" and left it to his son, Charles B. Coleman, and he in turn left it to his daughter, Caroline, who married first Major Snowden and second Mr. Selden, and she sold it out of the family.

Sarah E. Coleman married David Chalmers and went to live with him at "Rose Hill," near News Ferry. Later Dr. Chalmers inherited his father's estate, "Springfield," and moved to it, replacing the original frame dwelling with a brick colonial one in 1842. Afterwards "Springfield" became the home of Henry Embry Coleman, son of E. A. Coleman, and his wife, Sally (Crump) Coleman, the granddaughter of David Chalmers, then it came into possession of their son, Oliver C. Coleman.

When Dr. Ethelbert A. Coleman, son of Henry Embry Coleman, married Miss Elizabeth Simms, he bought "Rose Hill" from David Chalmers, his brother-in-law, and lived there until his second marriage to Martha F. Ragsdale, when in 1841 or 1842 he built a brick colonial house not very far from the old frame dwelling at "Rose Hill" and called it "Creekside." This place was inherited by his son, Thomas G. Coleman.

Colonel Nathaniel R. Coleman, son of Ethelbert A. Coleman, inherited 'Riverside," the home of his mother's parents, where his widow, Mrs. Annie Nelson Page Coleman, remained after his death. It was purchased by Nathaniel Ragsdale, father of Martha F. Ragsdale Coleman, about 1810.

Nannie Coleman, daughter of E. A. Coleman, married Thomas Edmunds. They lived at "Elm Hill," a fine old brick house, surrounded by many acres, including the lands of the pre-Revolutionary "old Glebe Church." He inherited it from his father. "Elm Hill" was sold in 1894 to Mr. Harris.

Elizabeth Coleman, daughter of Ethelbert A. Coleman, married John Clark, who inherited "Banister Lodge." The first census of Virginia gives John Clark, of Halifax, four whites and fifty-eight slaves in the tax list, and the court records show original land grants surveyed March 7, 1750, 366 acres on branch of Runaway Creek and Bradley's Creek, transferred to Robert Weakley by order of Charles Coleman, August 5, 1771.

William Thompson, of Chesterfield County, sells to John Coleman, of Halifax County, on October 7, 1760, for 100 pounds, 400 acres on Piny branch of Difficult Creek. The records contain a number of deeds to and from John Coleman in the county.

Lieutenant John Coleman, from Halifax County, was in the Revolutionary War.

Many Colemans and Chalmers are buried in the church yard of the little church at News Ferry. *[A History of Halifax County, by Wirt Johnson Carrington, 1924]*

COLEMAN, Thomas G., Jr., was Junior 2nd Lieutenant and Acting Captain, Company K. 3rd Virginia Infantry, in the Civil War.

Thomas Gordon Coleman, Jr., was born June 29th, 1833, son of Thomas Gordon Coleman, Sr., of Halifax County, Virginia. In the autumn of 1853 — a few months after attaining his twentieth year — he matriculated as a student at the University of Virginia, and pursued his studies in that institution with creditable success during the sessions of 1853-54, '54-55, and '55-56. On the 25th of the following November he was married to Isabella, daughter of Hon. Alexander Rives.

On the 26th of April, 1861, he enlisted as a private in the "Halifax Light Infantry," Company K, 3rd Virginia regiment. His command was stationed near Richmond and at Ashland until the 18th of May, when it was ordered to the defense of the Peninsula. At Yorktown the troops were compelled to do hard manual labor in throwing up fortifications.

On the 10th of June the battle of Bethel was fought. A few days after the battle of Bethel, the 3rd Virginia was ordered to Williamsburg, and remained there until late in the fall.

About the 1st of December Company K went into winter-quarters at Smithfield, but in the spring it returned to the Peninsula, and took part in the frequent skirmishing about Yorktown. It was during their stay at Smithfield that Mr. Coleman was advanced by his comrades to the office of Junior Second Lieutenant.

In the month of April, 1862, Lieutenant Coleman's health gave way under the exposure in the low country, the effects of which were no doubt aggravated by excessive fatigue. At the house of a friend in Richmond, he was tenderly nursed through a dangerous attack of typhoid fever, from which, as soon as he was sufficiently recovered, he received a furlough to go home and recruit. He had scarcely recovered his strength when the battle of Seven Pines occurred; but being confident that the campaign had opened in earnest, he set out for the field against the advice of his friends, who thought him unfit for active service.

The 3rd Virginia was then in Pryor's Brigade, Longstreet's Division, and in all that series of seven days' battles around Richmond, in which Longstreet tore his laurels from the enemy, Lieutenant Coleman bore an honorable part. His regiment participated in all the charges of the 27th instant, except the last, from which it was withheld by the commanding General on account of exhaustion. On that day Captain West, of the "Halifax Light Infantry," was mortally wounded; and Pryor's Brigade, which went into its first battle fifteen hundred and forty-eight strong, lost during the seven days eight hundred and fifty-seven killed and wounded!

From Richmond, after the defeat of McClellan, the route of Longstreet soon led to Gordonsville, and thence at once to the support of Jackson, on the Rapidan. The history of Pope's continued retreat from that place, begun on the 18th of August, and culminating in the three days' battle of Second Manassas, is familiar to the reader. On the morning of the 29th, Longstreet forced his way through Thoroughfare Gap, and hurried to the aid of Jackson, who, having already fought the battle of the 28th, was now confronting the entire Federal army.

At that time Lieutenant Coleman was the only officer with Company K, and therefore had command of it. He passed safely through the ordeal of the 29th, in which his gallantry helped to purchase victory. On Saturday, August 30th, when at the head of his command, the whole brigade temporarily lost organization under a galling fire. Captain Coleman, in attempting to collect his men, leaped upon a stump, and waving his sword, cheered loudly to them to rally around him. He thus became only too sure a mark for the enemy's guns; and while exhibiting a coolness and daring, he fell, pierced by a ball, and expiring without a word, left his name. *[University Memorial Biographical Sketches of Alumni of the University of Virginia who fell in the Confederate War, by Rev. John Lipscomb Johnson]*

COLES family: John Coles came from Ireland to Virginia during the eighteenth century. He was an early settler in Richmond Town and, tradition has it, built one of the first houses there. He was senior warden of the parish, and dying in Richmond in 1747 was buried in the chancel of old St. John's Church. William Coles, a younger brother of John, and the grandfather of "Dolly Madison," followed his brother to Virginia and settled in Hanover County, where he built "Coles Hill."

Walter Coles, son of John Coles, settled in Halifax on a plantation which he named "Mildendo," after the metropolis of the imaginary country of "Lilliput" in "Gulliver's Travels." Mr. Coles died in 1780, leaving several sons and daughters. All of the sons died unmarried. One of the daughters, Mildred Howell Coles, married Mr. Carrington and had a number of sons. To these Carrington nephews, Isaac H. Coles, who died in 1814 and was the last surviving son of Walter Coles, left the bulk of his estate: "The Dan River tract" to Edward Carrington; "the Burch Skin" tract to Walter Carrington; The Cub Creek tract to Paul Carrington, and the Home House tract to William Carrington. Each of these plantations was fully provided with slaves and stock. The "Home House" tract, William Carrington's inheritance, was "Mildendo." The original house was burned long ago, and some time afterward William Carrington built a new one, modeling it after a cottage which had caught his fancy during a visit to England. It is only one story high and the windows upon one side open directly upon a lovely old flower garden, which slopes down to the Staunton River. The splendid oaks which surround the house were the original forest trees.

Mr. Carrington married a Miss Scott, who was a noted beauty and belle in her youth. From this couple, Mildendo passed to their son, Charles S. Carrington, president of the James River and Kanawha Canal Company, and his wife, who was Miss Susan McDowell, daughter of Governor James McDowell. Mildendo, after their time, passed from the Carrington family. *[Historic Virginia Homes and Churches, by Robert A. Lancaster, Jr.]*

"Mildendo"

COLLINS, Joel, was born 16 September, 1772, in Halifax County, Va., eldest of four children of Stephen Collins and wife. The family moved to Kentucky in 1779.

CONNALLY, James F., was born November 20, 1844, in the south part of Halifax County, close to the North Carolina state line. He is a son of George Franklin and Mildred (Lewis) Connally. The Connallys were of Irish stock, and came to America in Colonial times. One of them located at Connally Springs, North Carolina, near Asheville, another in Halifax County, Virginia, not far from Milton, North Carolina, and a third brother lived in Caswell County, North Carolina. The land granted to the Connallys in Halifax County by King George was in their possession continuously for a century and a half.

They were stanch Methodists, and were the principal founders of the Connally Methodist Church which James F. Connally attended as a boy. George Franklin Connally was born in Halifax County, and his wife in Charlotte County. He was a planter and slave owner, lived to the age of seventy, and started in life with his only capital consisting of a slave woman and a mule. The slave died and he lost the mule, but his energy and industry enabled him to build up a substantial property. His wife, who died at the age of sixty, was a member of the Baptist Church at Milton, North Carolina, not far from the Connally home in Halifax County. George F. Connally and wife had five sons and three daughters, the two still living in 1924 were James F. and his sister Mary, widow of John Lipscomb of Halifax. Of those deceased, Sarah was the wife of David Elliott. Walter became a Confederate soldier, at first in the Wise Legion, and after capture and parole he resumed fighting as a member of the Second Virginia Cavalry, under the command of Fitz Hugh Lee. Martha Ann became the wife of David Elliott, who married her sister. Henry, who was with the reserves, once was guarding a bridge and volunteered to cross the bridge under fire and convey ammunition to his comrades, carrying out this brave exploit unharmed, and after the war was a merchant at Leasburg, North Carolina, until his death in 1919. Robert became a farmer in Halifax County, and died in 1907. William H. was a farmer near Milton in Caswell County, North Carolina, and died in 1910.

James F. Connally had only a comparatively few-days to attend school. He was reared at the home farm in Halifax County, and for a time he attended school at Milton, North Carolina. The old Connally Church Building was used both for school as well as for religious purposes. Soon after the war between the states broke out his teacher left the school to go into the army, and that ended formal education for James F. Connally. He then worked on the farm, but he, too, soon went into the war, as a member of the Forty-fifth North Carolina Infantry, under General Daniels, which later became a part of Jackson's Corps, then under the command of General Ewell. He was on the advance line in the first day at Gettysburg, and was shot through the chin. He fell at a point where he was under fire from both sides, and the soldiers of both armies went back and forth over his body where he lay wounded. One bullet passed through the shoulder of his coat, another carried away his coat tail and another his haversack. It was on the fourth day following the close of the three days' battle, that he managed to crawl from the scene of battle, was picked up and placed in an ambulance, carried to the Potomac River and then walked 100 miles to Staunton. For ten days he was without food except a glass of milk. From Staunton he was sent to a hospital in Richmond, and after recovering he rejoined his command. His last battle was at Five Forks, where he was taken prisoner, but the war was soon over and he was confined at Point Lookout, Maryland, only a brief time.

In 1866 Mr. Connally moved to Charlotte County, where he engaged in farming two years. He then opened a store at his brother's mill on Turnip Creek, and was in business there six years. He had barely $5 in real capital when he engaged in business, and by strict attention to his work and an unfailing effort to fulfill all his obligations were the factors in making his business a steadily prosperous one. He remained there six years, and in 1874 came to Pamplin, where he is one of the oldest residents and business men. He was in business as a merchant here until 1914, a period of forty years. He put up the first brick store building after the fire which nearly destroyed the town in 1882, and was instrumental in securing an order of the Council to prohibit frame structures for business purposes. During the first six years he was at Pamplin he was a member of the firm Thornton & Connally, and subsequently was in business under his individual name until he retired. Mr. Connally was one of the organizers of the Bank of Pamplin, and for a number of years has effectively guided its destiny.

In 1895 he married Miss Alice W. Franklin, daughter of J. R. Franklin. Mrs. Connally was a member of the Methodist Church. Two children were born to them, both dying in infancy. *[History of Virginia, Vol. V, 1924]*

CRADDOCK family are of Welsh extraction (sometimes spelled Caradoc), and it appears that Granville Craddock was the first of the name in this county and is mentioned as a vestryman in Antrim Parish in 1753. *[Meade's "Old Churches and Families of Virginia."]*

We lose sight of the name until 1819, when one Granville Craddock makes his will naming his wife Eliza, sons William Townes Craddock and Charles James Fox Craddock, and a daughter, Sarah Cornelia Craddock, whom he does not wish under any circumstances to be placed under the guardianship of a stepfather in the event of his wife, Eliza, marrying again. Should his wife marry, then Sarah C. Craddock, his daughter, is to be placed in the custody of Mrs. Nancy Wimbish, her grandmother.

Eliza, the wife, did take a second husband, but she very wisely waited until Sarah Cornelia grew into woman-hood, when we find an indenture of marriage, May 2, 1837, between Abraham M. Poindexter, D. D. (Baptist minister), of the County of Wake, State of North Carolina, of the first part, and Eliza J. Craddock, widow and relict of Granville Craddock, late of Halifax County, Virginia, of the second part, and A. W. Wimbish, of the County of Campbell, State of Virginia, of the third part.

"Whereas, a marriage is shortly intended to be had, and solemnized by the permission of God, between the said Abraham M. Poindexter and the said Eliza J. Craddock, and whereas the said Eliza J. Craddock is possessed of considerable personal and real estate, consisting of all the land left her by her deceased mother, Mrs. Nancy Wimbish, excepting a portion of which she has given in trust for her children, the following household furniture, plantation utensils, stock, horses, hogs, cows and twenty slaves, etc."

John W. Craddock was born in Halifax County and married November 24, 1853, Mary B. Easley. His brother, Charles J. Craddock, married January 21, 1852, Fanny Y. Easley, a sister of his brother's wife. The Craddock brothers graduated in medicine and practiced their profession as partners in Halifax County for many years, prominent local physicians held in high esteem, loved and respected by all.

The children of Dr. John W. Craddock were:

(1) Charles Craddock.

(2) William Easley Craddock.

(3) John Bailey Craddock.

(4) Robert Owen Craddock.

(5) Frank Leigh Craddock.

(6) Edward C. Craddock, who married Mrs. Vaughan, daughter of Judge William R. Barksdale, and his first wife, Hallie Bailey (Craddock) Barksdale.

(7) Catherine Craddock, wife of D. L. Traynham.

(8) Eliza Craddock, wife of J. J. Lawson (children given under Lawson).

(9) Mary Craddock (married first Robert Lawson), wife of Lewis Johnson.

(10) Granville Craddock, who was one of the most efficient clerks that Halifax ever had. He married Martha Wyche, of Henderson, North Carolina, and left the following children, Elizabeth, Martha, Granville, and John.

(11) Miss Sarah Craddock.

Dr. Charles J. Craddock died at his residence near Halifax Court House, December 30, 1865, aged 47. His wife, Fanny. Y. Craddock, died in 1885. They left the following children:

(1) Dr. Thomas Easley Craddock, of Asheville, North Carolina.

(2) Abraham P. Craddock, of Lynchburg, Virginia.

(3) John Wimbish Craddock, born in Halifax County, August 14, 1858. Married December 6, 1886, Mary Peachy Gilmer, of Pittsylvania County. Mr. Craddock was president of the Craddock-Terry Shoe Co., of Lynchburg, Virginia, a man of progressive ability and "an influential and positive factor in the local business community, and in the shoe trade of the East and South."

The grave of Dr. John We Craddock is at "Cluster Springs" in the "God's Acre" of the old Thomas Easley home, where the Drs. Craddock found their wives. The hospitality of this old home is mentioned in Mrs, Phillips' letter, relating her trip to North Carolina, wherein she says: "At the appointed time we left home for Black Walnut, a village south of Dan, and stopped with Mrs. Easley, my mother's friend, a grand old lady, who gave us a most cordial reception. There I met her three children, Fannie, Mary and William (Thomas), a youth who in after years was a captain of a company of United States soldiers, in the war with Mexico, in the regime of Santa Anna. This handsome gallant officer was killed in that war."

In the graveyard, on the slab sacred to the memory of this handsome gallant young officer are these simple words: "Lieut. Thomas Easley, of the U. S. Army, fell at the Battle of Churubusco, near the city of Mexico, on the 20th day of August, in the 25th year of his age."

Another slab at the graveyard says, "Sacred to the memory of John W. Craddock. Born 1824, died 1884." "I heard a voice from heaven saying unto me, Write, blessed are the dead that die in the Lord. From henceforth, yea saith the spirit, that they may rest from their labors and their works do follow them."

Another slab was sacred to the memory of Thomas Easley, born 1780, died 1835. *[A History of Halifax County, by Wirt Johnson Carrington, 1924]*

CREWS family: Colonel George Reade came to Virginia in 1637, died 1671. Colonial secretary of Virginia. He married Elizabeth, daughter of Captain Nicholas Martin, of York County, Va.

Francis Reade (died 1694) married Jane, daughter of Colonel Edmund Chisman.

Elizabeth Reade, married before 1706, Paul Watlington, born May, 1678, of Abingdon Parish, Gloucester County.

Paul Watlington, born in Abingdon Parish, May 7, 1706. Died June 8, 1752. Married Elizabeth (Armstead?). (Abingdon Parish Register, Gloucester County, Va.)

Armstead Watlington, born in Abingdon Parish, December 27, 1730. Lived there in 1756. Married Susannah (born January 16, 1736), daughter of Thomas and Elizabeth Coleman, of Abingdon Parish, Gloucester County. Moved to Halifax County; Virginia, and was justice 1764 in Halifax. The census of 1782 for Halifax County gave him a family of six. He was appointed member of King's Council in Williamsburg, Virginia, December 19, 1764, and justice of the peace, 1776, in Pittsylvania County. [*Historical Magazine, Vol. XVI]*

Elizabeth Watlington, married in 1781, Peter Barksdale. [*Family Bible of Judge W. R. Barksdale and Halifax records.*]

William Peter Barksdale, born March 28, 1799, married Elvira Morton, March 3, 1824. She was born 1806. Issue:

- William A. Barksdale, unmarried.

- Elizabeth Barksdale, unmarried.

- Louisa Jane Frances Barksdale, married John Bullock Crews.

- Thomas Flournoy Barksdale, married first Emma Neal, second Nannie Cooper.

- James Peter Barksdale, married first Josie Johnson, second Mrs. Sarah Williams.

- Mary Virginia Barksdale, unmarried.

- Robert Morton Barksdale, unmarried.

- Alex. Sydnor Barksdale, married Ellen Martin.

- Charles Nelson Barksdale, unmarried.

Louisa Jane Frances Barksdale, born September 10, 1830; died August 28, 1907; married John Bullock Crews, January 13, 1858. Issue:

- William Henry Crews, married Emma Spigner.

- Elvira Randolph Crews.

- James Dabney Crews, married first Ella Grasty, second Sallie Holt.

- Elizabeth Virginia Crews, married Harrison Martin.

- Charles Crenshaw Crews, married Callie Woolfork, 1891. (their children: Helen Griffin Crews, married William Deloney Hull; Charles Richard Crews and Charlotte Crenshaw Crews.)

- Rosa Emaline Crews, married N. H. Hairston.

- Frances Sydnor Crews.

- Annie Laurie Crews.

- Mary Virginia Crews.

- John Bullock Crews.

- Louise Barksdale Crews.

Peter Barksdale was recommended for ensign to Captain Epaphroditus White's company of militia, February, 1779. [*Halifax Pleas, 9, 388.*]

William Sydnor was recommended as second lieutenant to Captain John Phelps company, Halifax militia, August, 1777. [*Halifax Pleas. 9, 233.*]

Nathaniel Barksdale served in the Revolutionary War.

Peter Barksdale was also in the Revolution.

[A History of Halifax County, by Wirt Johnson Carrington, 1924]

DABBS family: Josiah and Frances Elizabeth (Dabbs) Dabbs, both descendants of an old Colonial Virginia family. There was a Sir Richard Dabbs, one time Lord Mayor of London. Joseph Dabbs, an early settler in Virginia, was a Baptist minister, and was persecuted and imprisoned for preaching without authority from the established church.

Julia Frances Dabbs, daughter of Josiah and Frances Elizabeth Dabbs, was born in Halifax County, 21 November, 1829, and died 9 May, 1909. She married James Matthew Blanks, who was born in Charlotte County, Virginia, March 13, 1818. He was a farmer, and for many years lived at Clarksville, where he conducted a mercantile enterprise and was both postmaster and mayor of the town. *[History of Virginia, Vol. V, 1924]*

DeJARNETTE family: Will of Elias DeJarnette, 18 March 1784, Halifax County:

"My well beloved wife, Frances DeJarnette; daughters, Frances, Hannah, Sarah and Nancy DeJarnette; mother, Elizabeth DeJarnette, and sister, Annaker DeJarnette; my son, Reubin." Executors: Thomas DeJarnette, of Halifax, and James Rines, of Charlotte. Witnesses: Nathaniel, John and Ursley Hall.

Will of Daniel DeJarnette, 3 May 1831, Halifax County:

"I, Daniel DeJarnette, County of Halifax, State of Virginia, &c., do place in the hands of Richard Thornton as agent for my wife, Nancy DeJarnette, land and a good many slaves, some slaves to be hired to William Collins for mining purposes, together with the fishery. To my nephew, Daniel DeJarnette (son of George DeJarnette), slaves, &c. I also loan my wife during her widowhood one cery desk, one walnut burow, one bookcase, one bottle case, one chest of drawers, one large 'still,' and at her death I give them to the above Daniel DeJarnette. To James Pitts' wife (formerly Rebecca DeJarnette), $200.00. The residue of my estate to be sold, and from the proceeds thereof I give to Anney Sims (formerly Anney Betterton), $100.00, and the balance I want equally divided between my brother, James DeJarnette, and my sister, Susan Ranson, and my nephews, James, Thomas and Daniel DeJarnette, and sons of George DeJarnette."

Executor: William Collins.

Some DeJarnette marriages in Halifax County, Virginia:

Ann DeJarnette and James McAllister, 24 Oct. 1791.

D. DeJarnette (husband) and N. Smith, 6 Dec. 1794.

Daniel DeJarnette and E. Davis, 19 May 1853.

E. DeJarnette and Christopher Jennings, 10 July 1844.

Edna DeJarnett and Nathan Betterton, 26 Nov. 1798.

Edness E. DeJarnette and Thomas M. Purkins, 27 March 1851.

Edward DeJarnette and Martha Ann Forest, 21 Dec. 1843.

George DeJarnette and Sophia W. Waller, 15 Dec. 1852.

James DeJarnette and E. Pillar, 7 Sept. 1791.

Mary DeJarnette and Archer Williamson, 4 May 1802.

N. W. DeJarnette (wife) and Richard Forrest, 2 June 1853.

Voseline Degernette and Richard Ligon, 17 Dec. 1835.

DEWS, William, was a native of Virginia, where he passed his entire life and where he was an extensive and influential farmer.

He had a son, Samuel Stone, who was born in Halifax County, Virginia, in 1835. He was reared to the invigorating discipline of his father's farm and remained at the parental home until he had reached his twenty-fifth year, when he moved to West Virginia and located in the vicinity of Ansted, Fayette County. He served as captain of Company C, Twenty-second Virginia Infantry, Confederate army, and saw hard service throughout the entire period of the civil war, participating in many important battles marking the progress of hostilities. He was wounded twice, was prisoner of war for several months and was in the sanguinary Seven Days battle. He married Mollie Moore, who was also a native of Halifax County, Virginia. She is a daughter of William Moore, who was born in Virginia, where he lived until 1860 when he moved to West Virginia, where resided until his death, aged eighty-nine years; he was a farmer.

Mr. and Mrs. Dews became the parents of eight children: William; Nannie J., was a popular and successful teacher in the Mount Hope high school; Laura J.; Brackenridge; Robert S., maintained his home at Halifax, Virginia; May; Joseph H. and Mattie, who was the wife of B. W. Walker, of Caperton, West

Virginia. *[West Virginia and Its People, Volume 2, By Thomas Condit Miller, Hu Maxwell, 1913]*

DRINKARD family: There is an indenture in the court house between Robert Bromfield and John Drinkard, wherein Bromfield sells to Drinkard for the sum of two thousand pounds, "paid in hand," a parcel or tract of land, five hundred acres, lying on both sides of Bates' branch. The said tract of land later being in possession of Robert Bromfield and Peter Cruze, they both having plantations on the said tract, and the said premises are adjoining plantations and tracts of lands, to-wit: A tract of land formerly in the possession of Captain Epaphroditus White; a plantation or tract of land now in the possession of Richard North; a tract of land belonging to Simeon Holt and a tract belonging to John Hill, who sold and conveyed the same by proper deed of conveyance to the said Robert Bromfield, who conveyed to John Drinkard, his heirs, etc. Signed in the presence of William Oliver, Mary Oliver, Mel Spragins and Bernard McGuckin.

On the 6th day of April, 1781, William Bottom, of Amelia County, sells to John Drinkard, of Halifax County, four hundred and twenty-four and a half acres on Catawber creek, beginning at Ephraim White's line.

On June 17, 1784, John Drinkard, Sr., of Halifax County, sells to William Vasser three hundred acres in the Parish of Antrim, on Catawber creek.

There are many indentures of land sales and lands bought by John Drinkard in this county. Professor A. W. Drinkard, of the Agricultural Experiment Station of Blacksburg (V. P. I.), Virginia, is a descendant of this family of Drinkards. Among the marriage bonds there is a record of the marriage of Professor Drinkard's great-grandfather, Archibald Drinkard, to Edith Hawkins, of this county, September 21, 1802. Witness: Epaph Sydnor.

On August 3, 1802, Phil Hawkins takes to wife Elizabeth Drinkard, of this county. Witness: J. Wimbish.

[A History of Halifax County, by Wirt Johnson Carrington, 1924]

EASLEY family of Halifax County are very numerous, and only those who are individually interested would undertake to straighten out and connect the various lines. They may have all sprung from the same original source, but not from the same head in this county. Through the numerous wills and deeds recorded herein the descendants can place their ancestral lines without difficulty.

In 1786, January 12, we find recorded the will of Daniel Easley, wife Elizabeth, sons Daniel, Jr., Isaac, daughters Ann Easley, Mary Ann Parker and

Phoebe Adams. Grandchildren, Robert and Elizabeth Easley, children of John Easley. In 1782 an inventory of John Easley's estate was taken and Daniel Easley was appointed guardian of the two children, Robert and Elizabeth. This Daniel died in 1786, and his son, Isaac, was appointed their guardian, and in 1790 he renders an account of their expenses in part, viz.:

"To cash paid Philomon Hurt, for boarding, clothes, and schooling of Elizabeth and Robert Easley." Isaac, their guardian, hired out their slaves and rented the plantation. Among the small articles he bought for Elizabeth, now about grown, was numberless yards of ribbon, "lute string" and satin. We conclude that Elizabeth was pretty and dressed accordingly.

In 1812, October 26, the administration of Daniel Easley's will, with the will annexed, was granted to Thomas Easley.

In 1823, March 2, the will of Drury Easley was probated. Wife, Susannah; children, Edward, Milley and Albert S. Easley; daughter, Jane Watkins. One-fifth of his estate put in trust in the hands of his son, William B. Easley, for benefit of Jane Watkins.

In 1810, Isaac Easley leaves a will. Wife, Judith; sons, Isaac and John. He leaves to John the tract of land on Dan River. To son, William, the land he bought from Thomas Easley, on the north side of the road leading from Meadville to Halifax Court House.

Dr. Henry Easley, of Cluster Springs, married a Miss Bennett, a descendant of the emigrant Bennett, who lived near Mayo. Dr. Henry Easley married for his second wife (had no children by the first) Miss Ann Rebecca Louise Watkins, daughter of William Watkins, and had the following children:

(1) Andrew Easley served in the War Between the States and was severely wounded in the head.

(2) Thomas Easley served in the War Between the States. He was clerk of Halifax court for several years. His first wife, by whom he had no children, was Miss Mary Moon. For his second wife he married Hallie Owen, daughter of Mr. William L. Owen. They had the following children: Helen, wife of Rev. Stimson; Dr. Henry Easley, who married Miss Yuille, and Hallie Easley.

(3) Henry Easley was born at Cluster Springs, 15 December, 1847, and at the age of 17 entered the War Between the States. Joined Poague's battalion of light artillery and served until the surrender at Appomattox. Colonel Henry Easley has held many offices of trust in the town, county and State, and was one of the leading citizens of South Boston. He married August 15, 1873, Miss Nannie Preston Owen, who was born in Halifax County, daughter of Thomas E. Owen, who was also born in Halifax County. They had the following children: Irving Easley, wife of Howard Edmunds; Owen, who

married Susan Morton; Annie, wife of Dr. H. S. Belt; Mamie, wife of Wiltze Willingham; Henry; Thomas and William Preston, who died 29 May, 1887.

(4) John Watkins Easley (Jack) was born 22 October, 1849, in Halifax County. He married first Miss Sallie Irving Owen, daughter of Mr. Thomas E. Owen, a sister of Mrs. Henry Easley and a half-sister of Mrs. Robert E. Jordan Sr., and Mrs. Joseph Stebbins. They had one child, Mrs. Preston (Easley) Mulford. After his first wife died on 2 August, 1881, Mr. Jack Easley married a second time on 15 January, 1885, to Miss Jennie Owen, daughter of Mr. John Owen, a son of Mr. Robert E. Owen, and had the following children:

(1) John W. Easley, who married his first cousin, Willie Easley (daughter of Thornton Easley).

(2) Elizabeth Easley, wife of Charles Skinner.

(3) Marie Easley, wife of Bruce Pendleton.

(4) Henry Alex. Easley, married Miss Florine Irby.

(5) William P. Easley.

(6) Virginia Carrington Easley, wife of Carl Taylor.

(7) Robert M. Easley.

(5) Fannie Easley, wife of Robert A. Penick (children given under Penick).

(6) Louise Easley, wife of Maurice Penick; second, of Moses Bendall.

(7) Bettie Easley, wife of Dr. Thompson.

(8) Mattie Easley, wife of William E. Owen (son of Thomas E. Owen), a daughter, Louise, wife of Rev. David Lewis.

(9) Hallie Easley, wife of Mr. St. Claire (one daughter).

(10) Thornton Easley, who married Emma Jordan (daughter of R. E. Jordan, Sr.)

The Easleys of the town of Halifax do not claim relationship with the above Easleys, but we have discovered from a very old member of the family that they did "cousin" each other fifty years ago.

Robert Easley was born in Pittsylvania County March 3,1781. He married Nancy, born November 6, 1783. They lived near the old town of Peytonsburg. He died September 10, 1859. His son, James S. Easley, was born March 27, 1802, in Pittsylvania County. He married Miss Holt.

Robert Holt Easley, son of above, married Miss Louise Edmonia Gilmer, November 3, 1879, in Chatham, Pittsylvania County. They moved to Halifax. They had the following children: (1) Elizabeth Easley. (2) Florence Leigh Easley. (3) James Stone Easley. (4) George Gilmer Easley. (5) Louise Easley.

Mr. James Stone Easley, son of above, was a prominent lawyer and Commonwealth's attorney for the county. He married Miss Margaret Lyle, of Rogersville, Tennessee.

In 1681, a Robert Easley lived in Henrico County, Virginia. He died in 1711, leaving five hundred acres to his three children, viz.: John, Warham and Margaret (wife of Thomas Duprey). He mentions three younger children, Elizabeth, William and Robert. This Robert Easley may have been the progenitor of the Halifax and Pittsylvania Easleys. The Pittsylvania Easleys were in Halifax before the county was cut off in 1767.

We learn from the records that the first court was held at "Hampton Wade's house," and the tradition is that it was held at Peytonsburg, therefore we conclude that Hampton Wade lived at Peytonsburg, then Halifax County, now in Pittsylvania County. Marcellus French refers to it in his letter as a venerable place with few contemporaries.

Mr. Charles B. Easley, of Halifax County, Va., married October 16, 1877, a daughter of William Andrew Horsley, of "Rock Cliff," Nelson County, and his wife, Eliza G. Perkins, daughter of George and Eliza Richardson Perkins, of Cumberland County.

Letter From General George E. Pickett to Mr. William A. Owens, of Black Walnut, in Regard to the death of Lieutenant Easley.

"Mexico, Dec. 7, 1847.

"Dear Sir:

"As this is the first and in fact the only opportunity that has occurred since the reception of your letter by General Twiggs, I have taken advantage of it to answer as far as I am able some of the inquiries concerning one of my best friends, Lieutenant Easley. We have been together for more than five years, classmates at West Point and in the same regiment after graduating. From constant association, the hardships we have undergone, and the struggles shared together, being from the same State and having so many interests in common, I had for a long time regarded him, I may say, as an elder brother and from the many kindnesses and little attentions he had shown me always and on all occasions when necessary, and could be appreciated, I had for a long time been well aware that the feeling was reciprocated. I therefore considered it my melancholy duty to write to his relatives and should have done so had not Lieutenant Jones, of his own regiment, informed me that he had done so, also as he had charge of his effects, papers, &c.

"As far as regards his standing and reputation in the army I can give it to you in a few words. He was thought by all to be one of the most active, gallant and promising young officers in the service. His extreme bravery is shown by the manner of his death. He, Lieutenant Jones and fifteen men were together in front or face of the worst of Churubusco, advancing towards it under a heavy fire from it, when a company of deserters from our ranks, who had enlisted in the Mexican service and were at that time defending the works, fired a whole volley right amongst them, killing my poor friend Easley dead, and killing or wounding the fifteen men, leaving Lieutenant Jones alone standing.

"Lieutenant Easley was shot through the head, the ball inclining downward, and he must have died instantly. I believe he was more generally beloved than any other officer with us. It could not have been otherwise, for he combined such an amiable disposition with so much firmness and decision of character that no one could know him a week and not appreciate his character. He was a general favorite in my regiment, to which he formerly belonged, the Eighth, and we all felt his loss when he left us to join the Second, but I can not tell you how deeply grieved we were when we learned of his untimely fate. Every one knew he had lost a friend, and the service a gallant officer. I assure you this is not the only place where his loss is felt. He was known and loved by every member of my family. He, of course, was always with me in passing through Richmond and consequently became well known to both my father and mother; and in an answer to one of my letters my mother in speaking of him says she felt just as if she had lost a near and dear relative, and that my poor little note had caused as much sorrow as if he had been her brother. She and my sister had known us to be together so much and had heard me speak so often and so affectionately of him that they had grown to believe that he was my guardian saint, and the last remark my mother made was that she felt but little anxiety on my account during my journey, as Mr. Easley was going with me. That was when we left Virginia to join our regiment.

"Should you go to Richmond you will do me a kindness by calling on my father, and I will insure you of a sincere and hospitable welcome. He would feel most hurt did he know you had been there and he not known of it. Lieutenant Easley's trunk is in the hands of the quartermaster at New _____ (illegible) and can be obtained by applying to Colonel Hunt, the quartermaster at that place, with the military directions. The rest of his effects are now in the hands of Lieutenant Jones and will be forwarded by train which will leave within a few days.

"I must now bide you farewell, sir, with the hope that we may meet at some future time, when this disastrous and bloody war has closed, and we may then have an opportunity of conversing upon a melancholy though dear and interesting subject to us both.

"With my kindest regards to his mother and sisters, I remain,

"Yours, etc.,

"Geo. E. Pickett."

"Dear Sir:

"The remains of the lamented Easley have been taken up and properly enclosed for transportation to his native place. They will go to Vera Cruz, by train that leaves tomorrow, in charge of Captain Kingsbury. They will be shipped from there at the first opportunity. While there they will be in charge of Lieutenant Patrick, Second Infantry. Some of his effects, with the greater part of mine, were lost while coming into the city. The rest I have packed up and will send, as above stated. If you have not received my first letter, write me and I will again give you the particulars of the death of my best friend. This I write you on a vacant space in Pickett's letter. He would have written by the first train, but knew that I had done so. Lieutenant Pickett, though not with us in the battle, was doing honor to his State in another part of the field.

"Yours sincerely,

"D. R. Jones."

The above was the celebrated General George E. Pickett, of "Pickett's Charge" at Gettysburg, and who was so prominent in the battles of Fredericksburg, Petersburg and Five Forks. He was born in Richmond, Virginia, January 25, 1825, graduated at West Point in 1846, served in the Mexican War as lieutenant in 1847, was made captain in 1855. In 1861 he left the service of the United States and joined the Confederate army. He was commissioned brigadier-general and was distinguished throughout the war for bravery and activity. He died in Norfolk, Virginia, July 30, 1875. *[A History of Halifax County, by Wirt Johnson Carrington, 1924]*

EASLEY, William H., of Halifax County, was the youngest brother of Lieut. Thomas Easley. He was Captain in Company "C," 3rd Virginia Cavalry in the Civil War. William H. Easley, the youngest son of Captain Thomas Easley, of Halifax County, Va., was born the 16th of April, 1832. His father was widely known and highly respected in his county, which he represented in the Virginia Legislature in the days when it was an honor to be elected to serve in her halls. Captain Thomas E. died in 1835, leaving a widow with six children, —three sons and three daughters. The mother, whose maiden name was Harriet Bailey, faithfully discharged the duties devolving on her in training and educating her children. Her eldest son, Thomas Easley, was the first graduate at West Point of his Congressional district. "He fell, fighting most gallantly, at the head of his men," in the battle of Churubusco, the last engagement of the Mexican War. The following spring the body of Thomas E. was brought from its temporary resting-place in a foreign soil to be laid in the family burying-ground. The military funeral, which drew together a vast crowd, seemed a mockery of grief to the older members of the family, but the ardent boy, William, was thrilled with dreams of glory. When the time came for going to college, he earnestly begged to be allowed to go to West Point; but his mother, who blamed herself for the military education of the older son, would not consent. Finally, as a compromise, he proposed the Virginia Military Institute, assuring his mother, if war came, he would fight for his country, and it would be better as an officer than as a private soldier.

He entered the Institute in January, 1853; remained until July, 1856, when he graduated. William was of a frank, genial nature, and from boyhood to manhood exercised a charm over his associates. He had fine abilities, and the best, most generous heart that ever beat. After leaving the Institute, for a year or so he lived with his mother, attending to her farm. At this time his social disposition led him into such company and habits as made his friends very unhappy, but through the mercy of God he was led to see and repent of his folly. He made a profession of religion, and joined the Presbyterian Church. He bought a farm, and was living on it, respected and beloved by a large circle of friends, when the late unhappy war called him to other scenes.

A volunteer company was raised in the neighborhood, and he was given command of it. This company, the "Black Walnut Light Dragoons," was composed of noble young men from the best families, who willingly gave up the comforts and luxuries of life to repel the invader. When congratulated on having the command of such a company, he replied, "I am proud of my men; no promotion would tempt me to leave them; but we will have a hard struggle, and when I think of what is before us, I wish they were mere soldiers, not 'friends and kinsmen" Captain Easley went into camp early in May, 1861, and daily exercised them in such drills as would make them more efficient in service. On the 24th of May the company left Black Walnut, and was marched into service in Richmond on the 29th, and assigned to duty in the Peninsula, near Yorktown. It was Co. "C," 3rd Regiment Virginia Cavalry, at first commanded by Major Hood (afterwards major-general). When the regiment was filled, General Johnson was placed in command. This regiment did a good deal of picket and scout duty, being the only cavalry regiment on the Peninsula for some time. They also pushed the enemy in their retreat from the battle of Bethel. Captain Easley filled all the duties of his office till November, 1861, when he was taken sick at the Half-Way House. His brother-in-law, Dr. C.,. was there at the time, and persuaded him to accompany him on his return to Halifax, where his chances of a speedy recovery would be much greater than at the noisy station. But his disease baffled the skill of physicians and the tender nursing of loving hearts that gathered around his bedside. On the night of the 10th of December, it became apparent that he must soon die. All night long his mind wandered,—most frequently he was in camp, giving orders to his men; then he would fancy he was in action, and describe a bloody engagement. As morning broke, his sister, who had watched and listened in agony to his wanderings, asked if he would not try to call his mind from such bloody scenes and fix them on Christ, who had died for him. He looked earnestly at her, and said, "I will try to pray, and you must pray for me." Then folding his hands on his breast and closing his eyes, he remained awhile apparently in prayer. Looking around after this, and seeing his mother weeping at the foot of the bed, and his servant kneeling near, sobbing as if his heart would break, he asked his mother, and then the servant, if he was dying; and, as they did not reply, he turned to his sister and repeated the question, "Am I dying?" The two physicians in attendance told her to tell him the truth; but one fearing she would not have nerve to speak the sad words, left to call the minister. His sister told him he was dying, but since Christ had died for sinners, none that trusted in Him need fear death. His face became calm, and he repeated, "Yea, though I walk through the valley of the shadow of death, I will fear no evil, Thy rod and Thy staff they comfort me." Pausing a moment, he said, with a tone of awe, "Then I will soon be dead, *dead*?" His sister replied, "Dead to earth, alive to the glories of Heaven." "Yes, I will soon be home," pointing and looking upward. Then he repeated, "Glory to God in the highest, peace on earth, good will to men," with an expression so bright, that his mother, clasping her hands, repeated, "Glory! glory!" The minister coming in, and not knowing what had passed, told him he must die. He said, "I know it; I had hoped to lead a useful life, but it's God's will; I'm resigned." He then asked the minister to pray for him, after which he requested to be left with his sister and servant. He was now so weak as to be able to speak only a few words connectedly, but he delivered a last message, for human love is strong even in death. Then he told his servant to hand him a shaving-glass from the mantel. It was strange the quiet look he gave, and the comment, "I look very natural." One of his company, who was on furlough and hearing of his illness, called just then to see his captain. When asked if he wished to see Dick Adams, he replied, emphatically, "Yes, I wish to see him." And when the poor fellow came in, and, after shaking hands and telling his captain, with choking voice, he was sorry to find him so sick, would have shrunk back to hide his emotion, he said, "Adams, you must—tell me farewell. Tell all the—boys—farewell. Tell them if" his sister, to help his failing voice, said, "if I have been too strict —" Looking in her face, he said, "Not that,—I *wasn't too strict*. If I have— hurt their feelings—forgive me—remember me. I remembered—them—to the last."

As calmly as an infant going to sleep, in a few moments more his spirit passed away, the 11th of December, 1861, as truly a sacrifice to the war as any who fell on the field of battle. *[Memorial, Virginia Military Institute, 1875]*

EASLEY, Dr. William D., was born in Halifax County, Va., in 1832. He was a graduate of the University of Virginia and took his medical course at the University of Pennsylvania at Philadelphia. Dr. Easley practiced medicine at Cannelton, West Virginia. He married Betty, daughter of John S. and Adeline Chaffin, of Virginia. Dr. and Mrs. Easley had a son, Edwin H., who was born 19 May, 1865, in Amelia County, Virginia. Dr. Easley was killed, in 1877, in a railroad accident in Kanawha County, West Virginia. *[West Virginia and Its People, Volume 2, By Thomas Condit Miller, Hu Maxwell, 1913]*

EDMONDSON / EDMUNDSON, family: Will of Samuel Edmundson, 3 Feb. 1819, Halifax County -- Wife, Caroline; sons, Samuel and Richard, "all lands in the counties of Halifax and Mecklenburg counties"; daughters, Margaret and Susannah, Lucinda, Nancy Hamner, Rachel Phillips, Patsy Anderson and Polly White. Two faithful old servants to the care of son, Richard, neither to be hired out or sold. Executors: Sons, William, Banister, Samuel and Richard Edmundson,

Major Henry, A. Edmondson descends from families seated in Halifax County in the eighteenth century. He was born in this county, on October 20, 1833, the son of Richard Edmondson, who was born in this county, and who died in November, 1857, aged 74 years. His mother, Miss Susan Howell Chastain, daughter of Rene Chastain, a descendant of the Huguenots.

His wife was born in Halifax County, Sallie A., daughter of Nathaniel H. Poindexter, and they were married at Halifax C. H., on May 21, 1857. Their children were born in the order named: Mary J., Susan H., Francis W., Anna H., Robert H., Rosa L., Lula H., Lizzie A., Willie L., Sallie A., and Frank. Their son, Henry A., died in August, 1865, aged seven years.

Mrs. Edmondson's father was born in Halifax County, and died in 1859, aged fifty-one years. Her mother, who was Miss Mary Johnson before marriage, died in 1883, aged seventy-two years.

Mr. Edmondson received his education in the schools of Halifax County. From 1852 to 1857 he clerked for Estes & Avery, general store. In April, 1861, he entered the Confederate States Army, in Company A, Montague's Battalion, and served till the close of the war, twice slightly wounded. He was promoted first lieutenant; later was commissioned major of the 53rd Virginia Infantry, a regiment of Pickett's division. Among the battles in which he took part were: Bethel, Seven Pines, Malvern Hill, second Manassas, Fredericksburg, Gettysburg, those around Petersburg, Sailors Creek, Five Forks.

After the war, Major Edmondson returned to Halifax County, where he engaged in farming until, in 1869, he was elected high sheriff of the county, which office he filled until 1887. He also dealt extensively in tobacco since

1872, was owner of the Edmondson Warehouse and interested in the Flag Warehouse, both at South Boston; was also a partner in the general store of Edmondson & Shepherd, South Boston. *[Virginia and Virginians, Vol. II]*

F. R. Edmondson, the representative of the Edmondson family in South Boston, was a progressive and influential business man, with extensive tobacco interests in the re-drying department, and a leading member of the Co-operative Tobacco Association.

He is the son of Major H. A Edmondson and his wife, Sally Owen (Poindexter) Edmondson. Major H. A. Edmondson was son of Richard and Susan (Chastain) Edmondson.

Major H. A. Edmondson had the following children:

Henry Archer.

Mary Johnson, wife of Edward G. Dorsey.

Susan Howell, wife of Captain Henry Edmunds.

Ann, wife of Joseph Farrall.

Fanny O'Connor, wife of James M. Faulkner.

Robert Hurt, married Sarah Glenn Hudman.

Rosa Lee, wife of A. P. Craddock

Lula Howard.

Elizabeth Archer, wife of Frank Willingham.

Willie Leander, wife of Thomas Barksdale Johnson.

Sallie.

Frank R. Edmondson, married Sarah Ridley Green, daughter of Alex. R. and Elizabeth (Wauhop) Green. They had four children: Archer, Frank, Lizzie and Sallie. Mr. Edmondson had one of the handsomest and most perfectly equipped and furnished homes in South Boston, from which they extend a lavish hospitality to their many friends and acquaintances. They were staunch members of the Episcopal Church and Mrs. Green, the mother of Mrs. Edmondson, was the organist for many years.

The Edmondsons have intermarried with so many of the prominent people of Halifax that their kinship is intricate and interesting, and runs in lines reaching through many States. They were not wanting in courage or valor, for the Revolutionary roster contains many of the name, and eight fought in the Battle of King's Mountain. Lieutenant Robert Edmondson, Sr., fought to his death, Robert E., Jr., was wounded, Captain William Edmondson was killed. Andrew, Sr., Andrew, Jr., John and Samuel were privates. We do not know if there is any relationship between those bravest of the brave soldiers and the

Edmondsons of Halifax, but we are inclined to think there was. [A History of Halifax County, by Wirt Johnson Carrington, 1924]

Howell Chastain Edmondson, the sixth son of Richard and Susan H. Edmondson, was born on the 25th of January, 1845, in the County of Halifax, Virginia, and died at Chimborazo Hospital, Richmond, on the 24th of June, 1864, of typhoid fever.

While but a boy Howell Chastain was possessed of qualities which, if his life had been spared, would have developed themselves into a noble Christian manhood. There was something so pure in his nature, so tender and considerate in his disposition, and withal so quietly brave in his bearing among men, that all who knew him were unconsciously forced to respect and love him. There are many who can remember his sweet-toned voice in the choir of old St. John's Church, and when he left, in 1859, to enter the Virginia Military Institute, all who were intimate with him felt sure that his devoted and pious mother had instilled such Christian principles into his young heart as would enable him to be true and manly and moral amid all the new temptations of college life,—principles which took deeper root and grew stronger in the face of those temptations, and which finally led him to embrace the Christian religion, and unreservedly to give his heart to the loving Savior.

He remained at the Virginia Military Institute until it was broken up by the war,—during which time he was once in active service with the Cadet Corps. Immediately after he left the Institute, in 1862, he joined the 1st Company of Howitzers, and remained in service until his death, never returning alive to his home in Halifax County.

Although but a youth,—only seventeen years of age when he entered the army,—he bore the hardships and privations of war without a murmur or a word of regret. He marched abreast with the strongest and the hardiest soldier, and his conduct in battle was that of a heroic and Christian patriot.

One incident in his career as a soldier is mentioned by one of his comrades, which the writer of this brief memoir cannot omit, as it exhibits both his coolness and his reliance upon God in the midst of danger. In one of the battles around Richmond, while the enemy was making a fierce assault, a comrade turned to Howell and asked him how he felt. Although under fire at the time, he calmly replied, "I fear no evil, whatever, for I have long made my peace with God."

In order to show in what esteem he was held by his fellow soldiers, we quote the following extract from the resolutions passed by the 1st Company of Richmond Howitzers: "In the death of this, our brother, though tender in years, the company has lost a pious and exemplary member, and the country a brave and patriotic defender. Stimulated by the desire to share the dangers with his brothers in the field, he came without any compulsion from his quiet studies at the Virginia Military Institute, and enlisted in his country's service. But, alas! the unrelenting hand of death has snatched him from existence; yet will his memory live, and the incidents connected with our long and pleasant association with him be the most pleasing recollections of after-life."

Yes, "his memory will live," for he was of a most loving and affectionate disposition. The youngest scion of his father's house, he was the pride and pet of his family, and all words are idle to convey an adequate expression of the grief which his untimely death caused in his bereft household. But, though gentle and affectionate, he was no less brave and ardent in the defense of his country. *[Memorial, Virginia Military Institute, 1875]*

EDMUNDS family came from the Eastern Shore to Charlotte County, and from Charlotte County to Halifax, where we find Henry Edmunds, of "Elm Hill." His son is John R. Edmunds, of "Redfield," a grand old home built before the War Between the States by the slaves on the plantation with brick made by them and wood from the surrounding forest. It was colonial style, contained fourteen rooms, with closets, etc., and situated in beautiful surroundings.

John R. Edmunds married Mildred Coles, daughter of Isaac Coles, Sr., and his wife, Lightfoot Carrington, of "Springwood," near Meadville. Their children were (1) Paul, (2) Nannie C., (3) Henry, (4) John R., (5) Lizzie Lightfoot and (6) Sallie Edmunds.

Captain Henry Edmunds, of "Elm Hill," married Martha Morton, and their children were:

(1) Susan Edmunds, wife of Robert Gaines, of Charlotte County.

(2) John R. Edmunds, who married Mildred Coles.

(3) Charlotte A. Edmunds, wife of George W. Read, of Charlotte County.

(4) Major Littlejohn Edmunds, who married Sallie White (daughter of Dr. White).

(5) Sterling Edmunds, who married Mary J. Claiborne.

(6) Elizabeth Edmunds, wife of Dr. Robert Jennings.

(7) Sarah Edmunds, wife of Thomas Barksdale.

(8) Joseph N. Edmunds (Charlotte County), married Bettie Hodge.

John R. Edmunds was a wealthy man before the Civil War, a staunch sympathizer with the South, and among the many conspicuous services that he did was the building for the Confederate government that section of the

Southern Railway lying between Danville and Greensboro. He owned many slaves and other property and was also a large land owner.

Hon. Paul Carrington Edmunds (son of John R. Edmunds) married Phoebe Ann Easley, and they were the parents of Mr. Henry Edmunds, who, ever zealous of good works, established a home for orphan girls near the town of Halifax. It flourished for a good many years, with some shall help from the churches and charitable organizations, but as the inmates increased the expenses also increased, and what to do with these girls after several years of training was a perplexing question and one that gave Mr. Edmunds a good deal of concern. The responsibility was very great, there were no homes in which they could be placed, to work and to live, and after due consideration Mr. Edmunds turned the matter over to the church and the church converted the home into a community house. We do not know what disposition the church made of the girls in the home at that time. Mr. Edmunds named the home as a memorial to his mother, "The Phoebe Ann" Home. He loved the work, and no doubt would have pursued it but for the force of circumstances and the best of reasons. Mr. Henry Edmunds married December 16, 1892, Miss Louise Gilmer Riely, daughter of Colonel John W. Riely (C. S. A.), attorney-at-law and member of Virginia Court of Appeals. They had the following children:

(1) Emma Cabell Edmunds, wife of Rev. Locke White, missionary to China.

(2) John Riely Edmunds.

(3) Elizabeth Holt Edmunds

(4) Margaret Carrington Edmunds.

(5) Louis Henry Edmunds.

(6) Richard Coles Edmunds.

(7) Phoebe Easley Edmunds.

(8) Paul Carrington Edmunds.

(9) Robert Holt Edmunds.

Among the first land grants and surveys was one made for Nicholas Edmunds of 2,435 acres.

There is a tradition in the family that Isaac Coles, Sr., died broken-hearted after the death of his beautiful wife, Lightfoot Carrington. They had three children: Mildred Coles, who married John R. Edmunds; Elizabeth Coles, who married Willis Walker (of Charlotte), and Isaac Coles, Jr., who married Fannie Green, and were the parents of Eliza Coles, who married Norman Spragins, and of Miss Eliza Burton Coles. It is very seldom that we hear of a broken-hearted man, but Halifax has had more than one woman who died of a broken heart, if we must believe some of its records. *[A History of Halifax County, by Wirt Johnson Carrington, 1924]*

EDMUNDS. J. E., Esq., was born in July, 1860, in Halifax County, Va., the eldest son of Paul C. and Phoebe (Easley) Edmunds.

His father, Hon. Paul Carrington Edmunds, was born 1 November, 1836, in Halifax County, Virginia. He was educated by a private tutor at home, and was three years at the University of Virginia, and graduated in law at William and Mary College, at Williamsburg, Virginia. He practiced law for nearly two years in Jefferson City, Missouri, but returned to Virginia in 1858, and engaged in agriculture on his farm in Halifax County. He was elected to the Senate of Virginia in 1881. After honorable service in the Virginia Senate for eight years, he was elected to the United States Congress from the Sixth District of Virginia.

His mother, Mrs. Phoebe (Easley) Edmunds, was daughter of James A. Easley, Esq., a wealthy and prominent business man of Halifax County.

Mr. J. E. Edmunds graduated at the Virginia Military Institute in the class of 1880, and, after teaching at Locust Dale Academy, studied law at the University of Virginia, receiving the degree of B. L. After completing his studies he located in Lynchburg, Va. *[South-West Virginia and the Valley, A. D. Smith & Co., 1892]*

FARMER family: The first we find of the name of Farmer is an inventory of the estate of Frederick Farmer, deceased, March 12, 1782. The county has many worthy families by the name of Farmer, most of them members of the old "Pleasant Grove Church," where for generations they have worshipped, and there in the old churchyard have laid their dead to rest. They have been well-to-do land and slave owners, and some of them have grown rich by economy and persistence.

In Halifax County will book 15, Will of David Farmer, 16 December 1825:

"My wife, Jane Farmer; son, Obediah; grandson, Henry Farmer; granddaughter, Polly Farmer. Balance of my estate divided between Hannah East, Ruth Famer and my granddaughter, Polly Ragland. Executor, my son, Obediah Farmer.

"David Farmer."

Witnesses: Archer Farmer and Jeremiah Farmer. Recorded Aug. 24, 1831.

Will of Archer Farmer, 24 March 1856:

Wife, Nancy; son, Joseph E. Farmer; grandson, John Harrison Farmer, "when he arrives at the age of 21." Confirmed what he had already given (which was very liberal) to Lucy A. Farmer, William W. Farmer, Elizabeth Russell, Harriett C. Chappell, Archer Farmer and James R. Farmer. Remainder of property to be equally divided among the last named six children.

"My will and desire is that my old negro man Gilbert and his wife Nancy shall have the privilege of choosing their master or mistress from among my children, said master or mistress to pay their appraised value. I appoint my son, William W. Farmer, or Archer H. Farmer, my executor and request that the court will not require security.

"Archer Farmer."

Witnesses: D. Chalmers, John Hughes, William Holt. (Archer H. Farmer gave bond for $60,000 without security.)

FAULKNER family: Dr. Leander Faulkner was born in Halifax County, November 11, 1818. After receiving the ordinary school education of those days, he attended lectures in Philadelphia in the University of Pennsylvania, and received therefrom a diploma of doctor of medicine, April 3, 1820. He returned to Halifax and began the practice of medicine. On the 14th day of January, 1846, he married Miss Sarah Elizabeth Green, the daughter of Thomas Jefferson Green and his wife, Frances Keeling (Burton) Green. Of this marriage there were born seven children, viz.: Thomas G. Faulkner, Charles James Faulkner (born July, 1849, in Halifax Co., Va.), Mary Elizabeth Faulkner, Mrs. T. W. Leigh, Leander Faulkner, Garland Estes Faulkner, Frank Faulkner and John Minge Faulkner.

Thomas Faulkner, the first of the name in the Colony, came in 1622 and settled in Elizabeth City County.

The first we find in Halifax County was Benjamin Faulkner (the great-grandfather of Leander Faulkner). He was born December 17, 1714, being the eleventh and last child of Thomas and Mary Faulkner, of King and Queen County. He was married twice. By his first marriage he had three children, of whom Jacob Faulkner, the grandfather of Leander Faulkner, was the eldest.

Benjamin Faulkner was in Halifax County in 1780, as we find from the census of that year, in which he was listed as head of family of ten (whites) and eleven (slaves).

His son, Jacob Faulkner, did not come with him at the time he moved to Halifax, but came later and settled in Halifax and was for a number of years the county surveyor, and as such laid off the first town of South Boston (which was then called Boston and later Old Boston), on the south side of the river. Jacob Faulkner married Catherine Howerton.

Benjamin Faulkner married the second time, and of that marriage there were eight children, three sons and five daughters. One of the sons, Joseph Faulkner, was the grandfather of Mr. R. E. Jordan, Sr., and others of the Jordan family.

The will of Benjamin Faulkner, dated October 20, 1783, is recorded in Halifax County, July 15, 1784, and Jacob Faulkner was one of the executors.

James Faulkner was married three times—first, February 10, 1804, to Martha Jane Jordan; second, July 16, 1816, to Mrs. Obedience Major, a widow. She was a Hamlet, of Charlotte County, before her marriage to Major. He married, thirdly, December 28, 1837, Mary Averett. There were children of all of those marriages. Leander Faulkner, the subject of this sketch, was the first child of the second marriage to Mrs. Obedience Major. He continued to practice medicine in Halifax County until 1900, when he received a sunstroke and remained in bad health until 1902, when he died and was buried in St. John's church yard, Halifax, Virginia, of which church he had been a most consistent member and a vestryman for about fifty years.

Dr. Leander Faulkner was no ordinary country doctor, but a prototype for those who succeeded him. He was the first physician in this county to diagnose the disease, myxoedemer, and prescribe thyroid for it, when other doctors in Richmond, Lynchburg and in this county were treating the case for heart disease; and when the patient was taken to Dr. Osler, then of John Hopkins, Dr. Faulkner's diagnosis was confirmed and the same treatment prescribed. He was an intense student and always so deeply interested in his cases as to read everything he could obtain concerning them. He loved his profession so well that he not only ministered to the sick, but contributed to their necessities as well. He was a "country doctor" after the order of "Weelum MacLure," and gathered the love of his clients as he worked among them, counting their friendship as the gift of God.

When he left the University he was very anxious to go to China as a medical missionary, and it was a blessed thing for Halifax County that his wife was not willing to give up her home and all she held dear here, to accompany him, and so he fought, like St. Paul, a good fight here, and laid down his armor after a long and useful life.

His daughter, Mrs. T. W. Leigh, had the following children:

(1) Sarah Leigh.

(2) Mary Grammer Leigh, wife of John Taylor.

(3) William Leigh.

(4) Thomas Leigh, married Louise Carrington (of Charlotte).

(5) Rebecca Leigh, wife of William Channing Harrison.

(6) Leander Leigh, married Bessie Monroe (of Brookneal).

[A History of Halifax County, by Wirt Johnson Carrington, 1924]

FERRELL, Peter W., was born May 31, 1832, in Halifax County, Virginia, where his father and mother were born, and where they were honored residents through life. His father, Bird L. Ferrell, born in 1798, died in 1871. His mother, Ann D. Reeves, born in 1797, died in 1872. His brother, Edwin R., who was a soldier in the Confederate States Army, died in 1885. Peter W. Ferrell attended schools in Halifax County, and finished his studies at Richmond College. In 1856 and 1857 he taught school in Halifax County; in 1858 removed to Danville and began business as a tobacco manufacturer, firm of Sutherlin & Ferrell. In 1865 this firm dissolved, and Mr. Ferrell continued business alone, as a leaf tobacco dealer, until 1878 when he entered into a partnership business again, firm of Farrell & Flinn. In the fall of 1885 he again began business for himself, leaf tobacco broker, place of business corner of Craghead and Loyal Streets. For eight years, 1871-9, Mr. Ferrell was president of the Danville Tobacco Association. In Danville, March 24, 1862, Rev. C. C. Chaplin officiating, he married Lucy C. Neal, of Danville. They had three children: Lena M., Thomas N. and Rosa A., and have buried two daughters: Nannie R. and Loula F. Mrs. Ferrell is the daughter of Thomas D. and Louisa F. (Carter) Neal.

Thomas D. Neal, was born in October, 1812, in Pittsylvania County, and died 21 June, 1884, in Richmond. Thomas D. Neal's wife was Louisa F. Carter, born in 1821, in Halifax County, Virginia, daughter of Col. Samuel Carter, of Halifax County. *[Virginia and Virginians, Vol. II]*

FLING, Richard, was born 25 May, 1783, in Halifax County (?), Virginia. He was a private in Capt. Joseph Sandford's Company, 69th Regiment, Virginia Militia, (Halifax County) 27 June, 1813, to 19 August 1813, also private in Capt. John A. Burd's Company, Col. Laval's Regiment, U. S. Light Dragoons, War of 1812. (In Battle of North Point, 14 September, 1814, wounded, discharged 1 May, 1815, received pension.) He settled at Bloomington, Illinois, about 1836, where he died on 28 September, 1855. He was buried in the old City Cemetery, in Bloomington, Illinois. Richard Fling's wife was Elizabeth (Wilkinson) Fling. Children were: Richard Fling, Jr., Owen Fling, Thomas Fling, Ann E. (Fling) Williams, Angeline A. (Fling) Heller.

FLOURNOY family: The inventory of Matthew Flournoy's (wife, Elizabeth) estate, in 1761, was large and comprehensive, slaves, lands, etc. Among other things was "Liquor for Charles Smith's funeral." He had large interests in Prince Edward as well.

The estate of Charles Smith, also a large estate, was wound up the same year, but does not indicate what relationship he bore to the Flournoys.

To Elizabeth Flournoy, one-third part.

To the orphans, two-thirds.

To orphans of Charles Smith, the balance due from Matthew Flournoy to the orphans.

One negro named Jacob, one named Dick, one named Hannah (Flournoy's choice).

Thirty-two head of cattle, one-third part left on the plantation of the orphans, one-third part of which belongs to Mrs. Flournoy, and two-thirds to the orphans.

August 19, 1761.

Witnesses: Robert Wade, William Stokes, Abram Maury.

Settlement of the estate of Charles Smith, deceased, due to Flournoy, etc.

Thomas S. Flournoy was born in Prince Edward County, December 15, 1811. He was married, January 1, 1835, at General Edward C. Carrington's in Halifax County, Virginia, by the Rev. Mr. Montgomery to Miss Susan Ann Love, daughter of Allen Love, Esq., a distinguished lawyer.

Alexander Brown says of Thomas S. Flournoy: "As a criminal lawyer Colonel Flournoy had few, if any, superiors in the State, and his power in swaying a crowd from the stump was second only to his effectiveness before a jury." He died March 12, 1883, at his residence in Halifax County. He had by this marriage six children.

Thomas S. Flournoy married the second time, July 22, 1852, at "Cole's Hill" (by Rev. John A. Scott) Mildred H. Coles, daughter of Hon. Walter Coles, of Pittsylvania County, and his wife, Lettice, daughter of Judge Paul Carrington, the elder, of Charlotte County (by his second wife, Priscilla Sims), and by this wife he had seven children.

The Flournoy family has been thoroughly written up, from its emigrant and origin to the present time. They did not belong to this county, except the names given above. The old Matthew Flournoy home was situated on a beautiful elevation commanding an almost unsurpassed view. At the foot of a long sloping hill is the Flournoy graveyard, the thick undergrowth of shrubs, flowers, weeds and brambles would not admit of close inspection, but through the tangle could be seen some marble tombstones, and on a cleared spot was the grave of a soldier of '61, the name and inscription too faded out of the painted board that marked the head to be deciphered. *[A History of Halifax County, by Wirt Johnson Carrington, 1924]*

FOURQUREAN family were among the Huguenots who settled in Halifax at an early date, as well as the La Grands, Fontaines, Chastains, Flournoys and many others.

The Fourqureans came from the Huguenot colony of South Carolina to Halifax. To tell their whole story we would have to begin with Susanne Rochette, the little Huguenot girl who escaped from France to Holland in a sugar cask (hogshead) and was called in her family "Little Nightcap." (The history of her marvelous escape has been written up by Dr. Morton in the Religious Herald, Richmond, Va.)

Susanne Rochette married in Amsterdam, Holland, a Huguenot named Abraham Michaux. Their daughter, Jane Michaux, married Pierre LeGrand. Their son, John LeGrand, married Bettie___; their daughter, Hannah Le Grand, married Elias Palmer; their daughter, Elizabeth Palmer, married Thomas Fourqurean; their son, Reuben Fourqurean, married Mary Baynham Boxley; their daughter, Elizabeth Baynham Fourqurean, married Robert E. Jordan, Sr., and their son, Robert E. Jordan, Jr., married Hallie LaFayette Turner.

No Huguenot ever came to the Colony or the county rich, but the Fourqureans accumulated very comfortable estates in slaves and lands. In the old "Cherry Hill" church yard is a section with the marble slabs of a half dozen Fourqureans, amongst them:

William Fourqurean, born 1812, died 1880.

Mrs. Parthenia Fourqurean, died 1851.

M. W. Fourqurean, born Oct., 1815, died April 15, 1836.

Daniel W. Fourqurean, born 1788, died Dec. 3, 1854.

Elizabeth Eggleston Boxley, born 1822, died 1875.

Near Black Walnut is a small stone enclosure in which are two slabs: "Sacred to the memory of Reuben Fourqurean, born Feb., 1812, and his wife, Mary Baynham (Boxley) Fourqurean, born Nov. 7, 1818, died April 15, 1868."

In this stone enclosure is also a monument, "sacred to the memory of Thomas E. Owen, who married the widow of Reuben Fourqurean."

The children of Reuben D. Fourqurean and Mary Baynham Boxley were:

(1) Elizabeth B. Fourqurean, wife of R. E. Jordan, Sr.

(2) Mary F., wife of Capt. John Fry (parents of John D. Fry, of Richmond, and of Mamie Fry).

(3) Emma F., wife of William M. McCorkle (parents of Walter McCorkle, of Lynchburg, Va., and George McCorkle).

(4) Willie Fourqurean, wife of Joseph Stebbens, who was born June 14, 1850, in Petersburg, Va., and they married July 24, 1872. Their children were Joseph, born November 5, 1874, and Laura May, born September 16, 1878.

(5) Thomas Fourqurean, married first Miss Gavin, of Texas, married second Miss Johnson, of Texas.

(6) George F., married Miss Cousins (parents of Annie, Archie and Henry Fourqurean).

[A History of Halifax County, by Wirt Johnson Carrington, 1924]

FRENCH family: William French was born in Ireland, April 29, 1725, and he died May 2, 1792. He married Winifried, who was also born in Ireland, 1722, and died May 1, 1786. The children were: Katherine, born February 6, 1747; Elizabeth, born March 30, 1749; Susannah, born January 1, 1751; Mary, born January 22, 1753; Margaret, born January 9, 1754; James, born November 5, 1756 (James went to Kentucky and married Miss Calloway, and was the grandfather of General J. B. Hood, C. S. A.); William, born September 18, 1758, died July 20, 1760; Stephen, born March 1, 1760, died May 22, 1842 (married Elizabeth Helen, born June 7, 1764); and Kizzie French, born December 5, 1761.

Stephen French and Elizabeth Helen had Susannah French, born November 21, 1790, died May 25, 1795; William French, born April 26, 1793; James French, born March 18, 1801, died May 6, 1850 (married Sarah Scarborough Butler Henry, daughter of John Henry and Margaret Williams, and granddaughter of Judge James Henry, of Accomack County, Virginia, and his wife, Sarah Scarborough, who was a daughter of Sir Edmund Scarborough, of England); and Stephen French, born July 29, 1804.

James French and Sarah S. B. (Henry) French, had Marcellus French, born February 14, 1831, at Warrenton, Virginia, married Elizabeth H. Logan (daughter of Senator Richard Logan, of Halifax County, Virginia), October 28, 1857.

Matilda Caroline French, born July 26, 1833, married first Franklin Gray, second Samuel Hewes of California, and died January 3, 1887. (She had one daughter by first husband, Franklin French Gray.)

James Henry French was born at Warrenton, March 26, 1835, and died at San Antonio, Texas, September 26, 1893. He married Sarah Lorrinilla Webb in

San Antonio, October 15, 1856, and had Junius Rufus French, Olive Ann French, James Vasser French, Sarah Lorrinilla French and Franklin Gray French.

Junius Butler French was born at Warrenton, Va., August 7, 1837. He was killed at Gettysburg, July 1, 1863.

Rosalie Henry French was born August 4, 1839, and died in California, August 28, 1889. Married Arthur H. Brown.

Marcellus French and Elizabeth H. (Logan) French had the following children:

(1) Margaret Logan French, born in Halifax County, October 26, 1858, died January 29, 1879.

(2) James French, born in San Antonio, Texas, in 1860, died in Halifax County, August, 1861.

(3) Sarah Henry French, born July 29, 1861, married Charles C. Carrington, of Halifax County, Va., August 20, 1883.

(4) Charles R. French, born December 25, 1863, married Mrs. Letitia Thornton (nee Edmondson), of Halifax County.

(5) Marcellus French, born June, 1865, died 1865.

(6) Junius Butler French, born May 21, 1867; married first Hattie B. Dix, of Accomack County; married second, Miss Sadie Wyatt, of Chattanooga, Tenn.

(7) William Logan French, born April 19, 1869, in Pittsylvania County, Va.; married Sarah Lorrinilla French, of San Antonio, Texas, January 30, 1896.

(8) Julius Coleman French, born July 8, 1872; married Addie M. Sparrow, November 13, 1885.

[A History of Halifax County, by Wirt Johnson Carrington, 1924]

GREEN family dates back to an illustrious line of "Buckton," Northamptonshire, England. Berryman Green was born in Westmoreland County, Virginia, in 1754. He enlisted in the Revolutionary War as a private, in 1776, and served though the war as quartermaster on General Washington's staff. He was unfit for active service, being lame. He married Nancy Terry, daughter of Nathaniel Terry, gent., burgess of Halifax County. Mr. Green died in this county September 13, 1825. Nancy, his wife, died February 20, 1837. They were buried at the old "Thompson Place," near "Banister Lodge." Their children were, viz.:

(1) Elizabeth Dickerson Green, who married her cousin, Colonel Joe Coleman Terry.

(2) Berryman Green, Jr., married Ariana Vaughan.

(3) Mary Green (died).

(4) Sarah Green (died).

(5) Thomas Jefferson Green, married Frances Keeling Burton.

(6) Nathaniel Terry Green, married Annie Colquehoun.

From Colonel Berryman Green descended some of Halifax County's most honorable and substantial citizens.

This data given is from the family Bible.

Excerpts From the Family of Berryman Green, the Revolutionary Soldier.

Written by Mrs. Emma Green Phillips, as told her by her mother.

Francis Keeling Burton, born at "Nine Oaks," North Carolina, December 11, 1797, married October 5, 1818, at Chapel Hill to Thomas Jefferson Green, born in Halifax County, December 26, 1796, and had issue:

(1) Sarah Elizabeth Green, born July 7, 1819, at Chapel Hill, N. C.

(2) John Burton Green, born September 10, 1820, in Halifax, Virginia.

(3) James Minge Green, born February 23, 1822, died unmarried.

(4) Frances Keeling Green, born March 23, 1824.

(5) Berryman Green, born September 15, 1825 (the day after the death of his grandfather, Captain Berryman Green (Revolutionary soldier).

(6) Thomas Jefferson Green, born March 4, 1827.

(7) Nathaniel Terry Green, born March 17, 1829.

(8) Robert Bromfield Green, born December 28, 1830.

(9) William Leigh Green, born December 22, 1832.

(10) Emma Green, born January 16, 1835.

(11) Clarence Green, born September 12, 1838 (died in infancy).

(12) Alexander Ridley Green, born December 8, 1841, in Halifax County. He married at Halifax C. H., on 31 October, 1871, Miss Lizzie R. Wauhop, who was born at Memphis, Tenn., daughter of William and Sarah F. (Ragland) Wauhop. Her father died at Memphis in 1848; her mother died on October 3, 1874, aged fifty-four years. Mr. and Mrs. Alex. R. Green had the following children: Sallie R., born May 29, 1873; Thomas J., born May 4, 1876; Fannie B., born January 5, 1879, died June 6th following; Lizzie A., born June 3, 1887.

Alexander B. Green served in the War Between the States. He was in Company A, 53rd Virginia Infantry, Armistead's Brigade, Pickett's Division. In Pickett's grand charge at Gettysburg, he was shot through the right breast, by a minie-ball, and was disabled by the wound for nine months, returning then to his regiment and serving till the close of the war. He took part in battles of: Bethel, Seven Pines, Fredericksburg, Suffolk, Gettysburg, Cold Harbor, Drurys Bluff, Howlett Farm, Five Forks, Fort Harrison and Sailors Creek. His brother, Robert B., was wounded in service. The other brothers in service were: Thomas J., Nathaniel T. and William L. After the war Mr. Green clerked in store at Halifax C. H. until August, 1871, when he was appointed commissioner in chancery for county and circuit courts, which office he has continued to hold up to date. On July 1, 1879, he was elected treasurer of the county. *[Virginia and Virginians]*

I have given the names of the children of Thomas Jefferson Green and his wife, Frances Keeling Burton, because they belonged to Halifax County, and it was from her mother that Emma Green Phillips received the interesting reminiscences recorded.

"My father, Thomas Jefferson Green, gave to my brother, Robert Bromfield Green, a condensed history of our line as follows:

"There were six brothers (Greens) born in Northamptonshire, England, near Stratford-on-Avon and Sulgrave Church.

"During the reign of Charles II and the life of Cromwell there was a division of the family, some in favor of Cromwell and some for King Charles.

"About the year 1630 Sir William Green sailed 'on the ship Speedwell' for America and came to Virginia and settled on the Eastern Shore in Westmoreland County. In Bishop Meade's book, 'Old Churches and Families of Virginia,' he says of Westmoreland: 'It was called the Athens of Virginia because of the worth, talents and patriotism of its people.'

"Here my great-grandfather, Thomas Green, was a vestryman in Pohick Church and counsellor to King Charles II. He married Anna Berryman. Their son, Berryman Green, my grandfather, was named for his mother's father, Berryman.

"Judge Berryman Green, of Dandle, Virginia, bore the name, also the Rev. Berryman Green, of the Theological Seminary near Alexandria, Virginia. Some of the Greens were called 'White Greens' because of their fair complexion and light hair. My grandfather was of the fair Greens, but I have been told that he had a glint of red in his hair. One of the 'Red Greens' was Duff Green, of Orange County, Virginia.

"Mr. Berryman Green was captain of a company in the War of the Revolution. When General Washington, with his army, was in Pennsylvania, about the time of the Battle of Valley Forge, his men were in great need and suffering for food and supplies. He wrote an urgent call to General Lee to find him an energetic and trustworthy officer for quartermaster to look after the comfort of his men. General Lee wrote him he had found the right man for the work, Captain Berryman Green, but he hesitated about accepting the position, as it would put him out of line of promotion in the army. General Washington was so insistent that Captain Green resigned his position and went to aid him in relieving the suffering and the need of the army there. It was there Captain Green met his first wife, Anne Pritchard. Her parents were from England and loyal to the crown. General Washington ordered Captain Green to secure rooms for the officers. He found a large, comfortable house, and was making the rooms on the lower floor, on hearing someone open a door across the hall he doffed his hat and turning bowed to a lovely woman with black hair and eyes. She spurned his salute with a shrug and turned her back on him. But that day their fate was sealed. It proved to be love at first sight and they were soon after married. In those days there were no railroads or stage coaches, most of the travel was on horseback. My grandfather owned a splendid horse and his bride was a magnificent rider; so when he began his long trip to Virginia he proudly seated his beautiful bride on his charger and for his mount took a work horse; thus they happily jogged along through the wild country with 'saddle bags' to carry their clothing instead of trunks of the present day, and were half way to their Virginia home when the charger took fright and ran away, throwing his wife and breaking her leg above the knee. This happened near a farm house, where she was taken in and cared for until able to travel, when she was placed in an army wagon on a bed to finish their journey to their Westmoreland home, where they lived for some time. Then his first wife died, I do not know the date. She left five children. Anne, the oldest, married a Mr. Barksdale and moved to Ohio before the State was cut off from Virginia. Hulda (or Hilda) married Colonel James Thompson and lived in Halifax County. Lucy married Colonel Stephen Davenport, who owned a farm near Colonel Thompson's estate. Hannah died unmarried, and Anthony Wayne, named for 'Mad Anthony Wayne,' the fiery fighter. Uncle Anthony lived in Halifax County on the south side of Dan River, married and raised a family. When the mother of these children died, they being young and helpless, grandfather and children moved to Halifax County. He endeavored for some time to look after them, but found it absolutely necessary for their happiness and comfort for him to marry again. Colonel Nathaniel Terry, who fought at the Battle of Yorktown and was aide to General Washington, lived in Halifax, and Captain Green knew him intimately during the war, so he visited Colonel Terry to ask his advice. (This Colonel Terry was a member of the House of Burgesses at Yorktown, Virginia. There is a monument to the members of the House and his name is inscribed thereon.)

When my grandfather arrived at the home of Colonel Terry he found there three young ladies, the Misses Terry, his host's daughters. After becoming well acquainted with them, he asked permission to address his daughter. Colonel Terry answered, 'There are three of them, Captain, take your choice.' He chose Nancy, the eldest, and was accepted. They were married and his second wife proved to be the kindest and most affectionate stepmother to his first children, who loved her devotedly.

"Colonel Terry was a very influential and wealthy gentleman in Colonial days, and after the Revolutionary War had enormous land grants (extending along the Banister River from Pittsylvania County, down through Halifax for miles below 'Banister Lodge'), 'for services rendered in the war.' Nancy, who married Captain Green, must have fallen heir to some of it.

"I have not seen the Terry coat-of-arms, but the grandson of my aunt, Elizabeth Terry, Mr. David Webb, of Halifax County, has it.

"Captain Berryman Green moved with his family to a large fertile farm he owned about two miles from the county seat, then called 'Halifax Court House,' but there was no court house there then.

"Berryman Green was then deputy clerk, and seeing the need of more room than he then had, and also seeing the need of a room in which to hold court, he built a house, so large, so the country people then thought, that they called it 'Green's Folly,' but to my grandfather it seemed wisdom. After passing through a large front porch you entered a very spacious, high-pitched hall. This he intended to be, and was, used as a court room until the court house was built. On the right hand was a room for the jury, on the left his bedroom, back of this the nursery and back stairs, and back of the large jury room was the dining room; the main stairway led from the hall to the second floor.

"The house is still in good state of repair. In the front porch there now stands two long wooden benches that my grandfather had made of boards, four inches thick, with solid board legs, mortised in with solid wooden pegs, not a nail in them, and just as perfect as though made yesterday. These I saw in July, 1914, when I was taken there to see the dear old homestead by my niece and her husband, Mr. and Mrs. Charles Penick.

"Halifax Court House of olden days is now called 'Houston,' and the good people of Houston and South Boston bought the old seat of 'Green's Folly' and converted it into a beautiful 'club house.' Some changes were made, but the electric lights and baths were run by water from the splendid old well.

"The children of my grandfather, Berryman Green, and his second wife, Nancy Terry, were, viz.:

"(1) Elizabeth Dickerson Green, who married Colonel Joseph Coleman Terry (her cousin, Berryman Green, married Aria Vaughan).

"(2) Mary (Polly), never married.

"(3) Sarah (Sallie), died in girlhood.

"(4) Thomas Jefferson Green, married Frances Keeling Burton.

"(5) Nathaniel Terry Green, married Anne Colquehoun.

"My grandfather was careful that all of his children should be educated. Aunt Polly, being the youngest living daughter, was petted and kept at home and taught until grandfather said she must have better opportunities. So after much preparation of a suitable wardrobe, she was packed off to a first-class boarding school for higher studies. She went on a bright Monday morning, and on the following bright Saturday morning she came back and gave notice that she would 'never go back again,' and she never did. Being naturally bright and witty in conversation, with a sufficient tang of sarcasm to interest and amuse without offending, warm hearted and affectionate, she endeared herself to every one, and my father and mother were devoted to her.

"My father was the fifth child of Captain Berryman and Nancy (Terry) Green. He and Nathaniel Terry Green, about one year younger than my father, were as devoted to each other as twins. Their primary education was in some country school, for there were no free schools in those days. Then they went to a noted teacher in the higher branches of education, a Mr. Levi Holbrook, who prepared them for college.

"When my father was about eighteen years old, my grandfather and my father set out on horseback for a long jaunt through the wilds of colonial or old Virginia to survey and sell his land grants which he had received from General Washington 'for services rendered in the War of the Revolution,' in all four thousand acres (copied from General Survey in Land Office, Washington, D. C., September 22, 1910), as follows: In the counties of Fayette, Pickaway, Ross, Madison, Franklin, Pike and Fairfield; townships, Darby, Union, Monroe, Deer Creek, Perry, Deerfield, Wayne and Sunfish. Since that time the city of Cincinnati has been built on some of that land. All of the land, except what he gave to his first child, Ann Barksdale, he sold for four dollars an acre.

"On his return to Halifax he entered his two sons, Thomas Jefferson and Nathaniel Terry Green, in the University of North Carolina, called 'Chapel Hill.' He told them his chief reason for selling his lands was to have the means to give them a college education, and that they must study earnestly and do their utmost to distinguish themselves in later life.

"Grandfather's earnest admonition was kept in loving remembrance, and brought him rich reward in their brilliant success, both graduating with high honors at the same time—'Uncle Nat' choosing the medical profession and my father taking the law course. Both became eminent in their professions and won sincere respect and appreciation from all who knew them.

"My mother's parents were James Minge Burton and Elizabeth (Ridley) Burton. They had three sons, John, Robert and Broomfield Burton, and two daughters, Frances Keeling Burton and Martha (Patsy) Burton. They entered the two eldest boys in the University of North Carolina, 'Chapel Hill,' about the same time my father went there, and he knew the Burton boys and visited them in their home. There he met their sister, 'Frankie,' Miss Frances Keeling Burton, loved her on sight, for she was more than pretty, with lovely, gentle manners, and sang sweetly, so they were engaged before they left college, and a month or two after he graduated they were married in the hall of the University, October 5, 1818, to please the students and their many friends, as my grandmother's parlor was not large enough to accommodate half of the guests.

"They had a most cordial and affectionate invitation from my mother's uncle, James Hamilton, and Aunt Polly, his wife (formerly Mary Ridley), to come to New York and spend their honeymoon with them, but as he was anxious to begin in his new profession, he declined this invitation and started the next day for their new home in Virginia.

"She brought with her an offshoot of white jasmine (her favorite flower) and planted it near the garden gate of her new home in Halifax, and nourished it all through her life, and gave to her granddaughter, Frances Burton Coles, a slip from it, which is flourishing now at 'Riverside.' Frances Burton Coles and her youngest brother, James Alexander Coles, are living on the farm, both in very feeble health,

"In the year 1820 my father was elected to the House of Delegates, and while in Richmond he took grandfather there to be treated by noted physicians, but he did not improve. He returned home, his sufferings greatly increased, and he died September 14, 1825, and was buried in the family burying ground at the home of Uncle James Thompson and Aunt Hulda, his wife (one of grandfather's first Wife's daughters). Grandmother did not live long after grandfather's death, and at her death was buried beside him, and Aunt Polly, who died many years afterwards, asked to be buried at their feet. His youngest daughter, Sarah, was the only member of his family to be buried at the old home near Houston. I do not know who bought the place, but Captain Philip Howerton was living there in my young days, a splendid type of the 'Old Virginia Gentleman,' with a charming family of four daughters and one son—a place where the young people flocked for fun and jollity. After Captain Howerton's death it changed hands, and has changed many times since.

"While a delegate in Richmond, my father had his portrait painted, he said, 'that my children might know how I looked when I was young,' and he also had a miniature painted for a gift to my mother. It was a work of art and set in a frame of heavy red gold, oval in shape, with a lock of his hair under glass in the back. My mother said when he gave it to her there was a blue ribbon run through the ring and tied in a 'love knot,' that she might wear it on her neck. When mother died she gave it to my sister (Frances Keeling Coles), and when she died it went to Frances Burton Coles, who has now given it to her niece, Frances Keeling Coles (widow of Mr. Arthur Burroughs) and great-granddaughter of my mother.

"While my grandfather was in Richmond my father, fearing that he would not live long, had his miniature painted also and gave it to him, 'to do with just as he pleased.'

"When he died he willed that it be given to his oldest daughters and granddaughters through succeeding generations. It passed through the hands of all his daughters by his second wife, and their daughters, until it came to Cousin Emily Yancey, of Richmond, Virginia, and when she died she charged that it be sent to Aunt Polly Green, his last living child, and unmarried.

"When Aunt Polly Green died she left it to my sister, Sarah Elizabeth Faulkner. After its various wanderings, I saw it for the first time after I was married, when on a visit to my sister, she then told me of my grandfather's will in regard to it. She said she would give it to 'Mittie' for her lifetime, and then it would go to little 'Sadie,' Mittie's oldest child, and her grandmother's special pet.

"When my father was in Richmond, my mother was living a few miles from Halifax Court House, up the mountain road, with her two little children, Sarah, one year old, and John Burton, an infant. She had faithful, devoted servants, and felt secure, but one morning (I do not remember the exact date, but it was between 1820 and 1821) my mother was aroused early in the morning by the cook knocking at the door and calling in a frightened tone, 'Get up quick, Mis Frances, and dress. Oh, my poor dear mistis; the niggers is a risen, away down yander in Southampton, date ole Nat Turner done started de debbil's work, killin' de pore white folks.' My mother hastily dressed the children and herself, when Dick, the man my father had charged to take care of his mistress till he got home, appeared at the door and said, 'Missis, don't you be scared, ain't nobody gwinter hurt you, for I got a good place for you, you just give me a comfort and some pillows and blankets and I'll be back here by eleven o'clock.'

"My mother hung her treasured miniature around her neck, packed a basket of food, and with Dick carrying Sarah and the basket, and she with the baby boy, they soon reached the hiding place, which was a cave under the hill, the mouth concealed by bushes.

"Dick had swept it out, and with fresh dry leaves covered with an old rug had converted it into a very comfortable hiding place. He brought an old tin lantern and three tallow candles, and a box of matches, and it was there my mother said she spent her first night in a prehistoric home, many years before kerosene oil was heard or dreamed of.

" 'Des lay down and go to sleep, Mistis,' said the faithful Dick. 'Kass I ain't gwine to close my eyes dis night, and nobody ain't going to hurt you, tell dey pass over my dead body, and dat will be a long time from now.'

"There she spent a day and two nights; early in the morning after the second night, the faithful guard went to get breakfast for the cave dwellers and inquire if there was any news, when suddenly my father galloped to the door, his horse white with foam, and he nearly wild with fright, as he called to Dick, 'Where are my wife and babes?' 'Come on wid me, Mars Tomie, and I'll show you 'zactly whar dey is,' and on reaching the mouth of the cave, Dick pulled back the concealing branches, with a broad grin, said, 'Go right in dar, Mars Tom, my Mistis jest as well and purty as ever.'

"My father thought it was a dreadful experience. 'Yes,' said my mother, 'but I wore your miniature next to my heart, for I thought if I had to die I would have my dear husband's picture on my heart.'

"My father, it seems, had heard of the Nat Turner insurrection, and had traveled day and night without stopping, except to relay horses on the route.

"I do not know how long my father was in the Legislature; he had been Commonwealth's Attorney, long before I was born, until the Confederate war. After the war a Yankee wanted him to sign an oath that he had never given aid or comfort to the Confederate army; he answered, 'I will never swear to or sign my name to a lie, I had five sons, two sons-in-law, and one grandson in that army; I gave it all the aid and comfort I possibly could, and would continue to do so if it was necessary,' so his office was taken from him and given to a Yankee shyster lawyer. I do not know his name, but I know they could never strip him of the honors he had won, long before they invaded and devastated our beloved Southland, God bless her.

"In 1843, about October 1st, my mother received an invitation to visit her uncle, Dr. James Ridley, of Oxford, North Carolina; her youngest child, Alexander Ridley Green, was just two years of age.

"When my father came from Pittsylvania court, she gave him the letter to read. After reading the letter he insisted on her going, saying: 'The older boys are here to take care of the younger, the servants are here to wait on them; it is all right, even if I should have to leave them to attend court, so write your uncle to expect you, Emma and Baby Sandy week after next, and get yourself ready for the trip through the country.'

"At the appointed time we left home for Black Walnut, a village south of Dan River, and stopped with Mrs. Easley, my mother's friend, a grand old lady, who gave us a most cordial reception. There I met her three children, Fannie, Mary and William Easley, a youth who in after years was captain of a company of United States soldiers in the war with Mexico in the regime of Santa Anna; this handsome gallant officer was killed in that war.

"Her two daughters married two brothers, Drs. Charles and John Craddock.

"Early the next morning we left Mrs. Easley's on our journey to Oxford. We had fair weather until noon, when it clouded up and a steady rain set in, continuing until night, with increased violence and pitch darkness. Between 8 and 9 o'clock the horses came to a dead stop, and little Sandy, being by that time coughy and croupy, my mother said to the driver, almost in despair, 'What shall we do?'

"In a few minutes we heard the steps of a horse (mother had just given the baby a dose of cough syrup, measured in her thimble); a gentleman called out in the darkness, 'Who's there?' 'Kind sir,' my mother answered, "we are travelers, fast in the mire and darkness, with my little children and by baby threatened with the croup. My husband told me on leaving home that if I could reach the home of Dr. Tharp before the night of the second day I might feel assured of a warm welcome.' When asked her husband's name, she told him, 'Thomas Jefferson Green, of Halifax Court House, Virginia.' He said, 'Mrs. Green, how glad I am to have met you at this critical moment, for I am Dr. Tharp, and will soon have you in my home, just up the avenue there, in call.'

"Then he turned to Uncle Allen, the driver, and said, 'Well, old man, haven't you any light?' 'No, massa, I was dependin' on de moon, but she done zerted me de fust time, when I needed her de most."

" 'No one in the carriage to help you?"

" 'No, sar, massa, just my mistis and her two little children wid nuss gal, an' a nuss ain't no count 'ceptin' to hold a baby and de rattle.'

" 'That's right, old man,' said the doctor, laughing.

"Then the doctor gave a ferryman's call, and immediately an answer came from the house. 'Order supper for travelers,' he said, 'and bring a double team of mules and boys with torchlights.'

"In five minutes I heard the clanking of chains on the mule teams, and looking out had my first view of a parade of torchlights, not those of paper boxes on poles, as in the national capital, but Simonpure lightwood knots from giant pines of grand old North Carolina, held high in the hands of about twenty men and boys, flaming and flashing in the darkness as they marched down each side of the team.

"It was a beautiful sight to my young eyes; the jaded horses were taken out and the four mules hitched to the carriage, the drivers mounted their teams, and with Allen on the seat, moved off with as little effort as if the carriage had been a paper box.

"Up the avenue of cedars we moved with the 'light brigade' each side, escorting us, Dr. Tharp riding horseback near mamma.

"Mrs. Tharp and her two daughters met us in the front porch with lights and kind greetings. We were taken to a cheerful room with a blazing fire. The doctor treated little Sandy and we were invited in to a bountiful and hot supper. They all sat at the table with us and talked to mamma. After supper I was put to bed and knew nothing more until I was aroused for breakfast.

"The doctor and his wife wanted mamma to stop over and pay them a visit, but she was anxious to get to Oxford that day, so everything was made ready for the last lap of our trip.

"After saying 'farewell' to the ladies, my mother turned to the doctor to thank him and to say 'good-bye.' 'Not yet, Mrs. Green,' he said, 'I am going to Oxford with you to see that you do not have another such one as last night.'

"We were received with open arms by Uncle James and Aunt Betsy, and it seemed so strange to me to hear them call my mother 'Frankie,' as if she were but a little girl.

"Uncle James came in the next morning from the farm yard and said: 'Frankie, I must apologize to you for reproving your driver a few minutes ago for neglecting to wash the horses' legs last night after their long drive. I told him that was not the proper way to treat your carriage horses.' He seemed very sorry and humble, and said, 'Lor, Marse Jeems, I hope you don't think these is my mistuses' carriage horses. Sir, deese is de plow horses, and de traveling carriage. No, sir, Marse Jeems, my mistis' blooded horses is at home eatin' dey long corn, and her visitin' carriage is got de kiver on it in de carriage house, waitin' for her to go back home.'

"While Uncle James was telling this mamma's eyes opened wide with amazement and laughter. 'Is it possible that that scamp has concocted such a romance for your deception and his defense? He told the truth when he said they were the plow horses, and should have added, 'and for every other purpose.' You must excuse him, uncle, it is a habit among Virginia darkeys to brag on what they call 'our quality folks' when speaking of their masters and mistresses, as well as everything belonging to them.'

"Everybody laughed at Uncle Allen's expense over his amusing pride and pomposity." *[A History of Halifax County, by Wirt Johnson Carrington, 1924]*

HALL family: Will of Wilmouth Hall, 25 January 1808, Halifax County:

"My unmarried daughters, Sally J. Hall, Chloe Hall; sons, William, John, Robert and Thomas Hall; married daughter, Caty Miller. All liberally provided for. Son, William Hall, executor.
"Wilmouth Hall."

Witnesses: James Terry and Willis Yeates.

Will of Thomas Hall, 1819, Halifax County:

"I give to my loving wife, Mary Ann Hall, as her just right and title, land, &c.; to my children, James, Presilla, Mildred, Elizabeth and Mary Ann Hall; my sons, William and James B. Hall. Must pay all of my debts and divide the land among my children or sell it, if they prefer to live elsewhere, but bury me decently on my own land, as it will be the last favor I can ask of them in this world.

"Thomas Hall."

Witness: John and Thomas Neal.

HALLEBURTON, Thomas: Will of Thomas Halleburton, 15 October 1829, Halifax County.

"In the name of God, Amen. I, Thos. Halleburton, being of sound mind and memory, do make this my last will and testament, thereby revoking all others.

"I leave to my beloved wife, Sallie Frances Halleburton, all of my estate, real and personal, during her natural life after all my just debts are paid, and subject to the following legacies:

"I give to Nancy Taylor the sum of one hundred dollars, to be paid out of my estate as soon as convenient.

"I give to my brother, David Halleburton, my Napoleon colt, to him and his heirs forever.

"At the death of my wife I give to my sister, Martha Holloway, one-tenth part of my estate loaned my wife, both real and personal, to her and her heirs forever.

"At the death of my wife I give to my brother, John C. Halleburton, the remaining nine-tenths of my estate, both real and personal, to him and his heirs forever.

"I do hereby constitute and appoint Thos. Easley my executor of this my last will and testament. "In witness whereof I set my hand and seal, October 15, 1829.

"Thos. Halleburton."

Witnesses: Richard Wade, Henry Easley, Richard H. Owen.

December 23, 1829--Inventory of Thos. Halleburton:

Negro boy Lewis, $350; girl Susan, $250; girl, $175; boy, $100; boy, $150; boy, $100; woman, $50; man, $50; a long list of cattle, horses, household furniture, all amounting to $3,259.17. Signed--Allen Halleburton, Elisha Betts, Richard Wade, Sr.

Some Halleburton marriages in Halifax County, Virginia:

Allen Halliburton and Martha Pickett, 24 Nov. 1814.

Eliza Halliburton and William Wareen, 9 March 1840.

Reubin R. Haliburton and ___ Faulkner, 8 Sept. 1842.

Richard Haliburton and Susannah Pickett, 22 Nov. 1803.

Robert Halliburton and Mary C. Pate, 11 Nov. 1828.

HART family was once very prominent in Halifax County, owning large landed interests, and the tradition is that South Boston was built upon part of the Hart estate, which tradition is partly true, as there are many deeds on record from Anthony Hart to Thomas B. Jeffress, and we know that George Carrington was the founder of old South Boston on the south side of Dan River, and Captain E. B. Jeffress the founder of the present South Boston.

Anthony Hart was born in King and Queen County, Va., October 14, 1755. He died in Halifax County after 1832, as his pension claim was allowed at that date.

A Revolutionary soldier, he enlisted on February 10, 1776, fought in the battles of Gwynn's Island, Brandywine, and Germantown, and was honorably discharged in 1781. He fought under Captain Gregory Smith, Thomas Hill and William Lumpkin, Colonels William Nelson and Matthews.

He married Elizabeth ____ as by deed 1821 Anthony Hart, Sr., and wife, Elizabeth, sells to John Hart land in Halifax County for 86 pounds of current money of Virginia in 1823, and again Anthony Hart and wife, Elizabeth, sell to John Hart land in Halifax for seven hundred and ten dollars.

In 1807 Anthony Hart bought of Elizabeth Franklin land in Halifax County. He may have married this Elizabeth Franklin later. Anthony Hart had very large land interests in this county. His son, Ambrose Hart, born 1784, married Rebecca Carlton and emigrated to Missouri, where he died in 1858 and is buried in the old Hart cemetery in Calloway County.

Anthony Hart had sons, John Anthony, Jr., and perhaps others. The old Hart home of this county, near Bold Springs, was destroyed by fire many years ago, and the graveyard on the place has no gravestones or monuments of any kind. *[A History of Halifax County, by Wirt Johnson Carrington, 1924]*

HENRY family: Patrick Henry owned land in this county, but never lived on it. He was our next door neighbor in Charlotte, but he left numberless descendants through his sixteen children in this county to perpetuate his greatness. Patrick Henry was a great man, a celebrated man, but not entirely through inheritance, as some genealogists would have us believe. He sprang into greatness on the spur of the moment through the courage of his convictions. Opportunity makes the man; "if this be treason, make the most of it,"

There are Henrys and Henrys in this county, and it is of them we wish to write because they are close kin to Patrick, the orator.

Alexander and Jean (Robertson) Henry, of Aberdeen, Scotland, were the grandparents of Patrick Henry, and also of James Henry, of Accomack County, Virginia. This James Henry owned twenty thousand acres at one time in the counties of Halifax and Pittsylvania, just on the line, lying mostly on Sandy Creek (about five miles from Peytonsburg). This land was a vast wilderness when James Henry, of Accomack County, came into possession of it, but he had an eye to business almost equal to that of Mr. James Bruce (who came into this county years later), but he evidently did not purpose to live here, though he did visit his possessions from time to time, driving in his "coach and four," upon the doors of which coach his coat-of-arms was emblazoned. The mystery will ever be how he traveled over the Halifax roads in a coach, or having made one trip ever ventured on the second. We know by the records that he did make several journeys to Halifax, and the wildness of the backwoods not appealing to him, he finally employed as his agent a Mr. William Ryburn. We also find that James Henry had leases running from twenty to twenty-five years, with all specifications as to what was to be built and produced on the same in his contracts.

James Henry was a prominent man, member of the Continental Congress, House of Burgesses, and judge. He married Sarah Scarborough, daughter of Colonel Edmund Scarborough, also a man of affairs. Charles Henry, the son of Judge James Henry, inherited one of these plantations in Halifax, but refused to live in such a wild country, and traded it to his brother, John Henry, for his home in King and Queen County, and it was here that Charles Henry's son, Charles, "was stabbed by a man named Griffin" while on a visit to his Uncle John and "died in the little room back of the parlor," and was buried in the graveyard, at the east end of the then beautiful terraced garden at "Woodlawn," the name of John Henry's seat.

A tragedy to begin with, without a coroner or trial, an unquenchable desire to know why Griffin stabbed such a youth, so far from home, and what became of Griffin, filled our minds as we looked on the worn slab that covered his grave, but we do know that wherever he went he carried the mark of Cain.

James Henry the second (son of John, son of James) married twice; his first wife was a Miss Graves and his second wife was Mrs. Laura Graves (nee Willis), by whom he had Charles (1), Patrick (2), Jennie (3), Bettie (4), and Mattie (5).

James Henry (second) had brothers, Robert Henry (attorney in Richmond, Va.) and S. Hugh Henry (?).

Charles Henry (the son of James, second, and Mrs. Laura Graves) was born 1874 and died 1914. He left the old home to his widow, whose maiden name was Virginia Walton.

Patrick Henry, the brother of Charles, lives near on some of the same tract of land. He married Miss Mary Nash, a sister of Daniel Nash, of this county.

The "Woodlawn" graveyard has three generations of Henrys buried there, but only one stone could be read after many time-worn years:

"Samuel Hugh Henry, born February 11, 1812; departed this life, April 25, 1840."

What relation he bore to James and John Henry we do not know, but the court records show one Hugh Henry and his wife, Mary, who bought land as early as 1745 (before the county was taken from Lunenburg). *[A History of Halifax County, by Wirt Johnson Carrington, 1924]*

Samuel Hugh Henry was son of Judge James Henry and his wife, Sarah Scarborough. Samuel Hugh Henry married Mary Beale, daughter of Col. John Beale, of Chestnut Hill, Richmond County, Virginia. Issue:

(1) James Hugh Henry, married Ann Elizabeth Carter, daughter of Carter Braxton and Sarah Moore, granddaughter of Carter Braxton, one of the signers of the Declaration of Independence.

(2) Charles Scarborough Henry, a graduate of William and Mary College, settled in Halifax County, and was killed when he was about 21 years old.

Judge James Henry and his wife, Sarah Scarborough, also had sons, Edward Hugh Henry and Charles Scarborough Henry. Edward Hugh Henry, married, first, his cousin, Martha Catherine Henry, daughter of Patrick Henry and his second wife, Dorothea Dandridge, granddaughter of Governor Spottswood. He married, second, Elizabeth Washington Peyton, daughter of Dr. Valentine and Bettie Washington Peyton. Being the eldest son he inherited Fleet's Bay. *[Some Prominent Virginia Families, by Louise Pecquet du Bellet]*

HODGES family: One of the earliest American Colonists of the family was William Hodges. He was born in Kent, England, and came to Kent County, Maryland. From Maryland two of the sons came to Virginia, John and William.

The records of Prince William, Va., contain under date of June 5, 1780, the following: "To John Hodges, Gent., is due two thousand acres under the King's proclamation for services of a certain Francis Eppes during the last French wars who was a lieutenant in the Second Virginia Regiment and which said Eppes hath assigned to said Hodges."

In 1769 John Hodge, of Orange County, sells to Hedgeman Warren, 125 acres in Halifax County on his creek.

On 4 June, 1774, John Brooks, of Orange County, N. C., buys of John Hodges, of same county and State, land in Halifax County, Va.

On 2 April, 1788, Moza Hurt, of Bedford County; sells to Thomas Hodges, of Halifax County, 30 acres of land, being a part of Wilson Mattox's survey.

In the early records the name is variously spelled Hodges and Hodge, and is said by those in authority to have been originally the same name, and those in Virginia springing from the same root. The Hodge and the Hodges families of Maryland and Virginia bore the same coat-armor.

The earliest Hodge marriage in this county was that of Fleming Hodge to Betsy Powell in 1792, and in 1805 William Hodge to Mary Lax. The earliest Hodges was Thomas Hodges to Keziah Hawkins, 1798, and John Hodges to Lucy Overby, 1805, and the names of Hodge and Hodges have mingled and multiplied in Halifax since those dates and have intermarried with many of the county's prominent citizens. *[A History of Halifax County, by Wirt Johnson Carrington]*

HOWERTON, Thomas: Will of Thomas Howerton, 26 January 1829, Halifax County--Wife, Tabitha; sons, James H. Howerton and Robert W. Howerton (mentions young children by my present wife). "To my daughter, Mary Ann F. Howerton, one chest of drawers, one large folding table, one curtain bedstead, bed and furniture, which came to me by intermarriage with her mother; my sons, William Howerton and Thomas Howerton; my daughter, Jane Wayne; a large number of slaves, and at her death to be divided with their increase between all of her children by William Pointer, her former husband. To my daughter, Elizabeth Hester, ten slaves, &c.; to my daughter, Mary Ann F. Howerton, all the land I derived by intermarriage with my second wife, Elizabeth Graves, devised to her by her former husband, Howell Graves.

"Money bequeathed to my son, Thomas Howerton, to be equally divided between my five oldest children, viz.: Elizabeth Hester, Jane Wayne, William Howerton, Thomas Howerton and Robert W. Howerton.

"Wife, Tabitha (or Tulucha), executrix; William and Thomas Howerton and Robert Hester, executors." Witnesses: Daniel Shelton, James Howerton, John Blane and William Sydnor.

Some Howerton marriages in Halifax County, Virginia:

Ann Judith Howerton and George W. Purkins, 4 May 1847.

E. Howerton and Thomas St. John, 1 March 1816.

Elared Howerton and Ann Howerton, 9 April 1822.

Frances Howerton and John E. Dewberry, 3 Jan. 1842.

George Howerton and Frances Jones, 22 Dec. 1785.

James Howerton and Nancey Foster, 1 Feb. 1789.

James Howerton and Susan Ragland, 22 Feb. 1816.

Jane E. Howerton and John W. Lambeth, 21 Dec. 1843.

Rebecca A. Howerton and Sam'l P. Watkins, 28 Oct. 1840.

Robert Howerton and Mary Ann Howerton, 19 Jan. 1830.

Thomas Howerton and Tabitha Hunt, 27 March 1817.

HUDSON family: On the roadside between South Boston and Clover is a quaint old house with a history all its own, built so long ago the oldest representative of the builder cannot tell the date, but it was built by the father of Julius Caesar Hudson, and was one of the earliest inns of this county. His father, William Hudson (?), was the host for many years and entertained celebrated travelers in his day. He left it to his son, Julius Caesar, who married, February 25, 1813, M. Womack. They must have found the Womacks good housewives, for his son, William Royall Hudson, took to wife in 1841 Miss M. J. Womack. When the die was cast for Julius Caesar Hudson, and he crossed the Rubicon, the old inn fell into other and strange hands, but one who goes in it and observes the old-time balcony stairway, the closets and cuddies can conjure up many stories of its past, but none so interesting or thrilling as the real truths about celebrated men who have found rest and refreshment there a century ago. In a little walled-in, neatly kept square was found three large grave stones:

"William H. Hudson, born 1827, died 1878.

"Mary G. Hudson, born 1840, died 1883.

"Kate, wife of J. A. Craddock, born 1844, died 1883."

The Hudsons were very numerous in the county and have intermarried with the Betts, Seays, Thweatts, Allens, Wilkins, Burtons, Owens, Chandlers, Lloyds, Raglands, Abbotts, Lanes and Wades.

The emigrant Hudson came from England to the Eastern Shore. The first Hudson we find in Halifax County was William Hudson, who built the old Hudson Inn, mentioned above, lying on the right-hand side of the road that leads to Clover. He is buried on Dr. Carden's place near Clover. His son, Julius Caesar Hudson, lived in Old Boston for many years, then moved to Dry Branch, near Clover. His son, William Royal Hudson, lived and died near Scottsburg, and his brother, Horatius Alex. Hudson, lived and died at Paces.

Henry Calvin Hudson was born near Scottsburg, and at the age of thirty moved to Scottsburg, opened a store, and at one time owned almost the entire village. He later moved to Dry Bridge, Powhatan County.

William Hudson's Will.

Book 6, page 419, Nov. 18, 1802:

"I, William Hudson, etc., wife Mary Hudson, daughters Nancy Robins, Judith Billington, William Thornton Hudson, Robert Hudson, John B. Hudson, my brother Robert Hudson, five hundred acres of land in Halifax County, and ten slaves. Brother Robert Hudson from Amelia Co.

"William Hudson."

[A History of Halifax County, by Wirt Johnson Carrington, 1924]

HURT family: Philemon Hurt, one of the most approved and useful preachers of the Roanoke Association, was a native of Caroline County, Virginia. He was born October 6, 1758. When he was quite a youth his father removed to Bedford County. As early as his eighteenth year he entered the army, participating in many of the stirring scenes of the Revolution. He was engaged in several battles at the North, and won the praise of his superiors and fellow soldiers as a brave man. Having passed through his term of service, he again volunteered and took part in the eventful conflict at Guilford, North Carolina.

At the close of the war he settled in Halifax County. He soon entered the ministry. In 1793 he was called to the pastorate of Catawba Church, Halifax County. Whether he was permanently the pastor of any other church cannot be distinctly stated, but in connection with the above named body he was a laborious, active minister for more than thirty years.

His eldest son, Robert Hurt, was often permitted, in the same pulpit with his aged father, to preach the gospel.

His youngest son being about to remove to the western country, he determined to leave his native State in his old age. Accordingly, in the year 1827, he migrated to Carroll County, Tennessee. On the 19th of January his Divine Master called him. [Virginia Baptist Ministers, by James B. Taylor, published in New York by Sheldon & Co., 1860, second series, page 94.]

1782, April 10: "Know ye all present that we Moza Hurt & Philemon Hurt of County of Halifax are bound unto His Excellency Governor Benjamin Harrison for the sum of, etc.

"Whereas there is a marriage depending by God's permission between Moza Hurt and Phebe Mann of said county, etc.

"Signed   M. Hurt,

Phil, Hurt."

The records show many deeds, wills and marriages of the Hurt family, but Hon. Samuel L. Adams says: "The record of the Hurt family in Halifax County is rather meager considering the number of ministers it produced. I was surprised not to find a will of the Rev. William Hurt, the late Baptist patriarch, who seems to have died intestate. I have heard a great deal of him, and he was a giant physically as well as a man of considerable mental attainment.

"They still have his old large 'grandfather's chair' at 'Hunting Creek' Baptist Church, about six miles from Lenig. I inspected it carefully during the summer of 1909 while the Dan River Association was being held at that place. He was pastor of Hunting Creek and other Baptist churches in this county."

In 1800, August 12, Philemon Hurt's daughter, Sally, married John Robins Hall, and in 1803, his daughter, Patsy Hurt, married Nathaniel Barksdale, Jr. The witnesses were Armstead Barksdale, J. Wimbish and Randolph Vaughan.

"Liberty" Meeting House was on land purchased from Jacob Keys, nearly a hundred and fifty acres, also a small strip purchased from Moon, 130 acres, on Staunton River, and on the west side of the road leading to 'Hatt Creek,' in Campbell County.

Several of the Hurt families migrated to Southwest Virginia, Tennessee, and Texas, and other States, leaving many prominent descendants to represent them. They also distinguished themselves as soldiers of the Revolution and later wars. Among the most distinguished was John Hurt (chaplain) of the Continental line, one of the bravest of the brave. John Hurt, chaplain of Sixth

Virginia Regiment, October 1, 1776; brigade chaplain, August 18, 1778, to close of the war.

His Petition.

"To the Hon. Speaker of the House of Delegates, the petition of John Hurt, clerk, humbly showeth that he hath served as Chaplain to a Regt. or Brigade raised by the state and upon Continental Establishment, upwards of three years and there being no lands allowed by law to Chaplains he therefore humbly prays the Honorable House, that they may be allowed the like quantity of lands as given to the Commissioned Officers receiving the like pay and rations, upon serving the term required by law for officer and soldier.

"John Hurt."

In the Land Office, Military Records.

"I do certify that Mr. John Hurt is entitled to the proportion of land allowed a Brigade Chaplain of the Continental Line, who has served seven years.

"Signed   Thos. Meriwather,

Ben j. Harrison.

"Jan. 14, 1784."

James Hurt is entitled to the proportion of land allotted to a private in the Continental Line for three years' service. One hundred acres assigned to James Hurt, delivered to Joseph Anthony, November 7, 1808.

In 1854, John Linn Hurt was appointed deputy clerk for Halifax County, later he was clerk of the Circuit Court for Pittsylvania County, a position he filled for twelve years. In 1877 he was elected State senator. He was twice married, first, to Miss Nannie Kate Clement, of Pittsylvania; second, to Miss Sallie T. Douglas.

Many deeds, wills and marriages of the Hurts are recorded in this county.

[A History of Halifax County, by Wirt Johnson Carrington, 1924]

IRBY family: Upon the authority of Mr. W. G. Stanard, secretary of Virginia Historical Society, who has made a chart of the Irby family, we give the origin of the Irby family.

The chart begins with William De Irby, Knight, in 1251, and running through many generations brings us to the first Virginia emigrant, Dr. William Irby, who settled in Charles City County the latter part of the seventeenth century. He married a daughter of Baron Blunt, an English woman.

William Irby was granted by the King of England a very large concession of land in Charles City County and lived and died there on the grant, leaving by his will much valuable silver, especially plate. Judged by the standard of his times he was a man of very large wealth. He was related to the Baron of Boston, England, whose family name is Irby.

Dr. William Irby left one son, William Irby, and several daughters. His descendants moved to Charlotte County and then to Halifax County, where we find William Irby, Gent., one of the first magistrates of this county, in which he figures conspicuously in its early formation and affairs. He left no will, but a lengthy and explicit inventory covers several pages of the court records, indicating a man of considerable wealth.

Through his son, Anthony, and Anthony's son, William Irby, the Halifax Irbys descend from Samuel James Irby, who built a small and unpretentious house about a mile east of the present Halifax Court House.

His son, Morgan Irby, built the first part of the old Irby home, about a mile west on the Mountain Road, very close to the post office of Vernon Hill, in this county. Meade Adams Irby, the son of Morgan Irby, made additions to the house, and it remained in the name of his wife, Amanda Tanner (James) Irby, until her death. Then it went to her son, Thomas Ratcliff Irby.

The old place at one time consisted of a thousand acres, and when Meade Adams Irby inherited from his uncle, Jarrett Irby, who lived near Meadville in this county, six hundred acres of land, he sold it and made with the money received from the sale some improvements and additions to the home at Vernon Hill, which at the time of his death had been reduced to about five hundred acres.

Meade Adams Irby was the first person in Halifax County to learn the art of curing bright tobacco, and farmers sent to him from miles around to come to their places and give them the art of curing their tobacco bright, to which he gladly responded, making no charges for time and work expended.

According to the records, we find the Irbys thrifty, industrious land owners and planters. The War Between the States resulted in many losses to them, as to nearly every other land owner in Halifax County, but with their innate energy, perseverance and industry they are now in line with the prosperous, and some of them who left the county after the war have amassed fortunes. They have intermarried with many prominent families in the county and in other States. *[A History of Halifax County, by Wirt Johnson Carrington, 1924]*

IRVINE: Will of James Irvine, 17 December 1773, Halifax, Colony of Virginia.

"My dearly beloved wife, Jennett; my well beloved son, John; my second and well beloved son, James; my third and well beloved son, Samuel; my fourth and well beloved son, William; my fifth and well beloved son, Alexander, and my well beloved daughters, Mary, Margaret, Jane and Isabel; my son by law, Robert Sharmon."

(Signed) "James Irvine."

Witnesses: David Lawson, Joseph Johnston, John Shaw and William Kimsey.

Some Irvine marriages in Halifax County, Virginia:

Alexander Irvine and Mildred McCraw, 19 Oct. 1798.

Ann Irvine and John Lawson, 17 Feb. 1782.

Christopher Irvine and Prudence Echols, 1 Jan. 1785.

David Irvine and Tabitha Brandon, 14 Sept. 1826.

George Irvin and Rebecca Hunt, 3 Dec. 1805.

George W. Irvine and Mary B. Owen, 12 Jan. 1829.

Isbell Irvine and Moses Walker, 31 Dec. 1789.

J. Irvins (husband) and N. McCraw, 18 Feb. 1801.

James Irvine and Mary Malone, 29 Dec. 1791.

Jinney Irvine and Stephen Edwards, 22 Feb. 1796.

John Irvine and E. Lawson, 6 April 1775.

John D. Irvine and E. T. Crawley, 19 Nov. 1850.

M. Irvine and John McMichell, 1 Nov. 1781.

Margaret Irvine and Thomas Brandon, 19 Feb. 1782.

Samuel Irvin and Sally Easley, 7 April 1805.

JEFFRESS family: Edward Bedford Jeffress, known as the "Father of South Boston," was born in Lunenburg County, the extreme corner adjoining Nottoway and Prince Edward, in 1823. He married in 1846, Mary Harwood Harvey, born February 1, 1825. He died in 1891. They had the following children:

(1) Narcissa Jane, married P. H. Yancey.

(2) Drusilla Thomas, married J. D. Terry.

(3) Susan Ann, married E. B. Yancey.

(4) Thomas Warren Jeffress.

(5) William Edward Blanton Jeffress.

(6) Mary Catherine, married W. T. Carter.

(7) Charles James, married Maria Osborne (of North Carolina).

(8) Coleman Bedford Jeffress.

(9) Sarah Henry Jeffress, married J. W. Elliott, February 6, 1889.

(10) Martha Wyatt Jeffress, born October 6. 1868, married January 22, 1890, Charles L. Norwood, born March 5, 1869, died February 23, 1905. They had the following children: (1) George W. Norwood, born November 12, 1890; (2) Marie E. Norwood, born February 21, 1894, married October 18, 1919, Eugene Homer Riely; (3) Irene T. Norwood, born July 9, 1895, married Howard Edmunds, Jr.

The father of Edward Bedford Jeffress was Coleman Jeffress, born 1798, married 1819, Narcissa Hamlett, daughter of James Hamlett, born February 4, 1751, died October 20, 1819. He married November 11, 1772, Mary Bedford (died June 12, 1812), daughter of Thomas Bedford, Gent., of Goochland County, Va., born 1725, died 1785; married 1753 Mary Ligon Coleman.

Thomas Bedford was a member of the Committee of Safety in the Conventions of 1775-76 for Charlotte County. He was justice of the peace for Charlotte County up to 1778, when he resigned. He was justice of the peace in Cumberland County in 1749.

Hening's Statutes, Vol. 7, page 307: "Whereas it is necessary that trustees be appointed for towns erected in the counties of Halifax and Lunenburg, therefore enacted by the authority aforesaid, Thomas Bedford, Clement Read, Paul Carrington, and others be appointed."

The will of Thomas Bedford, recorded in Charlotte County, February 3, 1785, shows a large estate of slaves, lands and other commodities, which he divided equally amongst his fourteen children, giving each a handsome estate.

Obedience Hamlett (daughter of James and Mary Bedford Hamlett) married in Halifax County William Majors, her first husband, by whom she had two sons, Samuel Majors and Drewry Majors. She married second James Faulkner and had James Faulkner, Jr., Leander Faulkner, A. H. Faulkner and Mary E. Faulkner, who married James Bell, of Prince Edward County.

E. B. Jeffress' line runs back to Miles Cary (1) through Harwood Cary, Sr., of Prince Edward County, who married Mary Cardwell (died 1845), and had Elizabeth Cary (who married Thomas Harvey) and William Haynes Cary. [William (4), Harwood (3). William (2), Miles (1)], 1765-1852, of Prince Edward County.

William Hames Cary (1) married Lucy Cardwell and by her had Patsy Cary, born 1794, and married Wyatt Cardwell. He married second Esther Jackson and had five children, all of Prince Edward County.

Will of Thomas Bedford (in Charlotte County)

"I, Thomas Bedford the older, of Charlotte County.

"My dear faithful and beloved wife Drucilla (Coleman), son Stephen, married Jane Daniel; daughter Elizabeth, married Joseph Fuqua; daughter Mary, wife of James Hamlett; daughter Martha, wife of Charles Crenshaw; son Thomas Bedford, first lieutenant in Revolutionary War, married Anne Robertson (born 1735); Benjamin (went to Kentucky), sons Littlebury, Archibald, daughters Anne, Janey Flippen Bedford, married Colonel Lewis Thornton; Peggy Bedford, son Charles Westley Bedford, John Bedford; daughter Susannah Bedford, wife of Anthony Walke.

The county of Halifax has many worthy descendants of E. B. Jeffress, who was a man worthy of emulation in character and in business, for by integrity and uprightness he won for himself not only a good name, which is better than riches, but riches sufficient to leave his family more than comfortable. He owned hundreds and hundreds of acres of land that he bought from Anthony and Ambrose Hart, the land upon which South Boston is built, and through his mercantile business and various land sales he accumulated a fortune for his time.

A family chart has been prepared showing the lineal descendants of John Fitz-Geoffreys, who emigrated to this country from Ireland about the year 1700. From this chart the relationship of the various branches of the family may be accurately traced, the diagram giving as far as possible the names, dates of birth, marriages and deaths. The information from which this chart was compiled was furnished by members of the different branches most competent to know, and is the result of an extensive correspondence extending over a period of about four years. The Fitz was dropped and the spelling changed to Jeffress.

Sir Herbert Jeffries (Jeffery-Jeffress) died in Virginia in 1678. William Jeffries was in Middlesex County in 1772.

Alexander, Richard and John Jeffries were in the Revolutionary War.

[A History of Halifax County, by Wirt Johnson Carrington, 1924]

JONES, Tabitha, was born about 1790, daughter of Jane Jones. Jane Jones was daughter of Daniel Jones and his wife, Anna. Jane had twin daughters, Tabitha and Patience, with a man of mixed blood. Tabitha was considered Mulatto and unable, by law at the time, to marry the white man that she had children with. The father of her children was Royal Wyatt, who was born in 1787, son of John Wyatt, of Halifax County. Tabitha's sister, Patience, must have passed as white because she married Royal Wyatt's brother, John Wyatt, Jr., on 28 December, 1819.

The children of Tabitha Jones and Royal Wyatt were:

- Rebecca Jones, born about 1820.

- Marcus W. Jones, was born about 1822, in Halifax County, Virginia. He married Sarah Dunaway on 6 March, 1856, in Halifax County. Sarah was born about 1835, in Halifax County, Va., daughter of John and Sarah Dunaway (they were neighbors to the Jones').

- Thompson Jones

- Coleman Jones, born about 1822; wife, Margaret.

- Royal Jones, born about 1828; wife, Elizabeth F.

Dates of birth from 1850 census. Marcus' birth year is consistent with his marriage record.

There is a marriage record for Stanfield T. Jones, born about 1829, in Halifax County, Va., that married Margarett Ashby on 2 May, 1855, in Halifax County. Margarett was born about 1834, in Halifax County, Va., daughter of Whitfield and Mary Ashby. This Stanfield T. Jones was son of Royal Wyatt and Tabitha Jones. I'm uncertain if this is their son Thompson or another son. According to census records, Thompson's wife was Margarett, but his age doesn't match up (which is rather typical).

Several depositions were given on 24th of April, 1857, on behalf of Marcus, Thompson, Coleman and Royal Jones, as they were requesting from the courts to be given a certificate to state that they were not Negro to protect them from the penalties and disabilities to which free Negroes were subject to at the time. These depositions state that their father was a white man named Royal Wyatt, and their mother, Tabitha Jones, was the daughter of Jane Jones, a white woman, and a Mulatto man (nobody knew his name).

Stephanie Tayloe published a small piece on this family called "Wyatts of Carroll Co. Tennessee," which contained great sources verifying this information.

Royal Wyatt married Sarah Jones on 3 May 1828, in the neighboring Caswell County, North Carolina. She was daughter of William and Martha Jones, and she was cousin to Tabitha Jones (Tabitha's mother, Jane Jones, is sister of Sarah's father, William Jones). Royal and Sarah moved to Carroll County, Tennessee. They had the following children:

- Mary, who married a Mr. Morris.

- Paul, no issue

- Silas, no issue

William Jones (the father of Sarah Jones and uncle to Tabitha Jones) married, 9 October, 1776, Martha ____, in Halifax County, Virginia. William died 12 November, 1828, in Halifax County. After the death of William, Martha moved to Carroll County, Tennessee, where she died on 18 August, 1843. William and Martha Jones had eleven children. The names of the ones who survived the parents were:

- Mary, widow of John Chism (married 29 January, 1801, in Halifax County, Va.)

- Elizabeth Jones

- Jane Jones

- Temperance, wife of Lemuel Brown (married 22 March 1804, in Halifax County, Va.)

- Sarah, wife of Royal Wyatt

- William R. Jones

From Revolutionary War pension application and vital records. The marriage date of William and Martha Jones was given by Martha in the Revolutionary War pension application. Their son, William R. Jones, stated in that application, concerning his parents, "they were married by publishing the bans of matrimony as was the custom in Virginia at that time when they were married and not by license."

JORDAN family: Samuel Jordan started from England in the "Sea Adventurer," was wrecked on the "Vext Bermoothes," spent a year on that island. He landed in Jamestown in 1609; was member of the first Assembly of Virginia which met in Jamestown in 1619.

(2) Thomas Jordan (son of Samuel), born 1600 in England, married Lucy Corker, daughter of Captain Corker of Surry County, Va. (He was burgess in 1629-1632, was a soldier with Yardley.)

(3) Thomas Jordan, born 1634, married Margaret Brasseur (Brashear). She was born July, 1642, died October 7, 1698. He was s burgess, 1696-97, Nansemond County, Va. (See the Virginia Colonial Register, page 91.) His sons were Thomas (III), John, Robert, Benjamin, Matthew; *Samuel Jordan*, born February 15, 1679. (Called Colonel Samuel Jordan of Amelia). He married Elizabeth Fleming, daughter of Colonel Charles Fleming, of New Kent County, Va., October 10, 1703 (or 1713). (These Quaker records

preserved in Baltimore. His will dated 1760, and probated 1761 in Amelia County, Va.)

(4) William Jordan, married Mary ____. Issue: William, Granville, *Robert*.

(5) Robert Jordan, born 1717, married before 1749 Susanna. "On account of having to take the oath he did not fight in the Revolution" (this from family records), but was loyal to the King during that time and succeeded in keeping his son, Robert (the youngest son), out of the army; but his sons, William and Henry, were both soldiers of the Revolution, and also Granville. This Robert Jordan bought tobacco during the Revolutionary War. After its close the prices went up and he found that he had amassed a fortune, and his granddaughter writes: "At the time of his death he was immensely rich, besides leaving eighty Negroes."

(6) Robert Jordan, Sr. (Royalist), born 1755; married, in 1778, Elizabeth Church, daughter of Richard Church, of Amelia County. (Richard Church was the son of Leonidas and Judith Church.) He died in 1816. Issue: Robert, Richard, Samuel, Henry, Elam, John, Elijah, Mary, Elizabeth and Martha. (The six oldest sons were all soldiers in the War of 1812.)

(7) Elijah Jordan, born 1804, married Martha Faulkner. Both died in 1886. Issue: Robert, John, Joseph, William, Clement, Samuel, Lucy, Mattie and Caroline (two last died young). Lucy married William Slate.

(8) Robert Elijah Jordan, born March 3, 1828, married Elizabeth Baynham Fourqurean, daughter of Reuben D. Fourqurean and his wife, Mary Baynham Boxley, August 30, 1855. He died December 17, 1894. Issue:

(1) Mary R.. Jordan, born May 31, 1862; married October 26, 1880, Mr. Garland Faulkner. They have three children, viz.: Bessie, wife of Rev. James M. Owens; Dr. Garland E. Faulkner and Mr. Frank F. Faulkner, of Louisiana.

(2) Emma McC. Jordan, born November 9, 1865; married Mr. Thornton Easley. She died May 5, 1894. He died a few months later, 'tis said, of a broken heart. They left two children: Willie Jordan Easley, wife of John W. Easley, and Thornton Jordan Easley.

(3) Robert Elijah Jordan, born December 7, 1867; married January 6, 1892, Hallie Lafayette Turner, daughter of Mrs. Wirt Johnson Carrington by her first husband, Allen Howard Turner. R. E. Jordan departed this life April 2, 1920. Issue: Wirt Carrington Jordan, wife of Mr. Acree D. Irby (they have one son, James Morgan Irby); Elizabeth Baynham Jordan, Hallie Turner Jordan, Robert E. Jordan.

(4) Willie Jordan, born August 24, 1870; married Virginus L. Fowlkes, vice-president of Planters and Merchants National Bank of South Boston. Children: May Hyde Fowlkes, wife of Philip Howerton Kasey (two children,

Elizabeth Kasey and Virginus Kasey); Virginus Lee Fowlkes, wife of Watkins Hunt; Robert Jordan Fowlkes and Ola Fowlkes.

Mr. Virginus L. Fowlkes married for his second wife Miss Elizabeth Warrener, of Amelia County, who descended on her maternal side from William Cabell, of "Union Hill" (no children).

Robert Jordan, Jr., and Elizabeth (Church) Jordan had Elijah Jordan, married Martha Faulkner. Their son, John Jordan, married Susan Rebecca Chambers. Their son, Thomas Jordan, married Ella Young, daughter of Matthew Hubbard Young, son of Thomas Young, of Mississippi. Thomas and Ella (Young) Jordan had the following children: Herman Jordan, Hurt Jordan, Hugo Jordan, Hammett Jordan (married Fannie Reily, of Halifax, and had Carrington, Frances Reily, Mary Green and William Jordan), Nora Jordan (wife of Henry Milton Booth; had Charles B., who married Charline Hester; John R. and Mary Jordan Booth), Bessie Jordan.

Six of the sons of Elijah and Martha Jane (Faulkner) Jordan fought in the War Between the States and came out safely. In a letter received from Joseph E. Jordan, he says: "All six of the boys were in the Civil War—John M., Joseph E., W. I. and C. H. Jordan—from the first to the close. R. E. joined the company the second year of the war, and the youngest, S. H., when they called for the younger ones, and it seemed a miracle that we all came out safe and sound with no broken bones. The voice of our country was to us the voice of God."

John M., Robert E., William I. and Joseph E. Jordan enlisted in the Black Walnut Cavalry company and were mustered into service May, 1861, William Easley, captain Company "C," Third Virginia Regiment, Fitz Lee Brigade, Stuart's Division. C. H. Jordan belonged to the "Danville Grays," Pickett's Division.

Neither R. E. or John Jordan were wounded. Joseph was shot in the hip and W. I. was wounded in the left arm. He was courier for General LaFayette McLaws for fourteen months and was in many important battles. C. H. Jordan was wounded at the battle of Gettysburg. John M. was one of the youngest men in the Third Virginia Regiment. He started in as a private and soon rose to the rank of captain. He surrendered his company at Appomattox. The officers from South Boston were Colonel T. H. Owen, Lieutenant J. H. Chappelle and Lieutenant James W. Hall. The Jordan sons and soldiers were:

(1) Robert E. Jordan, married Elizabeth B. Fourqurean.

(2) Joseph Jordan, married Miss Yarbrough, of North Carolina.

(3) William I. Jordan, married Miss Lightfoot Hobson, of Danville, Va. Had one child, Lightfoot Jordan.

(4) Clement Jordan, married Miss Louise Slate.

(5) John Jordan.

(6) Samuel Jordan.

(7) Lucy Jordan, wife of Rev. William Slate. The children of Rev. William Slate and Lucy (Jordan) Slate were:

(1) W. Clem Slate, first wife Fannie Easley (thee children). He married second, Janie Ragland (five children).

(2) Samuel L. Slate, married Sarah Yonge, of Columbia, Ga.

(3) E. S. Slate.

(4) Lucy Slate, wife of Thomas Webb, manager of trust department in South Boston National Bank. Their children: Dorothy, Lucy, Ella, Thomas and William.

(5) Mary Slate, wife of Ratcliffe Irby.

(6) Gertie Slate, wife of F. J. McGranighan.

Rev. William Slate was pastor of Winn's Creek (Baptist) Church for twenty-five years or more, and was a faithful Christian worker at all times and in all places. Elijah Jordan, son of Robert Jordan, Jr. (the Royalist), and his wife, Elizabeth Church, had, among other children, three daughters, one of whom married a Jamieson. Their daughter, Mamie Jamieson, married J. H. Hickey, and James Hickey, their son, married Miss Cook.

Tribute to Robert E. Jordan, Sr.

"Robert E. Jordan, Sr., was born in Halifax County, Virginia.

"In his youth he entered the store of Mr. Jack Rogers at Woodsdale, N. C. From there he went to Black Walnut, Va., entering the employ of William L. Owen & Co.

"Upon the death of Mr. Reuben M. Fourqurean, in 1851, he was admitted into an interest in the business, and the firm was Owen, Jordan & Co.

"In 1855 he moved to Catawba, in which year he married Miss Bettie A. Fourqurean, whither he carried his bride, and where he remained until the breaking out of the war.

"Casting his lot with his native State, he became a member of Company "C," Third Virginia Cavalry, and although of feeble constitution and under great bodily suffering, he stood to his post and shared with his comrades the hardships and dangers of the marches and battles that shed such luster on Fitz Lee's cavalry.

"The close of the war found him shattered in health, and it was nearly a year before he could resume active business.

120

"Removing to Republican Grove about this time, he formed a business connection with his brother, William I. Jordan, which continued for a number of years.

"In 1869 he came to South Boston, Virginia, when it was a mere hamlet with two stores, and from then until the time of his death, a period of twenty-five years, he was closely identified with its business interests and an active factor in its development and growth.

"In 1875 he retired from mercantile life and opened the first bank in Halifax County after the war under the firm name of R. E. & W. I. Jordan, which in 1885 was merged with the Planters and Merchants Bank, of which institution he was an honored officer. The success of this bank is largely due to the confidence and esteem in which he was held by the public.

"In his private life he was gentle, tender, affectionate. As a Christian he was of deep humility, free from guile, and without envy or bitterness. Of him it may be truthfully said that he was one of the best men that ever lived.

"The large number that gathered at his funeral (among them many members of his old company) attested the love and esteem in which he was held.

"J. S."

The above tribute to R. E. Jordan, Sr., was written by one who knew him almost a lifetime. We are putting it in this history as most worthy for his descendants to honor and emulate.

Tribute (In Part) to R. E. Jordan, Jr.

'In the death of Robert Elijah Jordan, Halifax County has lost one of her most beloved and useful citizens, the Commonwealth of Virginia one of her must distinguished bankers, and the South a loyal son, true to her traditions of noble manhood and purity of character.

"He was the late president of the Planters and Merchants National Bank, a Mason of high rank, an esteemed vestryman in the Episcopal Church, and a beloved trustee of the local school.

"His was the wholesome natural life free from cant and pretense. He thought and spoke and lived the Christly life as unconsciously as he breathed. Small wonder then that all admired him, aye and loved him, and looked upon him as a bulwark and tower of strength. He was a fearless business man, recognized throughout his State as a man of sterling character, of keen business sagacity, of conservative principles; add to this the Christly spirit and what a man.

"Be it resolved, That this expression of our gratitude for his life and our affection for the man be spread upon the records of the vestry, a copy sent to the town papers and to the Southern Churchman, and that a copy be sent with our love and sympathy to his sorrowing family.

"R. A. PENICK, S. W.,
"T. C. WATKINS, Jr.,
"D. H. LEWIS, Rector."

"Entered into rest eternal at an early hour on Good Friday, April 2, 1920, in his fifty-third year, Robert Elijah Jordan, vestryman and junior warden of Trinity Church, South Boston, Va., and superintendent of the Sunday school."

[A History of Halifax County, by Wirt Johnson Carrington, 1924]

JORDAN, Thomas R., son of John and Susan R. (Chambers) Jordan, was born in Halifax County. His parents were also natives of this county and residents of same through life. His father died in 1871, his mother died in 1887. His wife is Mary E., daughter of M. H. and A. M. Young. She was born at Marengo, Alabama. Their marriage was solemnized on New Years Day, 1876, by Rev. J. B. Shearer, and their children are two daughters, Nora and Lizzie, and four sons, Hamet, Hurt, Hugo and Herman. The father of Mrs. Jordan was killed by a runaway slave in 1863. Thomas R. Jordan served through the late war in the Confederate States Army, three years in Company C, 3rd Virginia Cavalry, one year in Poague's Artillery Battalion. He was taken prisoner in the advance on Gettysburg, and held a time in Washington, at the Old Capitol. On July 1, 1879, he was elected clerk of the Halifax County court. *[Virginia and Virginians, Vol. II]*

JORDAN, Hon. William J. (or I.?), State Senator from Halifax County, and a resident of South Boston, was born in this county in the year 1839. His father was a large planter, and both father and mother were natives of Virginia. He received his early education in the schools of the county. While yet quite young, he began clerking for the firm of J. L. & F. Owen, remaining with them four years. In 1861 he enlisted in Company C, 3rd Virginia Cavalry, in which he served four years. He was wounded in the battle of Fort Cannon, and was in all the principal engagements in Virginia, acting as courier for Gen. McLaws for over a year. When the war closed he came to Halifax and entered business with his brother, Robert. One branch of their business being conducted in South Boston, and they started a private bank in 1872, which they conducted until about 1885, when they united with the Planters and Merchants Bank, which was organized in 1884. Mr. Jordan has also large land interests in the county. In November, 1884, he was elected to the State Legislature. Hon. Jordan was married in 1876, to Miss Elizabeth Buster, daughter of James S. Buster, of Charlotte County. *[South-West Virginia and the Valley, A. D. Smith & Co., 1892]*

LACY family: Ernest C. Lacy, clerk of the Circuit Court of Halifax County, is an ex-service man with a record in the aviation corps in France, and for a number of years before beginning his term in the clerk's office he was actively identified with banking in his native county.

Mr. Lacy was born in Scottsburg, Halifax County, September 2, 1888. His grandfather, Micajah Lacy, was a lifelong resident of Halifax County, owned and operated a large farm and also conducted a hardware business in Halifax for a number of years. The last ten years of his life he spent in retirement at Scottsburg. He entered the Confederate army, but was captured and spent most of his time as a prisoner at Point Lookout, Maryland.

James T. Lacy, Sr., father of the clerk of the Circuit Court, was born in Halifax Court House in 1865. His home has been in Scottsburg since about 1883, and he was active in business as a tobacconist until 1913. He owns farms to the aggregate of twelve hundred acres in Halifax County, and has had a very busy and successful career. His interests have extended into politics and into religious work. He served as a member of the House of Delegates, representing Halifax County two sessions and two sessions in the State Senate. In March, 1919, he was appointed clerk of the Circuit Court of Halifax County to fill out the unexpired term of Gran Craddock, and filled that office until May, 1921, when he resigned on account of ill health. In his younger years he acted as a colporter, selling Bibles and Sunday school literature, and has long been a prominent member of the Scottsburg Baptist Church, is a deacon, and for forty years was superintendent of the Sunday school. He is a member of the Masonic fraternity.

James T. Lacy, Sr., married Ada B. Crews, who was born in Chesterfield County in 1858. Of their children Ernest C. is the oldest; James T. Jr., is cashier of the Boston National Bank of South Boston; Ruth F. is the wife of Kenneth Patty, a lawyer and coal broker at Graham in Tazewell County; Miss Edith J. lives at home; Alton G. is deputy clerk of the Circuit Court under his brother; Marie died in infancy.

Ernest C. Lacy acquired his education in the public schools of Scottsburg, graduating from high school in 1907, and then from Hampden-Sidney College, where he completed the classical course and received the B. A. degree in 1910. After leaving college he acted as principal of the High School at Rodden, Virginia, a year, spent one year as bookkeeper for the State Bank of Charlotte County at Drakes Branch, and coming to Halifax was assistant cashier of the Bank of Halifax from 1912-1917. In 1917 he was promoted to cashier and served until May, 1918, when he resigned to begin his active military service. He had volunteered for the aviation corps, and in May, 1918, he went to France, becoming a member of the northern bombing squadron and was situated near Bruges, Belgium. He returned home January 1, 1919, and was relieved from active duty in March of that year and received his permanent discharge from U. S. N. R. F. in May, 1922.

In March, 1919, Mr. Lacy resumed his duties as cashier with the Bank of Halifax, and served in that capacity until August 1, 1920, when he was appointed deputy clerk of the Circuit Court of Halifax County under his father, and on May, 1921, succeeded his father, who resigned as clerk of the Circuit Court. His term extends to January 1, 1928. His offices are in the Court House of Halifax.

Mr. Lacy was a Democrat, a deacon and treasurer of the Beth Car Baptist Church of Halifax, is worshipful master of Halifax Lodge, No. 96, A. F. & A. M., a member of Halifax Chapter, No. 38, R. A. M., at South Boston, Lynchburg Lodge No, 321, B. P. O. Elks, Houston Council No. 202, Junior Order United American Mechanics, at Halifax, Halifax Camp No. 112, Woodmen of the World, and the Kiwanis Club of South Boston. Mr. Lacy was a director of the Bank of Halifax and owned one of the comfortable homes of that town.

Mr. Lacy married at Richmond, Va., December 8, 1917, Miss Marian E. Chalkley, daughter of Edward H. and Lula (McGruder) Chalkley, residents of Drakes Branch, Va., where her father was station agent for the Southern Railway Company. Mrs. Lacy is a graduate of the Drakes Branch High School and also of the Harrisonburg State Normal College. They had a son, Ernest C., Jr., born June 6, 1920.

(Copied From a Letter to Mr. James T. Lucy, Jr.)

"Lacys of Scottsburg, Halifax County, were descended from pure Anglo-Saxon stock. They came to this county before the War of 1812, and your great-grandfather Lacy was in that war." (We find in Heitman's list of 1812 soldiers from Virginia the name of Westwood Armstead Lacey, Virginia Cadet, M. A., September 18, 1817, second lieutenant, Fourth Infantry, July 1, 1822; died November 3, 1829. This may or may not be the great-grandfather Lacy of the Scottsburg Lacys.)

"Your grandfather Crews people also came from England; some of them settled out west."

"My great-grandfather was Jacques (James) Martin, one of the little colony of Huguenots who left France in 1698 because of religious persecution and settled in Manakin Town, on James River, in Powhatan County, Virginia. Beverly in his History of Virginia says of them: 'The French refugees sent in thither by the charitable exhibition of his late majesty, King William, are naturalized by a particular law for that purpose.' Those who went over first were advised to seat on a very rich piece of land about twenty miles above the falls of James River, which land was formerly the seat of a great and war-like nation of Indians, called Monacans. These refugees were freed from every public tax for several years. Some of their descendants are now living in this county. Many of them settled in Chesterfield and adjoining counties.

"William Martin, son of Jacques Martin, married Elizabeth Stratton. The Strattons were of Anglo-Saxon origin, and the first one of the name who came to America was Joseph Stratton, of Plymouth, England, who settled in James City County, Va., in 1628. He was burgess in 1629-32. He died in 1641, leaving large landed estate in England. In 1678 there were many Strattons living in Chesterfield County, and research there ought to establish the dates, etc., of the above lines connecting them with this Lacy family."

In the marriage list, which is always so helpful in seeking out lines, we find the marriage of one John Lacy, September 15, 1784, to Alice Sydnor, and in 1799, Moore Lacy to Dorothy Ragland; October 18, 1804, Thomas Lacy married Fanny Powell, and in July 5, 1843, Armistead M. Lacy married S. T. Barksdale. In 1849, Charles L. Lacy married Mary T. Baker, and in November 2, 1853, Melcajah T. Lacy married Martha F. Greenwood, and were the parents of James T. Lacy, Sr., of Scottsburg.

Of the Lacys of South Boston, a descendant writes: "Our great-grandfather, John Lacy, married in 1874, Alice Sydnor, a widow. They had three sons, John, Samuel and Robert. He owned a great deal of land on Millstone Road, and left each of his sons a home on that road. Our grandfather was Robert. He lived on land lying near Millstone Church. He had four sons, William, Alex, Charles and John, who was a missionary to Africa. Our father's name was Charles. He lived all his life in the old homestead, now owned by my brother, Dr. J. B. Lacy."

We can certainly vouch for the probity, honor and usefulness of most of them who settled in this county, as they have held some of its most important offices. Dr. W. T. Lacy and son, Dr. Malcolm Lacy, were dentists of South Boston. *[A History of Halifax County, by Wirt Johnson Carrington, 1924]*

LAWSON family belong to a very ancient family from England and Scotland, where they flourished centuries ago. There were many Lawsons in Yorkshire, England. There was a Rowland Lawson who died in Lancaster County, Va., in 1661. His children were Rowland, John, Henry, Letitia, and Elizabeth.

John Lawson, surveyor, came to North Carolina in 1700. He wrote a valuable history of the early Carolinas. They have always been staunch, determined church people, leaning mostly to the Scotch Presbyterianism.

The Lawsons who married in Halifax County were William Lawson, who married Jane Banks in 1758, May 24; John Lawson, who married Martha Bates, 1778, August 8; John Lawson, who married Ann Irvine, 1782,

February 17; Thomas Lawson, who married Hannah Fuqua, 1782, January 4; David Lawson, who married Winnie Dodson, 1794, October 12; John Lawson, who married Elizabeth Miller, 1786, April 24; Francie Lawson, who married Betsy Taylor, 1791, February 16; G. M. Lawson, who married Angelina Marshall, December 21, 1836; and James E. Lawson, who married Julia Ann Johnson, November 18, 1835.

David Lawson married Jane Bailey. Robert William Lawson (son of David) was born in the village of Harmony, Halifax County, 1853. He married Mary E. Craddock, daughter of Dr. John Craddock, of Black Walnut, November 16, 1898. By this marriage he left three children, Robert Lawson, J. J. Lawson, and Mary Elizabeth Lawson. His widow married Mr. Lewis Johnston, son of Rev. Lewis Johnston, and his wife, Miss Dupuy. They had a son, Lewis Johnston, Jr.

In the Revolutionary War Robert Lawson was major of the Fourth Virginia Regiment, later brigadier general, and commanded a brigade of Virginia troops under General Greene at the battle of Guilford. The Revolutionary roster is reeking with Lawsons. They were brave men, and it is said "they were set in their ways," which is all right if their ways were set for liberty and righteousness; for it's said also that there was never a time when there lacked a man of the Lawson name to stand before the Lord.

In 1812, October 12, one Thomas Brandon was guardian of Priscilla, John F. and Catherine D. Lawson, as recorded in Halifax.

John J. Lawson, brother of Robert Lawson, married Eliza Craddock, sister of Robert's wife. They had the following children:

- John Lawson, married Nancy Carrington, daughter of Henry Paul Carrington.

- Bessie Lawson, wife of Tyree Wright.

- Barksdale Lawson, married Sallie Williams.

- Janie Lawson, wife of Julian East.

- Venable Lawson, married Vivian Moseley.

- Marie Lawson, wife of Ernest Harding.

- Stebbens Lawson, married Elizabeth Houston.

- Katherine Lawson, wife of Thomas Sutherlin.

[A History of Halifax County, by Wirt Johnson Carrington, 1924]

LAWSON, John James, of South Boston, Halifax County, Virginia, banker, for many years a member of the town council of South Boston, was born at

Harmony, Halifax County, Virginia, on the 27th of August, 1849. His father, David Lawson, was a farmer, characterized by great energy, strong common sense, promptness and thrift, and a high sense of honor. His mother was Mrs. Jane (Bailey) Lawson.

Richard Lawson, who came from England, in 1654, is the earliest known American ancestor of the family. Brigadier-General Benjamin Lawson of the Revolutionary army, and his brother, Hugh Lawson, both settled near Norfolk, Virginia, where General Lawson remained. His brother, Hugh Lawson, went to North Carolina, dying in Rowan County, North Carolina, in 1764, and leaving a son named John, who removed to Caswell County, North Carolina, near the Virginia line. John Lawson, the second, grandfather of the subject of this sketch, was born in Caswell County, North Carolina. The family were thrifty farmers and merchants, well remembered for their good business judgment and their strong common sense.

In his boyhood he had excellent health, and was fond of hunting, fishing and other out-door sports. His school years were passed in a thickly settled country neighborhood. His opportunities for attending school were limited to a few seasons at country schools near his home, with one year's attendance at Horner's School, in North Carolina, after which he returned to his home, in 1865, to take a place in a country store.

On the 1st of October, 1865, he took a place as clerk in a store at Harmony, Virginia, his pay to be fifty dollars for the first year. He continued in that business until January 1st, 1871, on which day he became a partner in the firm of J. J. Lawson and Company. On the 1st of October, 1876, this company changed its place of business from Harmony to South Boston, Virginia. With his brother, R. W. Lawson, and Joseph Stebbins, he carried a general line of merchandise, under the firm name of Stebbins and Lawson. Mr. John James Lawson attended chiefly to the office work. They built up a large and successful mercantile business, which grew in importance with the rapid growth of the town of South Boston. Mr. Lawson was actively interested in organizing and promoting the Bank of South Boston, which opened for business on May 1st, 1887. Mr. Lawson was elected cashier of the bank—a position which he held for over twenty years.

In the meantime his business ability and his sound principles have been recognized by his election to numerous positions for the direction of banks and business enterprises. On October 1st, 1906, he was chosen president of the Boston National bank. He is a member of the wholesale dry goods firm of Stebbins, Lawson and Spraggins company; he was president of the South Boston Electric Light and Power company; a director of the R. W. Lawson Grocery company; president of the Bank of Virgilina; a director of the Barbour Buggy company; and a director of the South Boston Ice company.

By religious belief he is identified with the Presbyterian Church, South; and for many years was deacon in that church. In politics he is a Democrat, and he has never swerved in his allegiance to the principles and the nominees of that party.

He was always interested in farming, buying and selling many plantations. He was fond of dealing in real estate, buying largely for cash when prices were low, and never suffering property to deteriorate upon his hands although he may have held it for years. While banking was his first interest, he was also successful in raising horses, cattle, hogs, corn and grass.

On the 26th of September, 1883, Mr. Lawson married Miss Eliza Jasper Craddock, daughter of Dr. John W. Craddock of Black Walnut, Halifax County, Virginia. They had eight children, four sons and four daughters, all of whom are living in 1907. *[Men of Mark in Virginia, 1908]*

John James Lawson

LAWSON, Robert William, was born in Harmony, Halifax County, Virginia, September 28, 1853. His father was David Lawson, a farmer of Halifax County; his mother was Jane Bailey.

Mr. Lawson's earliest known ancestor in America was John Lawson, who was the first colonial surveyor general of North Carolina, and who was burned at the stake by the Indians. A later ancestor was General Robert Lawson, who was major of the 4th Virginia regiment in the War of the American Revolution, and later its colonel, and who commanded a brigade of Virginia troops under General Greene at the battle of Guilford.

Mr. Lawson's youth was spent in the country, where he worked on his father's farm except when at school. He attended the common schools of his county; but, possessing no particularly literary or scholastic inclination, he, after obtaining a common school education, began the active work of life in 1870 as salesman in a country store at Harmony.

Mr. Lawson has been a merchant, the president of the R. W. Lawson company, wholesale grocers, the president of the South Boston Electric Light and Power company, and a director in the Bank of South Boston.

In politics, Mr. Lawson is a Democrat. In church preference, he is a Baptist. Though not a politician, Mr. Lawson served on the town council of South Boston. He also served on the local school board, and rendered useful service in furnishing educational advantages to the children of his town.

On November 16, 1898, Mr. Lawson married Miss Mary E. Craddock, daughter of Dr. John Craddock, of Black Walnut, Halifax County, Virginia.

Mr. Lawson was a director in the following companies: The Century Cotton Mill of South Boston; the Boston National Bank, of South Boston; and the J. A. Mebane Electrical company, as well as in the Boston and Houston Brick company. He was interested in farming and stock raising. He was a stockholder in the new South Boston Ice and Lumber company. He was president of the Keystone Drug company of South Boston, manufacturing chemists and druggists, who did business that extended through fifteen states. He was a stockholder in the Barbour Buggy company.

The business of Stebbins and Lawson, general commission business, was started in 1876, the first business house of the kind in South Boston. In 1892, the work of the firm was subdivided. R. W. Lawson became president of the wholesale grocery department; J. J. Lawson became cashier of the Bank of South Boston, and was later elected president of the Boston National Bank. Joseph Stebbins, Sr., took charge of the wholesale dry goods business under the firm name of Stebbins and Lawson, which in 1907 has become Stebbins, Lawson and Spraggins. *[Men of Mark in Virginia, 1908]*

Robert William Lawson

LEIGH family: The tradition is that Benjamin Watkins (the youngest brother of Thos. Watkins of Chickahominy), the first clerk of Chesterfield County, an office he held to the end of his life, and a man of genius, though with little education in the schools, cultivated his excellent understanding assiduously and was regarded as an excellent scholar. However much he cultivated his "excellent understanding," he did not comprehend that the course of true love is not to be thwarted even if the parent did not relish the idea of his daughter marrying a poor English clergyman.

The Hon. Benjamin refused to accept the situation until the congregation of the Rev. William Leigh took the matter in hand and built a home and furnished it for the happy young couple; so in spite of father and fate, they started on life's highway happy and unfettered with life's financial cares.

The Rev. William Leigh was a royal character, with lion-hearted antecedents, and not to be downed, as his father-in-law soon learned, and repenting him of his course, did the proper thing by his son-in-law and beloved daughter, and all the ambition he could ever have had for his daughter culminated in his two grandsons, Benjamin Watkins Leigh and his brother, Judge William Leigh, who lived in Halifax County. It was said of him that for almost a quarter of a century in which he had been the judge of the Halifax court he had discharged each and every duty with a fidelity and ability equal to any other man in Virginia, and had won by universal consent the title of a "just and upright judge."

He was the friend and adviser of John Randolph of Roanoke, and the sole executor by his will of 1821, and he, with Henry St. George Tucker, were the final executors by the will of 1832.

No character stands out more clearly in this county for acumen, probity and pureness than that of Judge William Leigh, and his descendants would do well to honor his memory by emulating his virtues, for we shall not see his like again.

Two daughters of Thomas Watkins married the two Leighs. Mary Selden Watkins married Benjamin Watkins Leigh (his first wife), and Rebecca Watkins married William Leigh. Their sister, Hannah Cary Watkins, married Dr. John Barksdale, of Halifax. Their children were (1) Thomas W. Barksdale, (2) Alice S. Barksdale, (3) Benjamin Watkins Leigh Barksdale, and (4) Rebecca Barksdale.

[A History of Halifax County, by Wirt Johnson Carrington, 1924]

LIGON family: Will of Joseph Ligon, 27 January 1779, Halifax County:

"I lend unto my loving wife, Judith Ligon, one Negro slave named Nan and one Negro girl named Rachel... one Negro man named Abram.

"my son, Blackman Ligon, that part of my land on the west side of Wades Creek which my pattron calls Peters Creek.... In case my son, Blackman, is dead, or should die before he leaves the army, the land shall return to my son, John Ligon.

"to my son, John Ligon, one hundred acres of land which I bought of Philmer Green.

"to my son Joseph Ligon, one hundred and fifty acres of land...also one negro slave named Jenney, which I bought of Charles Wade.

"To my son, Joseph Ligon, &c., and it is my desire that he shall act in all things and dispose of his estate as if he was actually 21 years of age.

"unto my six sons Blackman Ligon, John Ligon, Thomas Ligon, James Ligon, Obediah Ligon and Henry Ligon, six Negroes, Peter, Jack, Yellow, Rachal, Sue, Jeane and Dick.

"when my son, John Ligon, comes to the age of 21 years.

"when my son, Thomas Ligon, comes to the age of 21 years.

"Joseph Ligon."

Witnesses: John Flinn, Jr., Robert Jordan, Elizabeth Jordan.

Proved at Court held for Halifax County the 18th of May, 1780.

Abstract of a letter to Gen. Robert F. Ligon, Jr., Montgomery, Ala., dated 10 Feb., 1914, from W. H. Ligon of Clarksville, Va.:

"I am the second oldest son of the late Henry R. Ligon, who was the youngest son of Obediah Ligon, who was a son of Joseph Ligon of Halifax County, Virginia. My great-grandfather Ligon settled in Halifax County in Colonial Times, his home being on the North side of the Dan River opposite the mouth of Aron's creek, which creek, is the line between Mecklenburg and Halifax Counties, south of the river.

"The code of Virginia of Colonial times shows that a charter was granted him to open and operate a ferry across the Dan River, at that place. The ferry was opened, and the road that he built from it is in a south westerly direction out by Midway, and the Red Bank in Halifax County, and towards Roxboro, N. C., known to this day as Ligon's Road. My great-grandfather was wealthy and raised several sons, all of whom were educated after the old English custom, i.e. they learned a trade in addition to their literary attainments. All of his sons, excepting my grandfather, went west, though some of them may have gone in a different direction." *[The Ligon Family and Connections, William D. Ligon, Jr., 1947]*

Blackman Ligon was a soldier in the Revolutionary War. He enlisted in Halifax County, Va., 12 February, 1776, served as a private in Captains Nathaniel Cocke and William Moseley's Companies, Colonels William Dangerfield and Alexander McClanahan's Seventh Virginia Regiment. He was in the battles of Brandywine and Germantown and at the "affair at Cootes' Bridge" and was discharged 12 February, 1780. In February 1781, he volunteered and was at the battle of Guilford, where he received a musket ball wound in the thigh.

He moved to Greenville District, South Carolina, where applied for pension for his service in the war. He died 3 May, 1831. His wife, Elizabeth, was born 28 April, 1753. She died 15 October, 1842. In 1821 the soldier referred to his children, John T., aged twenty-nine years; Elizabeth aged twenty-five years; and Blackman aged twenty-two years; and his grandsons, James B. Roseman, aged nine years, and Joseph Ligon, aged four years. His oldest child was a girl and his second was Mrs. Nancy T. Moore, or Moon, who was born 1 November 1784. *[Revolutionary War pension application]*

Joseph Ligon. Born Dec. 11, 1755, Halifax County, Va.; died Sept. 21, 1842, Montgomery County, Tenn. Joseph Ligon, jr., was the son of Joseph Ligon sr., of Halifax County, Va., who organized a company of militia in April, 1775. Joseph Ligon, jr., was commissioned ensign in his father's company, August, 1777, and lieutenant in October, 1777; later Joseph Ligon, jr., served as a private in Capt. John Thompkins's company, Col. Nathaniel Cocke's regiment, in Gen. Stephen's brigade. While in line of his duty in Stephen's brigade at the Battle of Guilford Court House, N. C., on Mar. 15, 1781, he was wounded by a musket ball passing through his right shoulder joint. He moved to Tennessee about 1796, and died there. On his tomb are these words: "Joseph Ligon, formerly of Halifax County, Va. Born Dec. 11, 1755. Died Sept. 21, 1842. Soldier of the Revolution. Wounded in the Battle of Guilford Court House." The grave is sadly neglected. Buried at Paris, Tex. *[Eighteenth Report of the National Society of the Daughters of the American Revolution]*

Some Ligon marriages in Halifax County, Virginia:

Blackman Ligon and E. Townes, 17 June 1782.

James Ligon and Judith Church, 25 June 1789.

John Ligon and Nancy Anderson, 12 Nov. 1782.

Joseph Ligon and Lettice Sims, 10 June 1784.

Joseph Ligon and Diana C. Clay, 10 April 1790.

Judith Ligon and Wiley Yancey, 20 Sept. 1797.

Marsten Ligon (husband) and E. Wood, 12 Jan. 1808.

Matthew Ligon and Judith Pleasants, 16 July 1806.

Michal Stuart Ligon and Henry Stokes, 9 Dec. 1799.

Obediah Ligon and Anne Isbell, 16 Oct. 1799.

Patsey Ligon and Robert Wilbourn, 12 Aug. 1802.

Polly Ligon and Richard Parker, 31 Jan. 1797.

Polly Ligon and Littlebury Farmer, 5 Oct. 1802.

Richard H. Ligon and Incy Welborn, 18 Oct. 1798.

Richard Ligon and Voseline Degernette, 17 Dec. 1835.

Sally Ligon and William Puryear, 30 Nov. 1802.

Susannah Ligon and Thomas Wilbourn, 22 Aug. 1799.

William Ligon and Mary Ann Good, 29 Jan. 1823.

LOGAN family went from Scotland to Ireland, and from Ireland to Philadelphia, Pa., where David Logan married. [See Americans of Royal Descent.] They were powerful feudal barons of Scotland.

From Pennsylvania David Logan and his wife came to Augusta County, Va., where their son, Benjamin Logan, was born, and baptized by the Rev. Mr. Craig, May 3, 1743. This Benjamin became the distinguished General Benjamin Logan of Kentucky.

There was a David Logan in the earliest records of Halifax.

Elizabeth H. Logan, daughter of Richard and Mary Margaret (Coleman) Logan, married Marcellus French. *[A History of Halifax County, by Wirt Johnson Carrington, 1924]*

Richard, Logan Jr., of Halifax County, Va., was Captain in Company "H," 14th Virginia Infantry in the Civil War. He third son of Richard and Margaret Logan, was born on the 3rd of December, 1829, in Halifax County, Virginia. His early education was received at the Academy at Halifax Court-House, Virginia, which school he continued to attend until the summer of 1846. In September of that year he was sent to the Virginia Military Institute,— entering the third class,—and remained there until 1849, when he graduated. On returning home he selected the profession of civil engineering, for which his education had so well fitted him, and was for some time engaged on railroads in Virginia. He was subsequently employed on a road in Ohio, but his health becoming impaired he returned to Virginia and devoted himself to agricultural pursuits, settling upon a plantation near the village of Meadville, in his native county.

He was a true son of Virginia, sensitively alive to all that concerned her honor or welfare. As soon, therefore, as it was ascertained that the State would probably secede from the Union a volunteer company was raised in his vicinity, to the command of which he was called by acclamation. He at once addressed himself with zeal and energy to the duties which his new position imposed, laboring earnestly to prepare his company for the stirring scenes in which it was destined to play so active and distinguished a part. But little time, however, was left for this. As soon as the note of war was sounded, and the call to arms went forth from the capital of the State to every city, town, and hamlet within her borders, this company was not slow to respond, but at once commenced active preparation for its departure, and soon repaired to Richmond, where, on the 1st of May, 1861, it was mustered into the service of the State. It was subsequently transferred, as were all the Virginia troops, to the service of the Confederate States, and on the organization of the 14th Virginia Regiment was assigned to it and designated as Co. "H." This regiment became a part of Armistead's Brigade, which was organized at Suffolk, Virginia, in the spring of 1862, and which was assigned successively to Huger's, Anderson's, and Pickett's Divisions, joining the latter at Culpeper

Court-House, Virginia, in the fall of that year. The regiment was first engaged at Seven Pines, and subsequently, with distinction, in the bloody battle of Malvern Hill,—Captain Logan being in command during the latter part of that engagement. On the organization of the Army of Northern Virginia, the division to which this brigade belonged was assigned to Longstreet's Corps, and was engaged in nearly all the great battles afterwards fought by this army, except the battle of Chancellorsville, at which time the division was investing Suffolk.

Captain Logan commanded his company in all these battles up to the day of his death,—second Manassas, Sharpsburg, Harper's Ferry, Fredericksburg, Suffolk, and, lastly, in the great battle of Gettysburg. He led his company in the celebrated charge of Pickett's Division, and on the ever-memorable 3rd of July, 1863, at the close of the action, after having aided in capturing the enemy's guns, fell facing the enemy, pierced by a ball, which passed entirely through his body about the region of the heart. He died instantly, without uttering a word.

His fall was for a long time in doubt, and though the most anxious forebodings were felt by his relatives and friends, it was yet hoped that he might be among the thousands of gallant men who, in the very hour of victory, were made prisoners. This hope, alas! was destined to be disappointed, certain information having been subsequently received making known the manner of his death as above detailed.

Richard Logan, Sr., the father of Captain Logan, was a distinguished member of the Halifax bar, known and respected far and near for his talents, his high character, his stern and unbending integrity. He was repeatedly elected by the people of his county to stations of high public trust, having been a member of the Convention of 1829-30, and frequently of the Senate of Virginia. Mrs. Logan was a daughter of Colonel Henry E. Coleman, of Halifax County, from whom the large, wealthy, and respectable family of that name, so well known in South-side Virginia, was descended.

Captain Logan inherited from his parents a mind distinguished by sound judgment and practical good sense, and a warm and affectionate heart, which made him friends wherever he was thrown, in school, at college, in camp. His sound judgment, his high and chivalrous courage, his perfect sincerity, his genial good nature and modest demeanor, commanded the respect and won the esteem and affection of all with whom he came in contact, and made him a favorite wherever He was known. He was singularly well fitted for command, by talents, character, and education, having that happy faculty which enabled him to enforce the necessary discipline without losing the respect and affection of his men.

He would have filled a much higher station in the service with credit to himself and advantage to the country, and would doubtless have been promoted had he or his friends exerted themselves to that end. He seems, however, to have been actuated rather by a sense of duty than a desire for personal distinction, and was content to perform faithfully the duties of the position to which he had been called by his company, and preferred to remain with those—the sons of his friends and neighbors—who had been, as it were, intrusted to his care.

It so happened that there were no vacancies in the regimental offices of the 14th until the battle of Gettysburg, which proved so destructive to that gallant regiment, and in which Captain Logan himself fell. Thus it was that he failed to reach the high official position which he so well merited. This, however, is a matter of but little moment. He was loved and respected for what he was and what he did,—his warm heart, his manly courage, his gallant bearing, his faithful performance of duty. A higher position might have opened to him a wider sphere of usefulness and influence; it could have added nothing to the esteem and affection with which he was regarded by those who knew and appreciated him, and who watched with just pride his honorable career from the day of its commencement to that of its close on the bloody field of Gettysburg. *[Memorial, Virginia Military Institute, 1875]*

The Logans of Halifax County intermarried with the Caldwells, Barksdales, Sydnors, Holts and Colemans.

LOVELACE family: As far back as 1783, we find William Lovelace joining himself in matrimony to Sally Frambrough, and in 1789, July 27, Charles Lovelace marries Rhoda Hart.

The emigrant Lovelace came to the Eastern Shore and his descendants scattered through the various counties, coming this way until 1825, when we find the marriage of James Lovelace to Elizabeth Paynor; in 1829, Charles Lovelace to Harriet R. Butler; and in 1845, June 11, John S. Lovelace married Amelia A. Baker. In 1849, November 22, James S. Lovelace married Martha Ann Barksdale.

The grandfather of Charles L. Lovelace, of South Boston, William Oldham Lovelace, married Miss Womack. His son, John Logan Lovelace, married America Baker, and our citizen, Charles L. Lovelace, married Miss Elizabeth Hodge, whose connections, Mortons, Edmunds, Jennings, etc., of this county, have so intermarried with the Charlotte families of same name that the lines are as intricate as the web around the Lady of Shalott; so we leave them to those who are most interested to untangle.

Charles L. Lovelace and Elizabeth (Hodge) Lovelace had the following children:

(1) Charles Branch Lovelace, married Mildred Skinner.

(2) Sallie J. Lovelace, wife of John O. Harris.

(3) Eva Lovelace, wife of Lester Lane Dillard.

(4) Margaret C. Lovelace

(5) William Henry Lovelace

[A History of Halifax County, by Wirt Johnson Carrington, 1924]

Some Lovelace marriages in Halifax County, Virginia:

Amey Lovelace and John Owen, 1794.

Charles Lovelace and Rhoda Hart, 27 July 1789.

Charles Lovelace and Harriett R. Butler, 15 Dec. 1829.

E. W. Lovelace and Jeremiah White, 19 Feb. 1839.

James Lovelace and Elizabeth Paynor, 15 Dec. 1825.

James Lovelace and Martha Browder, 20 Dec. 1832.

James C. Lovelace and Permela W. Maynard, 20 Dec. 1839.

James S. Lovelace and Martha Ann Barksdale, 22 Nov. 1849.

John S. Lovelace and Amelia A. Baker, 11 June 1845.

Martha Lovelace and James M. Kirby, 18 Jan. 1832.

Nancy Lovelace and James G. Davis, 6 July 1830.

Nathaniel Lovelace and Wilmuth Russell, 13 Dec. 1832.

Sarah C. Lovelace and William Waller, 8 Oct. 1834.

Tabitha Lovelace and James Collins, 28 Sept. 1795.

Tabitha Lovelace and Charles Harris, 17 Nov. 1798.

William Lovelace and Sally Fambrough, __ Feb. 1783.

MALONE: Will of Daniel Malone, 3 November 1795, Halifax County.

"To my daughter, Mary Irvine; daughter, Elizabzth Tranum; son, Thomas; son Nathaniel; daughter, Becky Andrews; sons, Drury, John, Jameson and Banister.

"Daniel (his X mark) Malone."

Executors: James Irvine, Clement Tranum and John Andrews. Witnesses: James Reynolds, Saml. Pate, Wm. Irvine, John Irvine, Burwell Grant.

Codcil to Daniel Malone's will:

"I give to my daughter, Polly Harding, one shilling.

"I give to my daughter, Susanna Reynolds (deceased), one shilling.

"I give to my son, Peter Malone, one shilling.

"Daniel (X) Malone."

Some Malone marriages in Halifax County, Virginia:

Daniel Malone and E. Whitlock, 1 May 1784.

Mary Malone and James Irvine, 29 Dec. 1791.

Sally Malone and Larkin Grant, 27 Jan. 1791.

Thomas Malone and Susannah Tuck, 28 July 1785.

William Malone and Ann H. Blankenship, __ Dec. 1848.

MAXEY, Radford, lived on the Dan River in Halifax County, Virginia. He was a Justice of Halifax County in 1767. He was a descendant of Edward and Susannah Maxey, who came to America around 1700, and settled in Henrico (now Powhatan) County, Virginia. Radford married Marie Elizabeth Fuqua, daughter of William Fuqua, Sr., and his wife, Marie Elizabeth Faure. Radford Maxey's will was drawn 24 January, 1771, and probated in March, 1771, in Halifax County, Virginia.

Radford and Marie Elizabeth (Fuqua) Maxey had four sons and four daughters, namely: Josiah, William, John, Edward, Susanna, Croshea, Elizabeth and Sally.

Their son, William, was born 11 February, 1759, in Halifax County. He was a soldier in the Revolutionary War, and at one time served as a substitute for his brother Josiah Maxey. On 9th of September, 1784, in Halifax County, Va., William Maxey married Nancy or Anna Williams, who was born 4 October, 1764, in Lunenburg County, Va., daughter of James and Anne Williams. William and Nancy (Williams) Maxey had nine sons and three daughters. William died 27 May, 1833, in Monroe County, Kentucky, where he settled in 1806.

MEDLEY family came from England, and were among the early settlers in Virginia, coming to Halifax County before 1851, when Isaac Medley (the first on record) left his will, with a very large estate in slaves, land, stock, etc., to his wife, Martha F. Medley, his three sons, James, Isaac and Granville C., and his four daughters, Martha Jackson, Mary A. Lea, Sarah Burke and Rebecca Ballou. He also mentions a brother, James T. Medley.

In 1805, the will of James Medley names three daughters, Jenny Atkisson, Lucy Medley and Mourning Medley; also mentions Polly Wood, and two sons, James Towles Medley and Isaac Medley. (This Isaac Medley may have been the one who made the above will in 1851.)

For three generations the James Medleys came down until they reached James H. Medley, deputy clerk of Halifax Court. James H. Medley was for over thirty years clerk and deputy clerk of this court. His father, James Medley, Jr., was born in Halifax County, Va., and married Miss Sallie Dix, of Accomack County, and had the following children:

- Margie M. Medley, married Captain Marcellus French (second wife).

- Granville C. Medley, married Lucy Booth; left two daughters, Kate C. and Nellie.

- Walter W. Medley.

- James H. Medley, married Lucy Walton Claytor.

[A History of Halifax County, by Wirt Johnson Carrington, 1924]

MOON family: Walter L. Moon was born in Halifax County, Va., on 3 January, 1843, son of Henry (who was born in Charlotte Co., Va.) and Jemima (Bailey) Moon. He was twice married. First to Mary H. Russell, of Halifax County, becoming his wife in March, 1865, and dying in 1868, leaving him two children, Helen V. and H. R. He married secondly, in 1872, Eliza C. Carrington, and their children were: Elizabeth, Walter, Annie, Mollie and Edward.

In April, 1861, Mr. Moon entered the Confederate States Army, in Company A, 53rd Virginia Infantry, private, promoted sergeant. In the second year of the war he went to the Virginia Military Institute, where he remained until early in 1864, when he again entered service in Company G, 6th Virginia Cavalry. In the battle of the Wilderness, May, 1864, he received a shell wound, taking off his right arm, just below the elbow. He was three weeks in Chimborazo hospital, Richmond, then returned home. He engaged in farming for several years after the close of the war, then was three years in the tobacco warehouse business at South Boston until, in July, 1887, he was elected high sheriff of Halifax County. *[Virginia and Virginians, Vol. II]*

Will of Parham Moon, 8 July, 1866, Halifax County:

"It is my will and desire that all of my property of whatsoever description be kept together until my youngest child becomes of age, then I wish said property to be divided between my wife and children according to law.

"I desire that the portion of my estate falling to my daughter, Mary Ann Graves, be held in trust for her benefit by her brother, James A. Moon, free from the claim or claims of any person whomsoever the same as if she had never married, and if she dies without legal heirs, issue of her body, then the portion falling to her I wish to revert back to my heirs at law. I have made advances to four of my children in Negroes and money, viz.: Thos. A., Jas. A., Edward B. and Mary Ann Graves. In the division of my property I do not require Mary Ann Graves to account for any advance heretofore made to her, but wish her to share equally with my younger children who have received nothing. And as the slaves given to the older sons have been liberated by law I do not require them to account for said slaves, as an advance of property from me to them.

"My sons, James A. Moon and Edward B. Moon, executors, and I request that the court will not require them to give security.

"Parham Moon."

Witnesses: W. T. Fourqurean, Jos. E. M. Palmer, Walter C. Carrington.

Some Moon marriages in Halifax County, Virginia:

Joseph G. Moon and Jane Cumbee, 3 Sept. 1853.

Mary S. Moon and Beverly R. Fleming, 1 May 1845.

Patrick Moon and Sarah H. Hunt, 27 Nov. 1845.

S. H. Moon and Joseph G. Sneed, 13 Sept. 1848.

Susan E. Moon and Alfred Blanks, 11 Aug. 1842.

Susan A. Moon and William H. Roby, 8 Nov. 1850.

Walter L. Moon and Eliza C. Carrington, 29 Oct. 1872.

MORTON, Rev. Paul Carrington, was born in Halifax County, Va., 17 October, 1837, son of William B. and Margaret Irene Morton. He was reared in a home of piety. Seven sons came from that home. Three of them became ministers of the Gospel. The other four became ruling elders in the Presbyterian Church. From this we can judge the training of that home.

Rev. Paul C. Morton attended the schools of his native county. He graduated from Washington College, later known as Washington and Lee University. He entered the Union Theological Seminary in 1860. But the storm of war called him from here and he at once joined the army, attaching himself to the 23rd Virginia Infantry. He came as an independent chaplain, but often volunteered for dangerous scouting, and uniformly fought in the ranks until wounded and dying needed his ministrations. He was later appointed a regular chaplain, holding that position until Appomattox. When Gen. Kemper was wounded at Gettysburg he remained with him and was captured. Thrown into Fort McHenry he managed to escape after swimming the river. A series of narrow escapes followed before he could rejoin his regiment in Virginia.

After the war he returned to the Seminary and completed his course. He was licensed in Virginia in 1867 and ordained in Georgia in 1868. His first work was as professor in Oglethorpe College. He served the churches at Clarksville, Woodstock, Bath and Waynesboro, and other places in Georgia.

At Lexington he met and married Miss Serena Cox, daughter of Col. Swepson H. Cox. From Georgia he went to Alabama and was pastor of the church at Tuskegee, and later was one of the Synod's Evangelists there. He went to Roxboro, N. C., in 1895, the to Immanuel Church, Wilmington; and for the last three years of his life he did general Evangelistic work within the bounds of Wilmington Presbytery.

On 28th of February, 1902, after a seemingly slight illness of ten days, he suddenly fell asleep from neuralgia of the heart. His remains were laid to rest in Oakdale cemetery. *[Minutes of the Eighty-Ninth Annual Session of the Synod of N. C., Oct., 1902]*

NANCE family: Will of William Nance, 28 October 1801, Halifax County:

"To my son, Thomas Vaughan Nance; his wife and six youngest children; to two grandsons, William Nance (son of Thomas and James Nance, son of Zachariah Nance), Zachariah Nance, and Daniel Palmer, trustees.

"To my daughter, Elizabeth Palmer; to my daughter, Sarah Tucker; to granddaughter, Lavinia Frances Bates; granddaughter, Mary Vaughan Winter Tucker; granddaughter, Mary Nance; granddaughter, Kitty Palmer; grandson, William Palmer; to James W. Bates, son of James Bates; granddaughter, Martha Vaughan (now deceased).

"Executor: Peter Barksdale.

"William (X) Nance."

Witnesses: William Sydnor, Anthony Sydnor and Josiah Clay.

E. Nance and Daniel Palmer, 16 Aug. 1781.

Frederick Nance and Mary Willingham, 23 March 1823.

Levina F. Nance and James Bates, 28 June 1793.

Mary Nance and John Dismukes, 4 Feb. 1804.

Rebecah Nance and Absalem Comer, 17 Sept. 1801.

Suz Nance and Harrison Stegall, 27 Aug. 1823.

OWEN family: The first Owen we find in the county was William Owen, whose will is of record 1752, at the organization of the county. The next Richard Owen 1753, wife Elizabeth, daughter Mary Nicholds, sons Richard, William, James and Ambrose.

We find the records teeming with deeds and sundry wills, etc., but the family is too extensive to give them in order and relationship. However, we will give the three brothers whose many descendants live in this county, active business men and women of worth to carry on the line. The three brothers, William L. Owen, Robert Easley Owen and Thomas E. Owen were considerable men in the making of Halifax.

Mr. William L. Owen, of Black Walnut, Halifax Co., married September 8, 1842, Miss Harriet Easley, of this county. He amassed a fortune in the mercantile business, always carrying a line of goods especially "fine silks" out of the usual in this county at that time. He was a good financier, and a shrewd, clean business man, and left his family not only well provided for but rich.

Following the Civil War he was one of a committee to visit President Lincoln and present a protest against the activities of the "Carpet Baggers" in Virginia and other Southern States, during the Reconstruction period.

The children of Mr. William L. Owen and his wife, Harriet (Easley) Owen, were as follows:

(1) Daniel W. Owen, president of the Planters and Merchants National Bank, married Miss Nannie E. Hundley. They had Fannie Craddock, William L., Sue Watkins, Charles Hundley, Dan Bailey, Edwin Edmunds and Fred Clement Owen.

(2) Arch A. Owen.

(3) Rufus Owen.

(4) J. Bailey Owen.

(5) Minnie Owen, wife of Dr. J. B. Brookes.

(6) Hallie B. Owen, wife of Thos. Easley.

(7) Frances Owen, wife of T. S. Wilson.

(8) Helen Owen, wife of Dr. F. S. Whaley.

Children of Frances Owen and Rev. Thornton S. Wilson (son of S. B. O. Wilson, of Albemarle County, Va.)

> (1) William Owen Wilson, married Ida Louise Nelle.
>
> (2) Thornton O. Wilson, married Elizabeth Raine.
>
> (3) Sallie B. Wilson, wife of Malcolm Campbell.
>
> (4) Samuel B. Wilson.
>
> (5) Arch A. Wilson.
>
> (6) Harriett E. Wilson, wife of Rev. Grayson Tucker.
>
> (7) Frank D. Wilson.

The Wilson family have carried on fourteen generations of Presbyterian ministers. "Ye shall how them by their works." In connection with his ministerial and other obligations, Rev. Thornton S. Wilson is also Chairman of the Halifax County School Board.

Robert Easley Owen, the owner of Mayo place and plantation, where he is buried beside his wife, Mary (Howerton) Easley, also owned a large estate and was considered a rich man. He built a modern house on the site of the old Mayo home that burned down. He left this plantation and home to his daughter Mary, who married Mark Harris, the grandfather of Mr. John Harris, and it was through the Owens that Mr. Harris fell heir to the beautiful summer home "Mayo," a name given to it when Major William Mayo, with William Byrd and others, made the dividing lines between Virginia and North Carolina.

Thomas E. Owen, who married the widow of Reuben D. Fourqurean, June 26, 1853, had the following children:

(1) Nannie Preston Owen, wife of Col. Henry Easley.

(2) William E. Owen, who married Mattie Easley, parents of Louise Owen, (wife of Rev. David Lewis).

(3) Irving Owen, the first wife of Mr. John (Jack) W. Easley.

[A History of Halifax County, by Wirt Johnson Carrington]

William Owen, was born and died in Halifax County, Virginia. At one time he owned extensive plantations and operated them with slaves, and in his time was a man of much consequence.

Dr. Thomas J. Owen, son of William Owen, was born in Halifax County, Virginia, in 1827, and died in Prince Edward County in 1897. He was graduated from Jefferson Medical College, Philadelphia, and for over forty years was an eminent member of the medical profession in Prince Edward County. He was also interested in farming, and owned a large body of land at the time of death. His political support was always given the democratic party, and in church membership he was a Baptist. He married Louisa Rudd, who was born in Prince Edward County in 1822, and died there in 1887. They became the parents of the following children: Mattie, wife of David L. Sublett, who died at Chattanooga, Tenn., while serving the Government as a civil engineer; Delia B.; Hon. John J., who was born August 27, 1859, in Prince Edward County; and Mary, wife of Samuel W. Coleman, a farmer in Prince Edward County. *[History of Virginia, Vol. IV, 1924]*

PALMER family were among the early settlers. Most of them came from the Eastern Shore, but their ancestors were originally from England. Meade, in his "Old Churches, Families and Ministers of Virginia," says on page 200, Vol. 1: "Another residence of Nathaniel Bacon must have been near Williamsburg, for his tombstone now lies in a field on Dr. Tinsley's farm, while the tombstones of the Palmer family are in the garden of that place."

William Palmer was one of the earliest recorded in this county, and Chillian Palmer was a vestryman in old Antrim Parish, as recorded in its first church records by Bishop Meade.

Chillian Palmer had seven sons and three daughters, and the descendants of those traced show men of talents, distinguished professors, physicians, surgeons and prominent officials throughout the Southern and Western States.

The will books of this county abound in various Palmer wills, some very interesting, giving evidence of wealth and culture. Many of them were Revolutionary soldiers, Elisha, Jeffrey, Thomas, William and Henry enlisting from this county, and some of them received bounty warrants for their services.

They intermarried with the LeGrands, Fourqureans, Christians, Hubbards, Hartwells, Pettus, and other prominent families.

Among the worthy descendants of Chillian and Luke Palmer, his brother, were Dabney Palmer, who married, went to Mobile, Alabama, where he amassed a large fortune. Having no children, he educated several orphans, and in his will he desired most of his slaves manumitted and sent North, and desired that the balance be treated humanely. Isaac Palmer, son of Chillian, went to Missouri; he married Martha Adams, of Halifax County, and his daughter married Judge Ryland, one of Missouri's most eminent jurists.

Dr. Thomas W. Palmer, president of Alabama College, had a son who lived in New York, who was attorney for the Standard Oil Company, having in charge the legal end of their business for South America, his work being entirely in Spanish-American law. Dr. Thomas W. Palmer's brother, Dr. R. D. Palmer, was the president of the Florida Medical Association, and was honored with all the positions in the medical fraternity. These are sons of Stephen Palmer and grandsons of Chillian Palmer, of Halifax County.

Martin Palmer, son of Chillian, settled in Monticello, Florida. His son, Martin Palmer, Jr., wrote the Constitution of Florida, and was a member of the Secession Convention. Sarah, the daughter of Chillian Palmer, Sr., married Rev. Chappell, and their grandson, Rev. E. B. Chappell, was editor of the Sunday School Magazine of the M. E. Church, South.

Frank Stockton, the, eminent writer of Philadelphia, descended from Martin Palmer, through his son, Luke, brother to Chillian Palmer, and William Cabell Palmer, mentioned in Lyon G. Tyler's genealogical work, is a descendant of William Palmer, the brother of Chillian.

The Palmers of the Eastern Shore, Maryland and North Carolina, and the Halifax, Virginia, Palmers, can all be traced back to Edward Palmer of Palmer's Island. *[A History of Halifax County, by Wirt Johnson Carrington, 1924]*

PALMER, Elias, of Halifax County, had wife, Hannah LeGrand, who was daughter of John LeGrand and his wife, Bettie. Elias and Hannah (LeGrand) Palmer had a son, Dr. Reuben Dejarnett Palmer, who was Surgeon and Lieutenant in the War of 1812. Dr. Palmer married Martha Patterson Christian, who was born 15 June, 1796, and died 18 May, 1829. Dr. Palmer died 20 March, 1861, in Appomattox County, Virginia. Their children were: William Henry; Samuel C. (died in infancy); Martha P. Christian (died in infancy); Edward Alfred; Reuben J., married Fannie Branch, daughter of Professor Robert Guerrant Branch, of Hampton-Sidney College, Va., and had Robert and Edward, who died without issue, and Cora, who married J. M. Blanding, of Texas.

PALMER, Dr. William Bradley, was born March 1___, at Furman, Wilcox County, Alabama; son of William and Rachael (Bradley) Palmer, the former a native of Alton, Halifax County, Va., who came with his parents to Furman, Wilcox County, later living at Ackerville, served as a private in Co. I, 2nd

Alabama cavalry, Ferguson's Brigade, Wheeler's Division, Army of Tennessee, was wounded three times, the last time in his right hand, shattering it and disabling him for further service; cousin of Dr. Thomas W. Palmer; grandson of Ely and Allie (Simpson) Bradley, pioneer settlers of Conecuh County; great-grandson of Samuel and Mary (Presswood) Bradley, both natives of South Carolina, later of Conecuh County, the former the daughter of a Revolutionary soldier. The Presswoods are of Welsh descent and the Bradleys were French Huguenots. Dr. Palmer received his early education in private schools; graduated with the degrees of B. A., 1889, and B. L., 1891, at the University of Alabama. His professional education was received at the University of Maryland, school of medicine, which he attended for two sessions; Tulane medical college, New Orleans, receiving the M. D. degree, 1898; post graduate course. New Orleans polyclinic, 1898-99; New York post graduate, 1906; and Chicago polyclinic, 1908. Since 1899 he has practiced at Furman. In 1915 he was health officer of Wilcox County, Alabama. He was a Democrat; a Baptist; Knight of Pythias; Columbian Woodman; Knight of Honor; and a member of the Phi Delta Theta college fraternity. He was one of the assistant editors of the "Palmer Genealogy." *[History of Alabama and Dictionary of Alabama Biography, Vol. 4]*

PENICK family: From the fly leaf of an old Bible belonging to the late Bishop Charles Clifton Penick, consecrated third bishop, missionary district of Liberia, February 13, 1877; resigned (because of ill health), October, 1883; died April 13, 1914.

Direct line:

Charles Clifton Penick, son of Edwin A. Penick and his wife, Mary M. (Hamner) Penick, who was the son of Charles Penick and Sallie (Foe) Penick, son of Charles Penick, who was the brother of William Penick, son of William Penick and Judith (Pate) Penick, son of William Penick of Wales, who married an Irish woman named Judith and settled in Hanover County, Virginia.

Charles Penick married Elizabeth Foe and had Edwin Anderson Penick, Sr., born February 24, 1820, who married Mary Maurice Hamner, and had the following children:

(1) Charles Clifton Penick, born December 9, 1843; married Mary Hoge, April 28, 1881.

(2) William E. Penick, born August 1, 1846.

(3) Robert A. Penick, born November 25, 1848; married Sallie Jones, January 4, 1871.

(4) Elizabeth Penick (died young).

(5) Edwin Anderson Penick, Jr., born October 8, 1851; married October 22, 1884, Mary Shipman.

(6) Maurice Hamner Penick, born March 16, 1854; married Louise Easley.

(7) Clara L. Penick, born February 5, 1857.

(8) Watkins Breedlove Penick, born July 14, 1861.

Robert A. Penick (3), born November 25, 1848; married first Sallie Tanner Jones and had:

(1) Elmer Maynard Penick, born September 9, 1871; married Ida Trent Vaughn and had Irvie, Maynard, Elizabeth, Charles and Robert.

(2) Clifton Hamner Penick, born February 2, 1873.

(3) William Lucas Penick, born October 2, 1874; married Lucy Morton and had Charlotte, Marcia and William.

(4) Charles Anderson Penick, born March 7, 1877; married Elizabeth A. Green and had Charles Anderson Penick, Jr.

Robert A. Penick, married second, August 26, 1880, Fannie A. Easley and had Henry E. Penick, Mary Louise Penick, Elizabeth Archer Penick, Robert Penick and Ruth Easley Penick, wife of Mr. Alexander Whaling.

On the records at the court house we find the will of Nathan Penick (captain in War of 1812). He moved to Halifax from Nottoway County and died in this county.

His daughter, Judith Penick, married Joel Hawkins (her first husband), and had two sons, William N. and Thomas M. Hawkins, who were left out of their grandfather's will for some unexplained reason.

Nathan Penick had sons, Thomas R. Penick, William Penick (who was "a noted Baptist minister") and Branch Penick; daughters, Louisa Penick, Mary Ann Smith, Elizabeth Robertson, Judith Owen (formerly Judith Penick Hawkins).

This will was probated November 12 1847. Witnesses, Thomas Averett, James F. Hill and Edward M. Carrington. Grandchildren, the children of Elizabeth Robertson, were Lucy Robertson, who also married an Owen; Edward J. Robertson and Robertson R. Robertson.

A witness in the will of James Bruce, dated September 28, 1836, was named William Penick, and James Bruce leaves a legacy of five hundred dollars each to his three friends, James Atkisson, William Penick and James S. Easley.

We find no connection between this line and Bishop Clifton Penick's line, but we do know that the Penicks were staunch members of the Episcopal Church, faithful workers in the spread of the kingdom, and have in this line the Right Rev. Edwin A. Penick, D. D., of Charlotte, N. C., the youngest Bishop on record in the Episcopal Church. *[A History of Halifax County, by Wirt Johnson Carrington, 1924]*

William Sydnor Penick: At "Oak Plain," Halifax County, Virginia, the plantation of his parents, William and Elizabeth Armistead Penick, on May 12, 1836, William Sydnor Penick, the third child of the home, was born. Until he was fifteen years old "he lived in the glad freedom of plantation life before-the-War," and shared, with his three brothers and two sisters, the careful training of Mr. Berryman Green and Mr. Rufus Murrell, cultured gentlemen who were tutors in this home. According to the custom of the day the tutor roomed in the "office," in the yard, with the boys, and instructed all the children in Latin, Greek, Mathematics, and the English branches. Doubtless "manners" and dancing were not omitted from the curriculum of this school. Mr. Penick was an ardent lover of the chase, and his son, Sydnor, at an early age, having a hunter of his own, imbibed a love for horses, dogs, and hunting, especially following the hounds, that went with him through life. Since the father and the tutor united in desiring that young Sydnor should become a lawyer, and since it was Mr. Penick's opinion that a business training was fundamental to that profession, the youth, at the age of fifteen, was "bound" for three years to a Mr. Marshall, a successful merchant in Charlotte County.

Since Mr. Penick was an ardent Episcopalian (he was also a Whig), it was a distinct disappointment to him when Sydnor, at the age of seventeen, was baptized, probably by Rev. James Longanacre, into the fellowship of the Catawba Baptist Church, his mother's church. Again the father was doomed to disappointment in his plans as to this son's education. When his engagement with Mr. Marshall was over, the young man set out in the stage for Charlottesville and the University of Virginia. On passing through Richmond he was persuaded by friends to enter Richmond College, and he took this step before consulting his father, his plan being to follow his course at the college by further study at the University, but alas, this plan was never carried out.

While at college he organized the Philologian Literary Society, being its first president, and in the hall of this society there hangs his portrait, which the society had painted in 1875. Mr. Penick graduated in 1858. After he left the college he kept up an interesting correspondence for many years with his professors, George E. Dabney and Robert Ryland, and, in 1866, when the question arose in the General Association as to the reopening of the college after the ravages of the War, the third speaker in the discussion which resulted in the recommencement of the college was Mr. Penick. In 1871 his alma mater conferred on him the degree of Master of Arts, and some years later the honorary degree of Doctor of Divinity.

Once again his father was disappointed when, at the close of his college course, he decided to be a minister of the gospel and not a lawyer. His ordination to the ministry took place at the church of his childhood, Catawba, in Halifax County.

With his ordination began a ministry of almost half a century. Before his work as a regular pastor was broken in upon by the War he served successfully a weak church at Chatham, the county-seat of Pittsylvania County, and, by building up a Sunday school of over two hundred scholars, laid the foundations for a strong church.

On November 2, 1859, he was married, at Chatham, to Miss Betty Tarpley Martin, a daughter of Dr. Chesley Martin and Rebecca White, and the granddaughter of Dr. Rawley White, of Pittsylvania.

In August, 1861, he went into the Confederate Army as Captain of the David Logan Guards, a militia company equipped by his friend and cousin, Mr. David Logan, of Halifax County. In 1868, sharing, with the vast majority of the Southern people, the deep poverty that was part of the heritage of the War, with his young wife and three children, he went as a missionary of the State Mission Board to Charles Town, W. Va. The meeting-house was in ruins, so a semi-monthly service Sunday morning was held in the courthouse, while for the afternoons of these days he preached at old Zoah, the first house of worship built in Jefferson County.

The other Sundays of the month were given to Mt. Zion, a large country church in Berkeley County, and to the cause at Martinsburg, where there was no Baptist Church. At this place, in the parlor of Mrs. Henry Kratz, he organized, with some five women, a Baptist Church. The outlook here was soon so promising that the Board had him give his whole time to Martinsburg.

After leaving Martinsburg he was pastor for seven years of the First Church of Alexandria, and then for four years of the High Street Church, Baltimore. While in Baltimore he supplied, during the summer, for churches in New York and Yonkers. About this time he had calls from churches in New York State and Brooklyn that were declined, while one from the First Church of Shreveport, La., was accepted. For thirteen years he was the beloved pastor of his church.

His literary culture and fine address led to his being much in demand for college commencements and other similar occasions, while his record during the Civil War gave him high rank among the Confederate Veteran organizations. In 1887 he established in Shreveport the Genevieve Orphanage.

In 1898 he resigned at Shreveport and became pastor at Elizabeth City, N. C, but after three years he returned to the First Church at Shreveport and continued his work there until forced by failing strength to give up the active work of so large a church. After this he ministered for two years to the Ardis Memorial, an offspring of the First Church. On Sunday, June 30, 1907, just at the hour when for almost half a century, week after week, he had pronounced the benediction at the close of the morning service, he passed to the service of the heavenly congregation that shall never break up. The funeral was conducted by Dr. H. A. Sumrell, pastor of the First Baptist Church, and Dr. Jasper K. Smith, pastor of the First Presbyterian Church, all of the pastors of the city taking part in the service. Along the streets to the Oakland Cemetery, where the body was laid to rest, the crowds stood silent and tearful as the procession passed, and the Confederate Veterans covered the grave with their flag.

His widow remained in New Orleans, and there were six surviving children, namely: Chesley, wife of James Burrows Johnson, Charlottesville, Va.; William Sydnor Penick, New Orleans (whose wife was Miss Otelia Jacobs); Dr. Raleigh Martin Penick, Shreveport, La. (whose wife was Miss Eugenia Elizabeth Carnal); Mary Louise, wife of James Polk Ford, New Orleans; Nathan Treadway Penick, New Orleans (whose wife was Miss Anne Stephenson); Martha Brantley, wife of Burr. D. Ilgenfritz. *[Virginia Baptist Ministers, by George Braxton Taylor]*

Junius Marshall Penick was born in Halifax County, Virginia, April 3, 1886, a son of William B. Penick, and a member of one of the old families of Virginia, of English stock. The grandfather, William Aaron Penick, was born in Prince Edward County, Virginia, and died in Halifax County, where he had spent practically all of his life, and where he was engaged in farming upon an extensive scale. When the Civil War broke out he espoused the cause of the South and fought in its behalf as a soldier in the Confederate Army. His wife, Susan Baker, was born in Halifax County in 1827, and died at Richmond in 1904. They reared a family of four sons and three daughters.

William B. Penick was born in Halifax County in 1857, and died at Richmond in October, 1912. He was reared in Halifax County, and there for years was very successfully engaged in farming, but moved to Chase City, Mecklenburg County, Virginia, in 1894, and went into the livery business there and made it his home until 1907, when he came to Richmond. After coming to this city he was connected with the Simpson-Bass Company, dealers in hay and grain. The democratic party had his earnest and effective support from the day he cast his first vote until his death. He was equally zealous in behalf of the Baptist Church, which he joined in his youth. William B. Penick married Miss Pattie Roberts in Charlotte County, Virginia, where she was born in 1860.

Their children were: Fleet, who married Robert J. Walker, a manufacturer of hosiery; Frank, who resided at New Orleans, Louisiana, was connected with the Cumberland Telephone & Telegraph Company; Junius Marshall, who is third in order of birth; George R., who was superintendent of the coal mines at Ramage, West Virginia; Pela, who lived at Norfolk, Virginia, married John Parkins, chemist for the Royster Fertilizer Corporation; Helen, who resided at Tarboro, North Carolina, married John Cheshire, a bookkeeper; William A., who was a veteran of the World War, served on the State Draft Board of Virginia, resided at Richmond, and was a traveling salesman for the Barber Asphalt Company; Ruby, who resides at Richmond, married John Kolbe, owner and operator of a gas appliance and fixture store; and Gordon, who resided at Richmond, was manager of the Tower-Binford Electric Manufacturing Company, Incorporated. *[History of Virginia, Vol. IV, 1924]*

POWELL: Will of Edward Powell, 18 July 1766--Wife, Elizabeth; sons, William, David, Mark and Luke Powell; "To my daughter, Jane Medlock; my daughter, Mary Tuck; grandson, Zachariah Medlock." Executors: William Powell and William, Gent.; Ed Powell. Witnesses: Anthony Colquitt, Christian Colquitt, James William, Gent.

1774--Inventory of the estate of Edward Powell (deceased), David Powell, William Powell, Luke Powell, Mark Powell, John Tuck, for his wife; Moore Matlock, for his wife.

RAGLAND family is of Welsh origin, but descended from Norman stock, which goes back to the Herberts who followed William the Conqueror to England. They settled in Monmouthshire, Wales, and some three hundred years after their coming to England one Robert, youngest son of Evan Thomas Herbert, had a son, John, who was brought up by his uncle, Sir William Thomas Herbert, of Raglan.

This Sir William Herbert was a contemporary of Sir Roger Vaughan, who with him was knighted by Henry V on the battlefield of Agincourt in 1415 before the battle was fought. Sir Roger Vaughan fell in the battle. His daughter, Elinor, married Robert Herbert, father of John, and John Herbert took the name of Raglan.

Raglan castle in Monmouthshire, one of the great strongholds of the Middle Ages, and one of the famous places of Great Britain, passed from the Herberts to the De Clares, from them to the Berkeleys, etc.

The family belonged in England to what is known as the gentry, and had a coat of arms which was brought to Virginia by the American founder of the family, John Ragland, who married his kinswoman, Anne Beaufort, in Wales.

They emigrated from Monmouthshire, Wales, to Virginia, probably about 1720, for in 1723 they were settled in "Ripping Hall" on Mechums Creek, near the mouth of the Chickahominy River, in Hanover County, Virginia. The old home was occupied up to the time of its destruction by fire in 1823. John Ragland took out land patents which aggregated over fifteen thousand acres in the counties of Hanover and Louisa.

John Ragland had by his wife, Anne Beaufort, six sons and three daughters. The sons appear to have been James, Samuel, Pettus, John, Evans and William. The three daughters married, one a Tinsley, one a Jones, and one a Bowe.

The Virginia roster of the Revolutionary soldiers shows eleven Raglans: David, Dudley, Evan, Edmund, Finch, Gideon, John, Pettus, Pettus Jr., Shelton and Thomas.

The late Major Robert L. Ragland worked out the family history in detail from John down, but we are especially concerned with the lines of Ragland in Halifax County, one of which was Joseph E. Ragland (better known as "Ned" Ragland).

Evan Ragland, son of John the emigrant, married Susannah Lipscomb, and moved from Louisa to Halifax County, settling on Banister River, a few miles above its confluence with the Dan River. They had five children: Nancy, Lipscomb, Evan, John and Anne. Two of his sons, Evan and John, were very zealous churchmen in the Episcopal Church of that day, and Evan was a gallant Revolutionary soldier, and was severely wounded in the war, his wounds never healing. He never married and bequeathed the bulk of his estate to Antrim Parish.

John, the son of Evan (grandson of John the emigrant), married his cousin, Elizabeth Pettus, and they had nine children: Susannah, Evan, Nancy, Dabney, John, Lipscomb, Anne, Martha and Samuel.

Dabney Ragland, son of John, married, December, 1822. Harriet Byron Faulkner and had six children, Robert Lipscomb, Samuel H., John Pettus, Joseph E., Elizabeth A., and Harriet D. Ragland. This makes Joseph Edward Ragland fifth in descent from John the emigrant.

John was a Revolutionary soldier. His son, Dabney, was a soldier in the War of 1812; and the four sons of Dabney were Confederate soldiers. There is evidently an old Roman strain in the family, because at the outbreak of the Civil War Dabney called his four sons together and told them that, it was their duty to go to fight for their country.

The coat-of-arms of John Ragland the emigrant is described thus:

"Argent, three unicorns passant in plae sable. Crest, a unicorn statant gules, armed, crined and enguiche (unguled?) or."

Mr. "Ned" Ragland began his business life at the age of fifteen (1853) as clerk in the store of his brother, the late Major Robert Lipscomb Ragland, in the village of Hyco. Later he became connected with the firm of Tucker, Chappell & Co. In 1859 he went with the firm of Owen, Jordan & Co., at Black Walnut, where he remained until March, 1860, when the firm name was changed to Owen, Ragland & Co., Mr. William L. Owen, one of the partners, retiring and Mr. Ragland taking his place.

The war clouds were even then lowering, and a few months later, in 1861, Mr. Ragland entered the Confederate army, was a member of Company C of the Third Virginia Cavalry, which company was then under the command of Captain John A. Chappell and Lieutenant John M. Jordan, who surrendered the company at Appomattox after Captain Chappell was killed at Winchester in 1864. From that time until the surrender of Lee's army at Appomattox on April 9, 1865, Mr. Ragland served gallantly and well as a private soldier, always at his post of duty, and was among the ragged survivors with Lee at the end.

Returning home after a short rest, he engaged in the mercantile business at Harmony, with T. B. Traynham and Mr. John M. Owen as partners. This firm continued in business until the death of Mr. Owen, in 1871, when Mr. Ragland returned to Hyco. His mercantile career, except in the four years interval of the war, covers a period of sixty-one years. He has not amassed a great fortune, but has gained a competency and the esteem of the people of a wide area. Speaking of his business history, he says: "I have tried to do my duty as I see it to my fellow men, and I have no regrets for the past in my dealings with my customers, doing unto them as I would be done by." That he has lived up to this creed is shown by the regard in which he is held by the people of his native county in which his long life has been spent.

A Democrat in his political beliefs, he has never sought office, but has served his people as notary public and postmaster of the village in which he lives for forty years, an office more useful to the people than lucrative to the holder. He has been a Mason since 1859, and for many years a trustee of the Southern Methodist Church of his locality.

He is an earnest and devoted advocate of the prohibition of the liquor traffic, and from time to time has contributed articles to the press of his section in advocacy of that cause. Through his long life his favorite reading has been the Bible, and for fifty years he has been a consistent follower of the Christian faith.

He has been twice married. His first wife was Mary S. Bailey, daughter of John and Elizabeth Bailey, of Person County, N. C., to whom he was married May 3, 1868. After a brief married life she died, leaving an infant boy, Charles Dabney Ragland.

On December 14, 1870, Mr. Ragland was married in Halifax County to Lucy A. Lawson, a daughter of David and Jane Lawson.

The child of his first marriage, Charles Dabney Ragland, was an unusually promising and brilliant young man. After receiving a liberal education he entered on his duties as professor of chemistry at Randolph-Macon College, but his useful life was cut short in his early prime, on October 30, 1900, when he passed away. This son married Miss Mary Fisher Luckett and had one daughter, Mary Bailey Ragland.

Of the second marriage there were two children:

Janie H. (married W. C. Slate, president of the Slate Seed Company). They had five children, Lucile, Mary Elizabeth, Joseph Edward, Martha and Elise Slate.

The son, David Lawson Ragland, married Mary W. Stovall. He was in business in Lynchburg. They had five children, Mary L., Charles Dabney, David L., Jonathan B., and William W. Ragland. *[A History of Halifax County, by Wirt Johnson Carrington, 1924]*

REDD: Will of Thomas Redd, 29 August 1823, Halifax County--Wife, Rebeckah, "all of my land or such as may fall to me hereafter in Halifax, Powhatan or Cumberland Counties, or lands that I may be entitled to of the estate of Ray Moss, of Mecklenburg County.

"My daughter, Eliza H. M. Redd, Sally Woodson, Amanda Mayo Redd, Ann Redd; sons, George William Redd, Rebeckah Redd, Thomas Redd, James Tucker Redd, Robert Hoyt Redd, Anderson Cocke Redd, and Martha James Redd.

"My wife, Rebeckah, executrix; my friends, William Thaxton, of Halifax, and Richard W. Mechaum, of Pittsylvania County; my brother, Robert Redd, of Mecklenburg County; my son-in-law, Thomas Jefferson Woodson, of Kentucky, my executors.

Witnesses: John P. Woodson, John F. Farley and James Faulkner.

His daughter, Sally W. Redd, married Jefferson J. Woodson on 8 April 1824, in Halifax County, Virginia.

ROBERTS: Will of John Roberts, 5 November 1774, Halifax County--"Loving wife, Jane." Sons, Francis, Moses, William, Daniel, Peter and Thomas. Daughters, Jane Wooldridge, Molly, Betsy and Sally Roberts. Executors: Francis and Moses Roberts. Witnesses: Reuben Ragland, John

Hughes and George Camp. Recorded 21 March 1776. Inventory shows a goodly estate and twenty slaves.

Will of Jane Roberts, 29 September 1794, Halifax County--Sons, William, Peter, Moses, Daniel and Thomas; daughters, Jane Wooldridge, Molly Anderton and Sally Fulkerson. Executors: William Roberts and Theo. Roberts. Witnesses: Thomas Dobson, William Chandler and Edward Hall.

Will of Francis Roberts, 23 December 1793, Halifax County--Daughters, Susannah, wife of John Bruce; Polly, wife of Josiah Chandler.

"My four children, Humphrey Roberts, Susannah Bruce, John Roberts and Polly Chandler, equal parts in my estate."

Executors: "My beloved brothers," William and Thomas Roberts. Witnesses: Thomas Dobson, Simon Holt and David Street.

Will of Peter Roberts, 30 April 1801, Halifax County--Wife, Sarah; daughters, Patsy, Betsy, Nancy Willingham (wife of Jarrell Willingham); sons, William and Peter. Executors: "Trusted and beloved friends," William Terry and George Camp. Witnesses: Joseph Allen and Charles Allen.

SCOTT family: Among the prominent Scotts of Halifax County was John Baytop Scott, born 1761 in this county. He ran away from Hampden-Sidney College when he was only 16 years of age to join General "Light Horse" Harry Lee's Legion, and became lieutenant. In April, 1805, he was made civil commandant of the District of Mississippi at Cape Girardeau, Mo. (See Army of the U. S.) He was captain of the "Silver Grays" in the War of 1812, and brigadier general of State troops in Governor Floyd's administration.

Member of the Cincinnati and candidate for Congress without opposition when he died, in 1813.

Mr. Scott married first Elizabeth, sister of Hon. Henry Coleman, of Halifax County, by whom he had no children. He married second Patsy, daughter of William and Rachel Thompson (a cousin to his first wife). They had nine children, viz.: Polly C., William T., John Watts, Thomas Baytop, James Baytop, Francis Tompkies, Martha A., Christopher Columbus and Elizabeth R. C. Scott.

In 1803, December 24, Polly C. Scott married John R. Cocke in this county and removed, in 1824, to Greene County, Alabama, where they had the following children: John, Lucy, Patsy and William. *[A History of Halifax County, by Wirt Johnson Carrington, 1924]*

STEBBENS family, of great antiquity, belong properly to Deerfield, Mass., from whence the progenitors of the Halifax County Stebbens came.

Joseph and Charles Stebbens were the sons of Joseph Stebbens, of Deerfield, Massachusetts. Joseph, the second, married Mary Grundy, of Petersburg, Virginia. Joseph Stebbens, the third, married Willie Fourqurean, of Halifax County. They had two children, Laura, wife of Dr. John Walker, and Joseph Stebbens, Jr. (attorney). Mr. Joseph Stebbens and his son, Joseph, Jr., were among the most prominent men of South Boston; the death of each was a tragedy. One in the prime of life and usefulness, the other just beginning his professional career, beloved and honored by every one, his passing seemed the "irony of fate." With the passing away of these two ended the male line of this family.

Charles Stebbens (son of Charles) married Charlotte Carter Walden (Chesterfield County, Virginia), and their son, Harvey Brokenbrough Stebbens, married Frederica Keeper (Smithfield, Va.) Their children were:

Charlotte Russell, wife of Dr. N. E. McDaniel, of Bath County (three children).

Julia Wilton Stebbens.

Charles Halifax Stebbens, married Margaret Logan Carrington (five children, Margaret C., Sallie French, Frederica Cary, Charlotte Carter and Charles Harvey Stebbens).

H. B. Stebbens, Jr.

Louise Cary Stebbens, wife of George C. Carrington (one son).

William Keeper Stebbens, wife of Edmund Wilcox Hubbard, Buckingham County (two children).

Rebecca Stebbens, wife of William Priddy Ingram.

Shirley B. Stebbens.

Edwin A. Stebbens.

Virginia Carter Stebbens, wife of James B. Ingram.

Miles Cary Stebbens, married Julia Strong Gale (Hampton, Va.).

Mr. Charles Halifax Stebbens, cashier of the Planters and Merchants National Bank, was one of South Boston's most honored and efficient citizens. *[A History of Halifax County, by Wirt Johnson Carrington, 1924]*

STEVENS family: James Stevens came to Virginia from Baldernock, near Glasgow, Scotland, engaged in the milling business in Halifax County. Toward the close of the Revolution, the British commander in America sent an expedition to the James River and vicinity, under General Phillips, whose second in command was Benedict Arnold, with instructions to destroy the mills, warehouses and sources of supplies drawn upon by the patriot army. Cornwallis, coming north from the Carolinas, accompanied by Tarleton and his dragoons, carried on the work of destruction in Halifax County. The work was carried out under the guise of military necessity, but when a sergeant and a comrade robbed a house and violated a young girl, Cornwallis promptly halted the column, arrested the criminals, held a drum head court martial and executed the sentence, immediately, by hanging the offenders at Halifax Court House.

James Stevens, as did other millers, relied upon Scotland as the source of mill supplies, especially burr stones, and his voyage was undertaken to repair the damage done by the British army.

The Stevens descendants intermarried widely with the older families of Halifax County. Two of James Stevens' daughters, Ann and Margaret married Alexander and Nathaniel Carter, sons of Theodrick Carter, who was sheriff of Halifax County from November 1799 to November 1801. Dr. Walter Bennett, of "Poplar Mount," Halifax County, left numerous descendants who intermarried with descendants of James Stevens and Theodrick Carter. Dr. Walter Bennett and Theodrick Carter were among the gentlemen designated to take the first census of Halifax County, since published by the government. Previous efforts had failed because of the belief that the census was connected with a scheme to increase taxes. *[The Virginia Magazine of History and Biography, Vol. XXX]*

STOKES family: In 1747, November 13, James Terry surveyed for David Stokes 400 acres on both sides of Grassy Creek, then Lunenburg (now Halifax) County.

William, Henry and Sylvanus Stokes each married in this county, but they seem to have migrated to other States. A great deal of investigation along the Stokes lines has been done by various genealogists and families, but very little is found in this county in regard to the Stokes family.

This excerpt from a letter written by Mr. Iverson Stokes, of Todd County, Ky., may be of help to some of the readers of this history:

"I am the son of David and Sarah Stokes. David Stokes was a native of North Carolina, as was also his wife.

"David's father was John Stokes, a native Englishman, who emigrated to America prior to the Revolutionary War, and was a soldier in that struggle.

"John Stokes was also of English descent on the maternal side, and his ancestors on that side also participated in the Revolutionary war.

"John Stokes settled in North Carolina; he had ten children—nine sons and one daughter.

"David Stokes, his son, grew to manhood in North Carolina, married there, and removed to Kentucky, where he followed farming. He raised a family of twelve children, seven sons and five daughters.

"In 1829 David Stokes emigrated to Illinois and settled in the extreme part of what is now Christian County, where he entered land from the government and improved a farm. He died November 14, 1844. His wife survived him twelve years."

The names of above David Stokes' children were, viz.: Gabriel, Armstrong, Rachel, Harmon, Elizabeth, Young, Robert, Susan, Ann, Allen and Iverson.

David's wife was named Sarah (tradition says Sarah Hopkins).

The celebrated John Stokes, of North Carolina, married Elizabeth Pearson, daughter of Richmond Pearson, and there is some evidence of David being his son, but it cannot be proven without searching the records of North Carolina.

Captain John Stokes, Revolutionary soldier of Virginia, received a bounty warrant for his services of 4666 2/3 acres of land, which was located in Ohio.

There are many of the name in Lunenburg County and in various counties in North Carolina. *[A History of Halifax County, by Wirt Johnson Carrington, 1924]*

SYDNOR, family: Will of William Sydnor, 20 December 1815, Halifax County--Wife, Judith, "to live in the house with my son, Anthony." Sons: Thomas, Abraham, Anthony. "My late son, Epaphroditus." Daughters: Nancy Logan, Elizabeth Sydnor, Ailcy and Judith Brockwell. Witnesses: Thomas Davenport, Samuel Lacy and Joel Neal. Recorded July 27, 1818.

He had a large estate in land, slaves and money. He gave his children land and each twenty slaves, with their increase.

Will of Elizabeth Sydnor, 18 February 1826, Halifax County:

"My sister, Ailcy Barksdale; my sister, Nancy Barksdale; my late sister, Judith W. Barksdale (wife of Armstead Barksdale); her children legatees, William S. Barksdale, Nathaniel Barksdale, John Barksdale, Elizabeth A. Barksdale, and Judith A. Barksdale. I appoint my brother-in-law, Armstead Barksdale, guardian of the infant children of my late sister, Judith W. Barksdale." Executors: Anthony and Abraham Sydnor

Some Sydnor marriages in Halifax County, Virginia:

Alice Sydnor and John Lacy, 15 Sept. 1784.

Alice Ann Sydnor and Charles B. Coleman, 29 April 1846.

Beverly Sydnor, Jr., and Emmiline P. Crews, 28 June 1841.

E. Sydnor and John C. McCraw, 6 Feb. 1797.

E. Sydnor (wife) and Ashey A. Nelson, 7 Dec. 1835.

Epaphroditus Sydnor and Alice Milner, 30 April 1770.

Frances W. Sydnor and J. Crews (husband), 23 July 1838.

Henry A. Sydnor and Margaret Mary Logan, 16 Oct. 1849.

Judith Sydnor and Armistead Barksdale, 1805.

Judith Sydnor and Josiah J. Crews, 8 Nov. 1842.

Mary W. Sydnor and Clement M. Adkinson, __ Jan. 1849.

Richard Sydnor and J. Wall, 13 Nov. 1826.

William Sydnor and Elizabeth J. Crews, 17 June 1835.

TERRY family: Nathaniel Terry was one of the justices of the first court held for Halifax County, 1752; justice of the peace, 1753-54; captain of militia and burgess for several sessions. He held all the offices and enjoyed all the honors that Halifax could offer, and when he died, ripe with years, he was buried in the old "Thompson burying ground" without a stone to mark his last resting place.

Nathaniel Terry, Gent., has left in Halifax County numberless worthy descendants, and his children's children are scattered throughout many States.

His son, James Terry, also a burgess, died suddenly while on duty in Richmond and is buried beside the church in old St. John's churchyard.

His daughter, Nancy, married Colonel Berryman Green, and, according to the statement of Mr. David Webb, a direct descendant, they are all buried in the old "Thompson graveyard." (No stones to verify it.)

The services of Nathaniel Terry, Gent., have furnished eligibility to Colonial Dames and Daughters of the American Revolution sufficient for his numerous descendants of four generations. Added to his many offices he was also sheriff of the county for several years. (A History of Halifax County, by Wirt Johnson Carrington, 1924)

Will of Nathaniel Terry, 10 June 1778, Halifax County: Wife, Sarah. Estate to be equally divided between his children, except his son, William, for whom he has already provided by giving him 400 acres of land, a horse, cattle, sheep, household furniture, and a negro man named Charles.

"I appoint my trusty and well beloved friends, Paul Carrington, William Terry and Nathaniel Cocke my executors.

"Nat Terry."

Witnesses: Evan Ragland and Isaac McCarty.

Will of William Terry, Sr., 22 December 1806: "My wife, Susanna; daughter, Sarah Royal Wooding; daughter, Rachel Coleman Terry; sons, Thompson, William Royall, Nathaniel and Henry Dickerson Terry.

"I do exclude my daughter, Elizabeth Green, or any person claiming under her from recovering any part of my estate, her husband, Peter Green, having wrongfully, unrighteously, unjustly, dishonorably and dishonestly recovered a negro man named Guilford of me, so that it is not meant or intended that my said daughter shall receive any part of my estate, directly or indirectly.

"I do constitute my brethren, General John B. Scott, administrator; Nathaniel Terry and my son, William Terry, executors.

"William Terry, Sr."

Witnesses: Robert Read, Robert Haskins, Edward M. Thompson and William F. Baker.

Recorded 1811.

THORNTON family: All of the Thorntons of Halifax descended from William Thornton, Gent., who emigrated to Virginia and settled in York County (now Gloucester County) in 1646. He built his house four miles north of Gloucester Point and called it "The Hills" after his English home.

Later in life he moved to Stafford County. He married three times, and is said to have had nineteen children.

Dr. Richard Thornton, of Halifax County, was the seventh child (a twin) of Francis Thornton, born August 22, 1747. Francis Thornton was a soldier of the Revolution, being a member of Lee's Battalion of Light Dragoons. He was the son of William Thornton (4) and is said to have married Miss Lacy.

Dr. Richard Thornton was born December 23, 1786. He married first Miss Smith and settled in Halifax County, about twenty miles from the county seat, where he lived and died. He is buried there by his first wife and two of his daughters.

We went to the old home place, it had been destroyed, and on the site was a small modern house, owned by a Mr. Marshall and rented to a tenant, who very kindly showed us

At the old home place was the family burying ground of the Thorntons. The stones, of which there were four (the inscription on one could not be deciphered), read:

"Rebecca, wife of Dr. D. T. C. Peters,
Daughter of Richard Thornton.
Born Nov. 7, 1816. Died Aug. 30, 1846."

"Mary L., wife of Dr. A. L. Peters,
Daughter of Richard Thornton.
Born May 18, 1820. Died Sept. 20, 1848."

"Charles S., son of Dr. Peters.
Died 1850."

"Pat Matthews, beloved son of
D. T. C. and Rebecca Peters.
Born June 5, 1841. Died May 31, 1853."

Don Peters and his brother, Dr. Alexander Lemuel Peters, were the sons of Elisha and Cynthia Peters, of Lynchburg, Virginia.

Dr. Lemuel Peters was born and raised in Bedford County, graduated at the University of Virginia, and located at Meadville, Halifax County, Va., where he followed the practice of his profession until his death in 1885.

Richard Thornton Peters (son of Dr. Alexander Peters) married Bettie White. They had several children, among them Rebecca, who married Henry Howard, of South Boston, Va., and had one child, Thomas O'Conner Howard.

It will be impossible to carry out the various Thornton family lines in this short space, so I will only mention the heads of the families in this county.

John Wyatt Thornton, brother of Dr. Richard T., was born October 14, 1775. He married Betsy Vawter.

Mary Jane Thornton, daughter of John Wyatt, married C. T. C. Carr, of Halifax County, Va., February 15, 1843, and their youngest daughter, Lola Jane Carr, married William Marion Bates, of Halifax County, September 13, 1882. He was the eldest son of James Madison and Martha (Owen) Bates.

Dr. John Lemuel Thornton, only son of John Wyatt and Betsy (Vawter) Thornton, of Charlotte County, was a surgeon in Carter's Company and served until his marriage, in 1862, to Saluda Garner. Among their twelve children was Dr. Richard Presley Thornton, born September 13, 1863, and married June 5, 1889, Lena Maud, daughter of C. H. and Lula (Slate) Jordan. They had nine children.

[A History of Halifax County, by Wirt Johnson Carrington, 1924]

VAUGHN, Edgar H., Esq., the popular County Court Clerk of Halifax County, was born in Amelia County in the year 1845. His parents were both natives of Virginia. His father was a planter and died in 1879. Edgar Vaughn came to Halifax in 1860, and the following year enlisted in Company G, 6th Virginia Cavalry and served four years. He was in most of the principal battles of this State. After the close of the war he returned to Halifax and accepted a position as a clerk in a store, and soon began business for himself at South Boston under the firm name of Yancey & Vaughn, and later as E. H. Vaughn & Co. He continued in this business until November, 1878, when he was elected Clerk of the County Court.

Mr. Edgar H. Vaughn married in December, 1867, to Miss Almyra Prover, of South Boston. They had six children. Mrs. Vaughn died in 1885 and he married again to Miss J. J. Rogers, of Halifax. *[South-West Virginia and the Valley, A. D. Smith & Co., 1892]*

VAUGHAN John, was born in 1801, in Halifax County, Va., son of Stephen Vaughan of Halifax County. John Vaughan moved to Kentucky, settling at Paintsville in 1844, where he died in 1885. He married Isabelle Griffin, who was born in 1810, in Halifax County, Va., daughter of Lewis Griffin. She died in 1883 in Paintsville, Kentucky. John and Isabelle (Griffin) Vaughan had the following children:

1. Henry Stephen Vaughan, born in 1826, in Halifax County, Va., and he died in 1910, in Paintsville, Kentucky.

2. William W. Vaughan, born 22 February 1826; died 9 February 1901.

3. Sandy Vaughan, born 5 September 1838; died 18 February 1911.

4. Rebecca E. (Becky) Vaughan, born 28 October 1845.

[History of Kentucky, Vol. III, 1922; and Johnson County, The Heart of Eastern Kentucky, 1928]

VAUGHAN, Paul Bedford, was born 13 October, 1847, in Halifax County, Va., son of Paulus Bedford Vaughan and Mary Jane Tuck, who were married 22 June, 1841, in Halifax County. Mr. Vaughan married 17 February, 1870, to Sarah Lucy White, who was born 28 November, 1840, daughter of Henry

Milton White, of Bedford County, Virginia. Sarah Lucy (White) Vaughan died 20 April, 1921. *[Our Kin, by Mary Denham Ackerly and Lula Eastman Jeter Parker, 1930]*

WADE family came from England and were among the earliest settlers in the Colony of Virginia. As far back as 1656 we find one Daniel Wade, of Surry County, petitioning Lieutenant Governor Francis Nicholson to remit a fine which had, according to law, been imposed for replanting tobacco after the first of July, the penalty being a fine of 10,000 pounds of tobacco. One object of the fine was to prevent an overproduction and the other to insure a better quality; the ultimate purpose was, of course, to maintain a high price on the product, on which the planter depended for his revenue.

The first marriage recorded in Halifax County was that of Elizabeth Wade and Nathaniel Hunt, and the first court was held "in the house of Hampton Wade."

In the old vestry books of Antrim Parish, 1752-53, we find the names of Edward and Andrew Wade. (Meade's Old Churches and Families of Virginia.) From these two brothers, through George and Robert Wade, descended the Wades of Halifax County and the South and West.

Richard, the son of George Wade, married Sarah, a daughter of John and Sarah (Dickie) Chappell, on September 4, 1806. Shortly after their marriage they settled on what was formerly known as the McPhaile plantation, one of the finest on Dan River, but later removed to their home, a few miles south of South Boston, where Richard Wade died and where his widow continued to live for thirty-two years until she passed away.

A descendant says of the old home: "The old house, which was her home for more than sixty years, is still standing, a monument to the honest workmanship of the mechanic of a century ago. It is of a quaint and antiquated appearance, plain and unassuming, as was the good woman who occupied it, but it was a Christian home, proverbial for its hospitality, and the latch-string always hung on the outside. The framing timbers of the home were of hewn oak, put together with mortise and tenon, and the weather-boarding of black walnut, was nailed on with wrought iron nails, evidently made by a country blacksmith. It is a story and a half high with an ell, and the rooms, which are unusually large, are square. At each end of the house stands a brick chimney, built on the outside in the old style, and the fireplaces, which were large enough to take in a six-foot back log, have over them hand carved mantels of unusual height. As if in contrast to the mantels, the windows are unusually small. On the outside of one of the chimneys is durably chiseled the year in which the house was built, 1801.

"Sarah Wade was born April 18, 1785, and passed away April 23, 1874. Her remains rest in the family cemetery, near the old house, which can be readily found from the large cluster of cedar trees surrounding it. Over her grave has been erected a large and beautiful monument as a memorial of the loving affection with which her memory is cherished by her descendants."

The Adams, Garlingtons, Comptons, Wades and Chappells were buried in the churchyard of the old "Bold Spring" Church.

[A History of Halifax County, by Wirt Johnson Carrington, 1924]

WADE, Henry, Jr., of Hanover County, born 1740, son of Henry, Sr., (died 1760), and Judith Wade. Married, in 1761, Lucy Turner, born 1740, Children:

Luke, born 1763, married, 1785, Martha Stanley, of Halifax County.

Oneida, born 1765, married, 1801, Richard Jones of Halifax.

Andrew, born 1770, married, 1790, 1st, Sarah Petty, of Halifax; married 2nd, 1795, Elizabeth Kimball of Anson County, N. C.

Zachfield, married, in 1799, Mary Johnson of Campbell.

Polly, married, 1797, Thos. Stokes of Lunenburg.

Henry, born 1778, married in 1806, 1st, Polly Stone of Halifax; married, 2nd, in 1810, Mary Waene of Halifax.

Sarah, born 1786, married, in 1811, 1st, Matthew Hobson; married, 2nd, _____ Sweeney of Lynchburg.

John, born 1782, married, 1812, Elizabeth Hobson of Halifax.

[Campbell Chronicles and Family Sketches, by R. H. Early, 1927]

WATKINS family of Halifax County are very extensive, and many of them are descendants of Thomas Watkins, of Chickahominy, "Swift Creek." A name like the ancestral "Joel" Watkins, almost in toto, known for honesty, integrity and uprightness.

Among the descendants are many professional men, scholars and patriots. It is said of "Joel" Watkins, of "Woodfork," Charlotte County, the third son of Thomas, of Chickahominy, that "he was the very best man that ever lived in this world, remarkable for plainness, benevolence and integrity, a friend to the friendless, comforter of the widow, father of the orphan, adviser of the youth, friend of the poor, and at his death mourned by all."

The roll of Virginia Revolutionary soldiers rife with the name of Watkins, it is something indeed to be proud of. Among the earliest of the county was Thomas Watkins of the county militia; Jesse Watkins, who later settled on his bounty lands in Tennessee; three William Watkins left wills recorded in

Halifax. Alexander Watkins built a magnificent home for that period (soon after the Revolutionary War).

I wish I had space here for the romantic wooing and winning of Mourning Watkins by the Rev. James King, of East Tennessee (now Bristol, Tenn.), who was anything else but reverent at the time of his courtship; but the charming little Mourning made it interesting for her guardian, Mr. Coleman, when he told her lover that he could not marry her unless his estate was equal to the amount of her dowry when she arrived at the proper age to marry. James King was already a rich man for his generation. He was the son of James King, "patriot of 1776." He doubled his riches and brought his bride to "Sapling Grove." "Parson" King, as he was called, was a staunch Presbyterian, but not a stern one, for through the gentle influence of his little "Church of England" wife he developed into the broadest, sweetest and most generous character, whom every one loved almost to adoration. He gave to Bristol, Tenn., King College, a school from which many young ministers and professional men have gone forth into the world and reflected honor upon their alma mater.

Henry Joel Watkins was born October 9, 1849, in Halifax County. His father, Richard Venable Watkins, of Charlotte County, moved to Halifax in the early thirties. He married first Miss Simms, of Halifax County, who lived only one year; married secondly Miss M. A. E. Baskerville, of Lombardy Grove, Mecklenburg County, Virginia; of her there were born thirteen children (twelve reached the years of maturity), six boys and six girls, H. J. Watkins being the youngest.

He was, on account of his youth, the only son that was not enlisted in the War Between the States. He was the first graduate of Cluster Springs High School and afterwards M. A. of Hampden-Sidney College; moved to Charlotte County in 1870, was made treasurer of the county, and subsequently superintendent of schools of Charlotte.

He moved back to Halifax in 1890, and actively engaged in public education, serving as trustee of the schools of South Boston for many years and as superintendent of schools of Halifax County. The grandparents of Mr. "Hal" Watkins, as he is more familiarly known, were Captain William M. Watkins, of Charlotte County, and his wife, Ann Venable.

Captain William M. Watkins was a contemporary of John Randolph of Roanoke, and served in the State Senate from the Charlotte district for two terms, and was a great rival of John Randolph in politics, being of opposite political faith. His home is known as "Do Well." Hon. Abram Venable, who served a number of years in the Congress of the United States from North Carolina, was a brother of Mrs. William M. Watkins.

Public education has been Mr. Hal Watkins' slogan all of his life, and public Christian education more nearly describes the nature of his life's work. For this he stands today and states in no uncertain language that it is the hope of the world. Mr. Watkins was a staunch advocate of Bible teaching in all public schools.

Mr. H. J. Watkins married Miss Rose Overby, who died in 1921, leaving the following children:

(1) Henry Joel Watkins, married Marguerite Richmond, of England.

(2) John Overby Watkins, married Eva Tuggle, of Texas (they had three children, Eva, John and Douglas).

(3) Richard Venable Watkins, married Christine Boog in Alaska.

(4) Imogene Watkins.

Dr. Henry Easley, of Cluster Springs, married Miss Louise Ann Rebecca Watkins, daughter of William Watkins, better known as "Billy" Watkins. The sons of Billy Watkins were Nathaniel and Samuel; the daughters, Susannah, Louise Ann Rebecca, Mary, Martha and Roxanna. This Samuel Watkins was the father of Mrs. G. J. Hunt and the grandfather of Watkins and Francis Hunt, merchants of South Boston. [A History of Halifax County, by Wirt Johnson Carrington, 1924]

William E. Watkins, son of Samuel P. Watkins, Esq., was born in Halifax County, in 1844; in August, 1860, became a cadet at the Virginia Military Institute, where he remained until the corps went to Richmond, in the spring of 1861, to serve as drill-masters. When the corps was disbanded, young Watkins, though under age, enlisted as a private in Alright's Battery,—an artillery company from his native county. With this battery he served during the whole war, having for his soldierly qualities been made orderly sergeant. The severe service of the last campaigns of the war brought on disease which proved fatal, taking him home just a few months after hostilities had ceased. One of his comrades says of him, " He was a noble boy, much beloved among us." *[Memorial, Virginia Military Institute, 1875]*

WATKINS, George P., son of William and Mary (Wharton) Watkins, and grandson of Thomas Watkins, was born in Halifax County, Virginia, March 10th, 1852. His father was born in Virginia, where the family has been long seated, and his mother was born in the State of Maine. His wife is Jimmie Lelia, daughter of Col. James W. and Mary Elizabeth (Jones) Watts. She was born in Bedford County, Virginia, and they were married by Dr. W. E. Edwards, at the Court Street M. E. Church, Lynchburg, December 22, 1880. Their children were Florence, Lucile and Lelia. Robert W. Watkins, brother of George P., served in the Civil War. His mother died in 1857, when he was five years old, and his father died in 1864, when he was twelve years old. After that he attended boarding school for two years, then entered on a business life in 1868 as clerk in a retail store in Halifax County, Virginia. In 1871 he went to Richmond as traveling salesman for the wholesale notion house of Yancey & Franklin; in 1875 went to Baltimore, traveling for a wholesale house. On July 1, 1878, became a partner in the wholesale boot and shoe firm of Witt & Watkins. Mr. Watkins was also a director in the National Exchange Bank of Lynchburg since its organization. *[Virginia and Virginians, Vol. II]*

WATKINS, W. Lafayette: The families from which Mr. Watkins is descended were Huguenots and in 1700 settled at Manakin Town, Virginia. He was born in Richmond, Virginia, on January 10, 1824, the son of Stephen D. Watkins, who was born in Halifax County, Virginia, January 27, 1778, and who died on July 13, 1862. Thomas Watkins, father of Stephen D., was born on November 15, 1748, and died July 28, 1816. He married Magdalene Dupuy, daughter of Jno. Bartholomew Dupuy (Huguenot). The mother of W. Lafayette, was Sarah H., daughter of Peter Dupuy. She was born January 20, 1800, and died on August 14, 1864. Her father was born July 1, 1760, and died August 29, 1826. Her mother was Margaret Martin, born November 6, 1768, died July 18, 1852.

Mr. Watkins received a collegiate education at William and Mary College, whence he was graduated on July 4, 1843. He studied law under Judge Thomas S. Gholson, of Petersburg, and received license to practice in 1846. Since that time he followed the profession of law continuously, practicing in Dinwiddie and adjoining counties and Court of Appeals.

His first wife was Maria S. Hall, born at Fredericksburg, Virginia, June 4, 1833, and died September 21, 1864, aged thirty-one years. They had seven children. Mr. Watkins married secondly, at Petersburg, October 9, 1866, Eliza Stringfellow, daughter of Rev. Horace Stringfellow; she was born at Washington, D. C., on September 19, 1845. *[Virginia and Virginians, Vol. II]*

WILBOURN family: 25 January, 1796, Estate of Gunnery Wilbourn, deceased. Wife, Judith; sons, John, Thomas, William and Robert Wilbourn; daughters, Nancy, Obediah and Jane Wilbourn, Sally Allen legatee; Charles Allen on the bond.

Inventory of Judith Wilbourn (wife of Gunnery Wilbourn), mentions sons, John, Thomas, William and Robert; daughters, Nancy, Obediah and Jane Wilbourn. Sally Allen legatee; Charles Allen legatee through wife, Sally.

10 August, 1799, Will of Lewis Wilbourn. Wife, Mary; son-in-law, John Whitlock, and Sary Whitlock, his wife, 100 acres of land, the old "Clays tract;" grandson, Richard Whitlock; son-in-law, Robert Page, and wife,

Elizabeth Page, 100 acres. Witnesses: Robert Wilbourn, Sary Whitlock and Elizabeth Page.

James B. Wilborn was one of the prominent men of South Boston, being a business man and the Mayor. Mr. Wilborn was born at Virgilina, in Halifax County, January 10, 1881. The Wilborn family came to Virginia in Colonial times from Ireland. His grandfather, William H. Wilborn, was born near South Boston in Halifax County, and spent all his life in this part of Virginia. During the Civil War he was a plantation overseer for the Confederate government, and after the war he conducted extensive farming interests of his own.

His wife was Elizabeth Childress, a native of Charlotte County, Virginia. Stephen M. Wilborn, father of the Mayor of South Boston, was born at South Boston, December 20, 1852, but has spent practically all his life in the Virgilina community and was a prosperous farmer with three hundred acres located four miles north of Virgilina. He held a number of local offices, was a democrat, and an active worker in the Baptist Church. Stephen M. Wilborn married Mary S. Tuck, who was born at Virgilina, September 15, 1856, and they became the parents of eleven children:

1. Julia, wife of David S. Bray, a tobacconist of Reidsville, North Carolina.

2. Philip T., a farmer at Virgilina.

3. James B.

4. Charles L., a merchant at South Boston.

5. Mary, wife of John Dalton, of Durham, North Carolina. Mr. Dalton was widely known as an inventor and he invented and operated the bag stringing machine for the Golden Belt Tobacco Company.

6. Lynn B., a farmer at Virgilina.

7. Jennie, wife of Charles Casada, a farmer at Halifax.

8. Naomi, wife of William Hudson, a farmer at Moffet, Virginia.

9. Zora, farmer at Virgilina, who served six months in France with the Field Artillery and was in the Chateau-Thierry campaign.

10. Truett, a farmer at Virgilina.

11. Tyler, who was in the United States Navy.

On June 27, 1907, at Henderson, N. C., Mr. James B. Wilborn married Miss Zulene Shanks, daughter of Henry T. and Maude (Jenkins) Shanks, of Henderson, where her father was a farmer. Mrs. Wilborn was a graduate of Oxford College, North Carolina. Four children were born to them: James, Jr., born February 16, 1910; Lillian, twin sister of James; Shanks, born September 6, 1917; and Frances, born June 27, 1922. *[History of Virginia, Vol. V, 1924]*

Some Wilbourn marriages in Halifax County, Virginia:

America H. Wilburn and William Adams, 16 Oct. 1839.

Edwin D. Wilburn and Araminta Price, 18 Nov. 1845.

Greenbury Wilbourne and Dicey Sales, 25 Aug. 1852.

Incy Welborn and Richard H. Ligon, 18 Oct. 1798.

J. Wilbourne (husband) and E. N. Spencer, 12 Jan. 1832.

John Wilborn and Judith Martin, 1 Nov. 1804.

John Wilburn and Martha Smith, 8 Aug. 1807.

John Wilburn and E. Chentham, 27 Sept. 1809.

John Wilbourn and Eliza W. Faulkner, 11 June 1828.

M. Wilbourn (wife) and Pascal Talley, 23 April 1840.

Martha W. Wilburn and Rednor W. Adams, __ Aug. 1847.

N. Wilburn and William Canaday, 21 Jan. 1808.

Obediah Wilborn and E. Martin, 26 Dec. 1805.

Robert Wilbourn and Patsey Ligon, 12 Aug. 1802.

Thomas Wilbourn and Susannah Ligon, 22 Aug. 1799.

William Wilbourn and Hanah Shelton, 13 July 1791.

WILLINGHAM family: We do not know the emigrant of the Willingham family, but we do know that they were not among Halifax County's earliest settlers. Who and whatever the emigrant Willingham was his descendants have illustrated the legacy he left them in character and brains.

Andrew Jackson Willingham, once a leading citizen of South Boston, married Miss Mildred Pollard, daughter of Isaac Pollard, and left the following children:

(1) William A. Willingham, of New York, who married Miss Manfell of English parentage.

(2) Mary Willingham, wife of W. A. Gray.

(3) E. Wiltse Willingham, married Miss Mamie Easley.

169

(4) Miss Susie Willingham.

The Willinghams were strong supporters of the Baptist Church in South Boston, and were known for their liberality in church and charitable work generally. Mr. William A Willingham was a prominent tobacconist, a financier and an all-round business man. He built one of the handsomest and most perfectly equipped homes in town for his mother. *[A History of Halifax County, by Wirt Johnson Carrington, 1924]*

Will of Jarrell Willingham, 6 October, 1790, Halifax County: "To my beloved wife, Mary;" sons, John, Jeremiah, Johnson and Jarrell Willingham, Jr. Executors: Jeremiah Willingham and Joshua Towles. Witnesses: Jeremiah Pate, Samuel Pate, John Malone and Daniel Malone.

Will of Johnson Willingham, 25 September 1809, Halifax County: "My wife, Polly Willingham" (names of children not stated, all under age). Witnesses: John Nance, Fred Nance, William Chandler and John Daniel.

Some Willingham marriages in Halifax County, Virginia:

Allen Willingham and M. J. Deupree, 7 Oct. 1835.

Fanney Willingham and Joshua Powell, 2 June 1787.

Jarrell Willingham and N. Roberts, 13 Jan. 1790.

Jeremiah Willingham and Tabitha Powell, 17 May 1790.

Jerrald Willingham and Rachel Boyd, 18 July 1793.

Johnson Willingham and Patsey Roberts, 22 Dec. 1801.

Johnson Willingham and Polly Roberts, 3 Jan. 1805.

Mary Willingham and Frederick Nance, 23 March 1823.

Nancy Willingham and Archer H. Boyd, 6 Nov. 1833.

Rebeckah Willingham and William Finch, 12 Dec. 1792.

Sally Willingham and James Fulkerson, 23 March 1825.

Tobitta Willingham and Jacob Robinson, 25 May 1836.

WILSON, Robert, was born a slave in Halifax County, Virginia. He was interviewed in the 1930's by the Federal Writers' Project. He was 101 years old and a resident of Pine Bluff, Arkansas.

"My name is Robert Wilson. I was born in Halifax County, Virginia. How old am I? Accordin' to my recollection I was twenty-three years old befo' the war started. Old master tole me how old I was. I'm a hundred and one now. Yes'm I knows I am.

"Yes'm I been sold. They put us up on the auction block jest like we was a hoss. They put me up and white man ax 'Who want to buy this boy?' One man say 'ten dollars' and then they run it up to a hundred. And they buy a girl to match you and raise you up together. When you want to get married you jump over the broomstick. I used to weigh one hundred and fifty-six pounds and a half, standin' weight. I could pick four and five hundred pounds of cotton in a day.

"When the Yankees come, old master make us boys take the sack of money and hide it in the big pond. Yes'm, we drove the buggy right in the water.

"Durin' the time of the war I used to ride 'long side of the Yankees. They give me a blue coat with brass buttons and a blue cap and brass-toed boots. I used to saddle and curry the bosses. I member Company Fifth and Sixth.

"They tole us the war was to make things better. We didn't know we was free till 'bout six months after the war was over. I didn't care whether I was free or not.

"'Bout slavery—well, I thinks like this. I think they fared better then. They didn't have to worry 'bout spenses. We had plenty chicken and everything. Nowdays when you pay the rent you ain't got nothin' left to buy somethin' to eat.

"Yes'm, I been to school. I'se a preacher (showing me his certificate of ordination). I lives close to the Lord. The Lord done left me here for a purpose.

"When we used to pray we put our heads under the wash pot to keep old master from hearin' us.

"You 'member when Grant took the fort at Vicksburg? I 'member he and that general on the white hoss—yes'm, General Lee, they eat dinner together and then after dinner they go to fightin'.

"Oh lord! Don't talk about them Ku Klux.

"After freedom my folks refugeed from Virginia to Tennessee so I went to Memphis. We got things from the Bureau. Yes, Lord! I had everything I wanted. I wouldn't care if that time would come back now.

"'Did you ever vote?' Me? Yes'm I voted. Never had no trouble 'tall. I voted for Garfield. I 'member when Garfield was shot. I was settln' out in the yard. The moon was in the 'clipse. I'll never forget it.

"I think the colored folks should have a legal right to vote, cause if ever they come another war—now listen—them darkies ain't never goin' to France again. The nigger ain't got no country—this is white man's town.

"What I been doin' since the war? Well, I'm a good cook. When I puts on the white apron, I knows what to do. Then I preaches. The Lord done revealed things to me.

WIMBISH family settled early in Halifax County, and in 1770, March 9, James Wimbish made his will. His wife was named Sarah, of whom he speaks as "My well beloved wife Sarah, and it is my will that my estate shall be kept together until my beloved son, John Wimbish, shall arrive of age." John was his only son. He makes Sarah, his wife, his executrix, and Samuel Wimbish and Elijah Hunt his executors. Witnesses: John Hunt, John Logan.

June 10, 1818, we find the will of John Wimbish:

"I, John Wimbish, of Halifax County, State of Virginia, parish of Antrim, etc.

"I give to my wife, Nancy, all my estate, both real and personal, of every description for her use, and to the end that she may dispose of it only to my children, to-wit: John H. Wimbish, Elizabeth Craddock, Abram Wimbish, Judith A. Wimbish and Mary Wimbish, to them and their heirs forever. (Nancy is vested with power to dispose of any part of the estate for the benefit of his children, and after her death all to be equally divided between the children. Nancy, his wife, executrix.)

"John Wimbish."

Witnesses: Robert Hurt, Catherine C. Vasser, Joseph M. Crews. Samuel Williams, C. H. C.

June 24, 1845, we find the inventory and appraisal of the estate of John H. Wimbish (deceased). The appraisers were James Holt, James Young and William Bailey. The estate consisted of eighty-five Negroes, a large plantation, mansion house, furniture, mahogany and walnut, piano and guitar, silver, cut-glass and china (a very long list), silver candlesticks, brass candlesticks, farm utensils and crops, cattle, horses, hogs, sheep, cows, a large crop of tobacco and several farming machines. The list covered several pages and showed him to have been in very comfortable circumstances, if not rich.

Mrs. Eliza (Wimbish) Poindexter, daughter of Major John Wimbish and Nancy (Williams) Wimbish, was born October 18, 1800, in Halifax County. She married in early life Dr. Granville Craddock, who left her a widow with two sons and two daughters. Afterwards she became the wife of Rev. A. M. Poindexter, D. D., in which relation she was the mother of one daughter and two sons.

Granville Craddock was chief presiding justice of the Court of Halifax and a most efficient and popular county treasurer. He was the grandfather of Mr. John W. and A. P. Craddock. He had a brother, William Craddock. *[A History of Halifax County, by Wirt Johnson Carrington, 1924]*

WOODING family: Will of Robert Wooding, 14 May 1796, Halifax County:

"I, Robert Wooding, of the county of Halifax, Parish of Antrim, being of sound mind and memory," &c.

Legatees: James and Mary Taylor, James Chappell (son-in-law), Elizabeth Hill, Thomas Hill (Wooding), John Wooding (brother).

To Benjamin Rodgers (husband of Nancy Hill) bequeathed five slaves, six silver spoons and silver ladle, to be delivered after the death of Mrs. Elizabeth Hill, who is to have the use of them during her lifetime.

To John Hill (son of Elizabeth Hill), 75 acres of land.

To Porterfield Kent, husband of Elizabeth Hill (the daughter), 50 pounds.

To Catherine Wooding (niece), 50 pounds.

To Sophia Wooding (niece), 50 pounds.

Thomas Hill (Wooding), executor.

Witnesses: John Stanley, Morris Roberts, Thomas Roberts, Thomas Hill (Wooding), on motion of the court, was appointed executor, giving security, amount of twenty thousand dollars, with Isaac Coles, George Carrington, Moses Roberts, Simon Holt and Benjamin Rodgers as bondsmen.

Some Wooding marriages in Halifax County, Virginia:

John Wooding and Sucky Hill, 24 Nov. 1774.

John Wooding and Susanna Johnson, 29 Feb. 1786.

Martha Wooding and James Chappell, 22 June 1781.

M. Wooding and James Taylor, 5 May 1788.

Robert Wooding and N. Williamson, 15 Dec. 1801.

Robert Wooding and S. Terry, 21 Feb. 1805.

WYATT, George W., was born 2 August, 1819, in Halifax County, Virginia. He married Catherine Mildred Gwatkin, who was born 8 July, 1837, eldest child of Charles B. and Charlotte Ann (Tinsley) Gwatkin, of Bedford County,

Virginia. Her first husband was Benjamin Steward. George Washington Wyatt enlisted April, 1861, at Lynchburg, Virginia, in Company C, Virginia Heavy Artillery, C. S. A. After the seven days fight around Richmond, was made Commissary Sergeant of 34th Virginia Infantry, C. S. A., and paroled at Appomattox at close of the war. He was a member of the Jno. N. Edwards Camp of Confederate Veterans at Higginsville, Missouri, until his death, which occurred at Higginsville, 29 September, 1905. His wife died 11 December, 1889. *[Our Kin, by Mary Denham Ackerly and Lula Eastman Jeter Parker, 1930]*

WYATT, John, presumably the son of William Edward and Lettice (Nichols) Wyatt, of Stafford County, Virginia, was the progenitor of the branch of Wyatts in Halifax County. He and his family were living on Birch Creek, in the upper part of this county as early as 1782, when the first United States Census was taken. Other county records show that his plantation adjoined the farm of Micajah Wyatt, son of William Edward and Frances (Newton) Wyatt, of Prince William County, Virginia, and that he was also a neighbor of William Wyatt, son of John and Jane Wyatt, of Caroline County. Both of these men were direct descendants of the Rev. Haute Wyatt. During those days it was not unusual for relatives to settle near each other when removing from one county to another.

Although John Wyatt, of Halifax, never lived in Henry County, official records at the Court House, in Martinsville, Virginia, show that he purchased 150 acres of land on Leatherwood Creek, for 25 pounds, current money of Virginia, in 1775. This land was sold later for a profit of 50 pounds.

John Wyatt died at his home in Halifax County, Virginia, about 1807, and his wife, Hannah (Vincent?), died about 1808. His will, drawn February 24, 1801, was probated in the county court at Halifax, February 22, 1808, naming his youngest son, Eliel, as Executor of his estate. To him he bequeathed the household furniture, stock and entire plantation after his wife's death. To the other children he bequeathed money. Children of John and Hannah Wyatt:

1. Vincent Wyatt, married Elizabeth Simpson, 23 February, 1787.

2. James Wyatt, married Milly Compton, 25 August, 1790.

3. Nancy Wyatt, married ___ Williams.

4. Lettice Wyatt, married David Hamrick, 9 February, 1788.

5. Sally Wyatt, married ___ Lovell.

6. Molly Wyatt, married William Cooksey.

7. Eliel Wyatt, married Martha Compton, 1803.

Vincent Wyatt, son of John and Hannah Wyatt, of Halifax County, Virginia, was born about 1766. He was married February 23, 1787 to Elizabeth Simpson, daughter of John and Hannah Simpson, of the same county.

In 1790 Vincent Wyatt purchased a farm in Halifax County, adjoining William Wyatt's estate. Later, he apparently purchased land in Spartanburg County, South Carolina, and resided there awhile with his family. About 1798 they removed to Henry County, Virginia, locating on Leatherwood Creek, near Horsepasture. County records show that he was a planter and the progenitor of the Wyatt clan in that county.

During the War of 1812, it appears, he enlisted on August 27, 1814, and served as a private in Captain George W. Jackson's Company, 36th Regiment (Renno's) Virginia Militia. He was discharged November 24, 1814.

After his demise in 1832, his son, John Posey Wyatt, was appointed Administrator of his estate and his widow was given a dower. After her death this land was sold at public auction July 18, 1838. Prior to this date official records show that he had deeded one hundred acres of his farm in Henry County to John Posey and fifty acres to his son, Craven. He had also deeded eighty acres of his farm in Spartanburg County, South Carolina, to Vincent, Jr., and another "tract of land" on Elder Creek in that State, to William. Children of Vincent and Elizabeth (Simpson) Wyatt:

1. Vincent Wyatt, Jr., married Mary Ann ____; settled in South Carolina; left many descendants in that State.

2. William Wyatt, untraced.

3. Lettice Wyatt, married George Davis.

4. John Posey Wyatt, married Agatha Richardson, 1816; settled in Henry County, Virginia.

5. Craven Wyatt, married Eleanor Richardson, 1823; settled in Henry County, Virginia.

6. Nancy Wyatt, married Daniel Lovell, 1823

7. Elijah Wyatt, born 1800.

8. Clay Wyatt, born 1803; married Betsy____; settled in Kentucky.

9. Eliel "Eli" Wyatt, born in 1806, near Horsepasture, Henry County, Virginia; about 1828, he was married to Ruhama Evans, of North Carolina, and removed to Pittsylvania County, Virginia; he died December, 15, 1890, at his home near Grady.

[The Wyatt Family Records, by Lucile Rebecca Douglass Wyatt.]

YEATES family: Will of John Yeates, 13 January 1846, Halifax County-- Sons, James and Gilderoy. "My daughter, Polly Hall; daughter, Christiana Brown; granddaughter, Sarah Thomas Whiteman; John Coates (husband of my daughter, Sally); to children of Willis Yeates (John Yeates and Betsy Hankla); Patsy Guthrie, James Yeates.

Executor: Gilderoy Yeates. Witnesses: Thos. C. Whitworth, David B. McGehee and Wm. H. McGehee.

Some Yeates marriages in Halifax County, Virginia:

Absolem Yates and Catherine Haley, 24 Jan. 1836.

Elizabeth Yates and Elisha Taylor, 15 Nov. 1794.

Gilderoy Yeates and Polly Throckmarton, 8 Sept. 1825.

Jas. Yeates and Elizabeth Nichols, 18 Jan. 1827.

Nancy Yates and Esau Coles, 9 Aug. 1788.

Polly Yates and Thomas Hall, 20 Dec. 1798.

Polly Yates and Richard Alderson, 22 Nov. 1827.

Sanoford Yeates and Mary T. Poindexter, 22 Nov. 1848.

Susannah Yeates and John Bohannon, 17 March 1797.

William Yates and Nelley Trammel, 1 Oct. 1790.

William Yeats and Diana Crawley, __ Jan. 1850.

Willis C. Yeates and Mildred Roberts, 20 Dec. 1815.

YUILLE family: Thomas Yuille figured at an early date in Halifax County. In 1792 he bought 500 acres of land on Childrey Creek from William Oliver (both of Halifax County). Witnesses to the sale were William H. Hurt, Elizabeth Hurt, Jr., David A. Rice, Samuel Clemens and James Clemens,

Account current of Thomas Yuille (deceased), taken November 9, 1843, Daniel B. Easley, administrator *de bonis non*, with the will annexed, of Thomas Yuille, deceased, we find the same administrator indebted to the estate of his testator in the sum of two thousand five hundred and seventy-four dollars, including interest to November 9, 1851. "All of which will more fully appear by reference to the foregoing statement which is submitted as a part of the report," which was recorded February 23, 1852.

At Williamsburg, in the old Bruton Churchyard, may be seen the following inscription on one of the tombstones:

"Here Lieth the Corpse of John Yuille (Merchant) son of Thomas Yuille of Darleith in the County of D— in Scotland, who died at Wm—burg, in Virginia upon the 2nd day of Oct, 1746, in the year 27 of age."

The Yuille coat of arms are on the tombs with description of same and this motto, "Numine et Virtute."

A stretch of one hundred and two years between the deaths of the two Yuilles. The name is an unusual one, they may have been related. Thomas Yuille, of this county, left descendants, and I find that some of them changed the spelling of the name to Ewell, so I have not traced the family further. *[A History of Halifax County, by Wirt Johnson Carrington, 1924]*

Charles Yuille (or Ewell, as a branch of this family is now called) came to Virginia from England in 1690 under contract to build the capital at Williamsburg, accompanied by two brothers, They were said to be sons of John Yuille, of the clan Buchanan. A stone in Bruton church-yard is inscribed to the memory of John, son of Thomas Yuille of Darleith, Scotland, Dumbarton County, John died in 1746, aged 27 years. Thomas; a descendant of Thomas Yuille of Darleith, married Lucy Fletcher, of England, settled at a place now called Clarkton, in Halifax County, Children:

Frances, born 1806.

George, built a home, "Prospect Cottage," at Lawyers in 1840; married Amanda V., daughter of John Payne, of "White Hall."

Jane, married Winston Henry, lived in Charlotte County, near Brookneal, Campbell County.

Mary, married _____ Hairston.

Antoinette, married Colonel John McCraw.

Melvina, married Colonel Daniel Easley.

Alexander, unmarried.

Children of George and Amanda V. Payne-Yuille:

William Murdock, married Lillian Winfree, lived in Lynchburg.

Thomas, married Miss Hunter and moved to Kansas; lived for some years in Campbell County, Va.

Sue, married Colonel Richard Burks of Rockbridge County.

Andrew, unmarried.

John Matteau (named for Dr. Matteau, friend of the family, of Prince Edward County), married, 1st, Susan Burks, of Rockbridge County; married, 2nd, Nancy Coleman Hundley (his first cousin) and lived in Halifax County; a son of the first marriage, Thomas Burks Yuille, of New York City, was vice-president of the American Tobacco Company, until its dissolution, and President of the Universal Tobacco Company.

Philip Payne, married Nannie Wyatt; lived near Lynch's Station.

Alexander Campbell, married, 1st, Sally Moon of Halifax County; married, 2nd, Sue Massie of Nelson.

Helen, married S. Flynn, of Culpeper County; lived in Danville and Washington, where she died.

Fletcher Campbell, married, 1st, Sally Butler Scott; married, 2nd, Addie Armistead, great-granddaughter of Patrick Henry.

John Matteau and Fletcher Campbell resided at "Prospect Cottage." John Matteau, Philip Payne and Alexander Campbell Yuille served in the Confederate army, and were in the engagements around Lynchburg; J. Matteau with General McCausland's command. *[Campbell Chronicles and Family Sketches, by R. H. Early, 1927]*

www.ingramcontent.com/pod-product-compliance
Lightning Source LLC
Chambersburg PA
CBHW070010300526
45794CB00001B/270